# Dynamics of Fitness and Health

Ninth Edition

## F. Compton Jenkins

*Bergen Community College*

KENDALL/HUNT PUBLISHING COMPANY
4050 Westmark Drive     Dubuque, Iowa 52002

13

# Contents

## 5 Cardiovascular Fitness and Health   141

## 6 Principles of Exercise   167

# Acknowledgments

Mary Pat Boron—Photographer in love with sport whose enthusiasm for both have allowed private exhibits, news photos, and publication in textbooks/instructional books for sport.

Robert R. Thompson—Professor and Program Director, Division of Allied Health and Physical Education at Bergen Community College. An outstanding person to whom I am indebted for advice about life, parenthood, the present and the future.

My Colleagues—Who share the responsibility of teaching about exercise and lifestyle choices with expertise and enthusiasm: Professors Doug Davis, Florio DeGaetano, Bernard Fuersich, Peter Martin, Elaine Mostow, Kathleen Pignatelli, Joan Szabo, and Paul Wolfe.

Tracey Arallo—A student in the Exercise Science program who aspires to greater achievements in body building through her hard work and dedication which is exemplary.

Dawn Colussi—A student in the Exercise Science program who enjoys swimming, teaching swimming and all outdoor activities. Future plans include personal training and a degree in Exercise Physiology.

Steve Duplessy—A student in the Exercise Science program who enjoys playing basketball and writing poetry. Future plans include consultancy work with college athletes.

Elizabeth Mayemich—A student in the Exercise Science program who enjoys all sports and looks forward to sharing this interest as a teacher and coach.

Margaret McGill—A student in the Exercise Science program who enjoys softball and rollerblading with a future involvement in athletic training.

Darren Reilly—A student in the Exercise Science program who aspires to professional body building status and a career with college or professional athletes as a coach with expertise in strength development.

Robert Schmetter—A student in the Exercise Science program who enjoys training, roller-hockey and flag football in particular. Future plans include being a strength and conditioning specialist for athletes.

Dena Spirito—A student in the Exercise Science program who enjoys volleyball, running and rollerblading. Future aspirations include a degree in Exercise Physiology applied to a business venture.

# Introduction

Since we have entered the 21$^{st}$ century, quality of life issues continue to be of great concern in our society. The emphasis on life-style behaviors brings these issues to a very personal level. There is a never-ending supply of recommendations that promote optimum well-being that include fitness, health, and an all encompassing idea of personal wellness. It is interesting to note that all approaches to optimum well-being emphasize individual responsibility in the practice of various life-style behaviors. Ultimately, the two behaviors that will affect someone more so than others are: what you do and what you eat—EXERCISE and DIET. Add exercise and everything else begins to fall into place. Regular physical activity has been shown to help in preventing and/or counteracting the effects of coronary heart disease, hypertension, obesity, non-insulin dependent diabetes, osteoporosis, stroke and mental health problems (depression, anxiety and low self-esteem). In addition, regular physical activity aids in maintaining functional independence for the elderly. Quality and quantity of life are definitively affected favorably. However, upon examination of the health status of members of our society, it is easily concluded that some major problems exist.

There has risen a critical interest in physical activity, which has been an aspect of life minimized by the age of technology. Many pieces of literature have been written that encourage people to participate in various forms of physical activity for a variety of avowed purposes.

This book acquaints readers with information with which they may construct a prudently self-administered exercise program as part of their life-styles. It must be recognized that the needs and interests of people vary. Yet all people share a mutual interest in maintaining their physical selves at an optimal level by using exercise: for the health of it.

The book explores the considerations necessary to develop a fitness level that impacts on health status. To achieve this purpose, chapter material includes information regarding:

- The role of exercise in contemporary life-styles
- The physical and psychosocial benefits of exercise
- Exercise principles and their application
- The nature of heart disease and its risk factors
- The nature and dangers of obesity

- The role of exercise in affecting body weight and heart disease
- Considerations regarding diet and calories
- The health promotion and disease prevention benefits of exercise

The material presented to the reader represents a condensation of an incredible amount of investigation dealing with exercise. Personal applications are included that help to reinforce concepts presented as well as to provide a better personal understanding of these ideas.

The design and intent of this text is such that an instructor may use the material without being forced into a particular format of presentation. The concepts and personal applications appearing at the end of chapters are those believed to be essential to a course of this nature in a situation with limited facilities, equipment and time.

It is hoped that the information presented will help in consideration of a part of life which is all too often neglected—Exercise: for the health of it.

# CHAPTER I

# Rationale for Physical Activity

## You and Fitness

Our society has become well-acquainted with the meaning and benefit of physical activity. The number of publications, health club memberships, sweat suits, sport shoes, treadmills, rowers and bicycles sold all support the curiosity of the American populace regarding exercise. It appears that active Americans—whether dancing, running, swimming, cycling, or pumping iron are driven by a common goal. They appear to be spurred onward by a belief that exercise transforms their lives in a meaningful and productive fashion. Interestingly, medical, clinical, epidemiological, and anecdotal evidence supports this notion.

Surveys support the belief that those who are exercising become more health conscious. Perhaps it is because there may be a distinct relationship between health status and physical fitness. This association may at last be making its impact on a society that cannot afford to sit complacently as the future so rapidly becomes the present.

Most people will acknowledge the need for exercise while at the same time doing little, if anything, to take advantage of what exercise has to offer. It is commonplace to find that most people take better care of and pay more attention to things they own—cars, wardrobe, HD TV's, IPODS, computers and the like—than to themselves. For some people the idea of physical fitness equates with a slim waistline and a suntan. One only has to look around to see that most have opted for the suntan.

The human organism needs physical activity. Unfortunately, present day society makes physical effort in life virtually nonexistent. In the past, physical effort was a requisite for life itself. Now, experts fear for the future because our present day society demands much less effort. Technological advancements have created a sedentary, disease-prone society. Degenerative diseases are common today and appear to be directly related to this sedentary existence. This is in keeping with a well-known biological adage that states *"use it or lose it."* Relative to physiological function—the less the body does, the less it can do, and thus it becomes more susceptible to disease and deterioration. The term *hypokinetic disease* is used by Kraus and Raab[1] to describe those afflictions which promote human deterioration through inactivity. The most dramatic example is heart disease, which continues to be the leading cause of death in our society. This is accompanied by other "diseases" that can be profoundly affected by exercise: obesity; low back syndrome; hypertension; diabetes; osteoporosis; and the effects of emotional stress, such as depression.

Ever-mounting evidence suggests that exercise and its corollary, physical fitness, can significantly enhance health status and well-being. Whether fitness can *guarantee* better health remains to be seen. Exercise can provide the basis of a "fitness for life" that may carry with it a greater health status. People are born with a 70-year warranty—*not* a guarantee. Exercise can aid in living a healthier, more abundant, more productive life.

"EXERCISE IS MEDICINE"—according to a survey of 1,750 primary care physicians conducted by the journal *The Physician and Sportsmedicine.* They prescribe exercise for weight control (95%), cardiac rehabilitation (94%), depression (85%), low back pain (83%), arthritis (80%), diabetes (80%), anxiety (60%), chronic obstructive pulmonary disease (58%), asthma (56%), and chemical dependence (43%).

The most frequently prescribed modes (types) of exercise are walking (97%), swimming (82%), bicycling (67%), strength training (67%), and running (46%).

One important consideration to bear in mind is that exercise need not mean engaging in competitive ventures like athletics. A distinct difference exists between what is now understood as *sports fitness* as opposed to *health-related fitness.*

If what you do in the form of "exercise" makes no strenuous demands on your body, requires little prolonged exertion or in no other way helps to improve your heart, lungs, and muscular system, your exercise is not contributing to health-related fitness—fitness for life.

The goal for most people should not be athletic excellence (that may never be achieved) but, rather, **physical conditioning for the demands of daily life**.

With each passing year your basic physical condition—fitness—becomes increasingly important. No one ever died from skinny legs or underdeveloped biceps, but thousands become victims of heart disease, the consequences of obesity, the ravages of stress, and generally poor physical condition.

Optimum well-being should be your most important consideration, and it can best be achieved when the body is strong and viable. It incorporates a balance of living that integrates mental, physical, and emotional optimums. Exercise is not a panacea for each individual's needs, but it does make an indispensable contribution. Very simply, exercise can make you look better, feel better, and function better.

*"If all you do is sit and read, all you get is smart and soft."*
*-Scott Carpenter, NASA Astronaut*

The importance of physical activity takes on additional dimension when agencies of the national government endorse it. As an example the Department of Health and Human Services has developed Year 2000 objectives for the Nation relative to promoting health and preventing disease. Consider the implications of the following selected objectives:

- Increase to 60 percent the proportion of people who participate in moderate physical activities 3 or more days per week for 20 or more minutes each session.
- Increase to 30 percent of people who participate in *vigorous* physical activities 3 or more days per week for 20 or more minutes each session.
- Increase to 50 percent of people who regularly perform physical activities that maintain muscular strength, muscular endurance and flexibility.
- Reduce to below 20 percent of the population those people who are overweight.
- Reduce to below 15 percent the occurrence of overweight among adolescents ages 12 - 17.
- Increase to 75 percent of overweight people who use scientific dietary practices *combined* with physical activity to achieve weight reduction.
- Increase to 80 percent the proportion of people who know that regular exercise reduces the risk of heart disease, helps maintain appropriate body weight, reduces symptoms of depression and anxiety and enhances self-esteem.

*Everyone needs exercise.*

- Increase to 25 percent the proportion of people who can identify cor-
  rectly the frequency and duration of exercise which most effectively
  promotes cardiorespiratory fitness.

## The Body–Mind Connection

In recent years research efforts have gone beyond documenting the physical benefits of exercise relative to health. Presently, there is good evidence
that exercise may do for the brain what it can do for the biceps, that is,
make it stronger. In part the results appear to be due to the effect of greater
oxygen supply to the brain as well as increases in some of the naturally
occurring hormones and enzymes.

In response to exercise, a variety of chemicals are released in the body.
Some, like IGF-1 (insulin like growth factor), cross the blood-brain barrier
and affect neurotransmitters in the brain (such as dopamine, serotonin, and
nonrepenephrine). One that is increased is BDNF (brain derived neu-
rotrophic factor) which affects almost all functions that lead to higher
thought. With regular exercise the levels of BDNF build up and allow the

# Examples of Exercise Training for Moderate and High Fitness

## *Longitudinal Study*

Figures 1 through 3 show age-adjusted death rates by physical fitness categories for all-causes, for cardiovascular disease, and for cancer. (Physical fitness was assessed by maximal exercise testing on a treadmill.) The low-fit category is comprised of the least fit 20%; the moderate-fit category is the middle 40%; and the high-fit category is the most fit 40%. [A reprint providing more details of the treadmill test and a description of the fitness categories may be obtained by sending a stamped, self-addressed envelope to S.N. Blair, Director of Epidemiology, Institute for Aerobics Research, 12330 Preston Road, Dallas, TX 75230.] The study group was 10,224 men and 3,120 women who were followed for approximately eight years. There were 240 deaths in men and 43 deaths in women during that time. Death rates show a striking decline across fitness categories in both men and women. Death rates in the low-fitness category are about twice as high as in the moderate-fitness category, and higher still when the low- and high-fitness categories are compared.

**29**

SPORTS SCIENCE EXCHANGE

Source: Gatorade Sports Science Institute

Figure 4 illustrates the relation between fitness and all-cause mortality in men with high levels of other risk factors. Men in the moderate-fitness category have much lower death rates than the low-fit men in each of the other risk factor groups. Even cigarette smokers are better off if they are fit than if they are unfit. Low physical fitness is an independent risk factor for early death. Furthermore, low fitness seems to be as important as the other major cardiovascular disease risk factors.

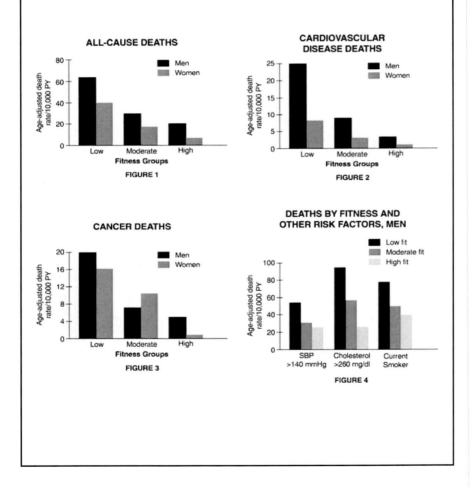

ALL-CAUSE DEATHS

FIGURE 1

CARDIOVASCULAR DISEASE DEATHS

FIGURE 2

CANCER DEATHS

FIGURE 3

DEATHS BY FITNESS AND OTHER RISK FACTORS, MEN

FIGURE 4

brains nerve cells to "talk" to each other in new ways. This is the process that creates learning.

Although, most research has been done with older individuals, there is little question that the same responses occur in children. Consequently, here is another reason to encourage exercise in young people. Perhaps more physical education programs should be required just as are other subjects in our nation's schools.

Researchers have been able to show that new nerve cells have grown in the brain, a process that was thought to be unlikely, by having subjects follow a three month aerobic program. Other researchers have found that vigorous exercise can create more dense interconnections in older nerve cells. There is evidence that exercise may help in slowing down the initial stages of Alzheimers. Apparently a strong, fit body is crucial to creating a strong, active mind.

## Physical Exercise and Stress

The pace of modern-day life may literally be killing us. This statement is a simplification of the theories developed by several noted individuals. Those in the medical profession include Drs. Meyer Friedman, Ray Rosenman, Hans Selye, and Thomas Holmes.

Dr. Hans Selye is the leader in the study of stress and its effect on the human body. He defines stress very simply as *"wear and tear on the body."* His studies have led to the formation of the **General Adaptation Syndrome** (GAS), which depicts the reaction by the body to a stress (real or imagined). The GAS has three phases: the **alarm stage**, which involves the immediate biochemical changes preparing you to deal with the stress; the **resistance stage**, which involves a "fight or flight" situation; and the **exhaustion stage**, which represents the inability to adjust to stress.

Under stress the body works in predictable ways. Sometimes these can cause discomfort:

- Adrenaline levels increase
- Breathing speeds up
- Heart rate speeds up
- Bloodflow decreases to the organs and increases to muscle
- Blood pressure rises

These reactions are in-born reactions creating a sort of extra gear we need during emergencies. Imagine walking in the woods and meeting a bear. Your body's reaction to stress helps get ready to fight for your life or make a run for your life ("fight or flight"). Most emergencies in life do not occur in the woods but rather include overbearing bosses; a slow commute; a job that feels out of control; a job transfer or loss of a job; the wedding of a family member and a multitude of other life problems.

Drs. Friedman and Rosenman believe that personality determines how an individual handles stress and in that light consider stress to be a cause of heart attacks. Their Type A personality displays hostility, aggressiveness, and impatience. Type A personalities seem to be in a hurry in speech patterns as well as action. They cannot relax or put thoughts of the job out of their minds. "In the absence of Type A Behavior Pattern, coronary heart disease almost never occurs before 70 years of age, regardless of the fatty foods eaten, the cigarettes smoked, or the lack of exercise. But when this behavior pattern is present, coronary heart disease can easily erupt in one's thirties or forties."[10] Type B personalities do not suffer from a sense of urgency and are not overly boastful. Their physical recreation is marked by a feeling of fun rather than overassertiveness. They relax easily and work without undue agitation.

The Type A personality has been found to be more vulnerable to heart attack. The effects of the emotional stressor in conjunction with the variables discussed in chapter 5 make the Type A a high-risk candidate.

Some characteristics of Type A personality are:

- explosively accentuate words in normal speech
- move, walk, eat rapidly
- exhibit impatience
- try to think or do two things at once (polyphasic thinking)
- control conversation to your own interests
- feel guilty when relaxing
- have no spare time
- try to do too much in too short a time
- display characteristic gestures or nervous tics

Dr. Thomas Holmes has devised a scale that quantifies stress. By accumulating "stress points" the chance of suffering poor health becomes greater. Holmes's "Social Readjustment Scale" helps to predict potential for physical illness as the result of emotional stressors. The death of a spouse, divorce, and loss of job would be significant contributors to potential ill health. Even vacations bring additional stress (see chapter activity for further consideration).

Stress may be regarded as anything that causes change in the body. There are psychological/emotional stresses that raise blood pressure, increase heart rate, create tension in muscle, and alter the chemical balance of the body. The responses are called **psychosomatic**, that is, the mind changing the body.

Exercise is also a form of stress, since it changes physical function in the body, that is, heart rate, blood pressure, chemicals, and muscle tension. These responses are short-lived, occurring during the exercise, and in the long run produce positive changes in function called the **training effect**. Exercise seems to relax the body so that the negative effects of psychological stress do not have the impact on function to the extent of creating harm (stage of exhaustion).

Exercise is important in lessening the damaging effect of emotional stress. Selye believes that disproportionate stress on one organ or system of the body can be equalized by distributing the stress over a wider part of the body through exercise. Keeping the body fit will help it to withstand external stresses, whether emotional or physical. Exercise and its resulting fitness seem to be able to change the mind; thus, a **somatopsychic** chain of events occurs, that is, the body changes the mind.

Regular exercise, which has been referred to as *"nature's best tranquilizer,"* clearly allows you to feel better. Feelings of well-being associated

*Everyone needs exercise.*

with exercise have been traced in part to naturally occurring hormones called **endorphins** (endogenous morphine). Both physiological and psychological mechanisms are in effect during exercise and it is difficult to distinguish the exact role that endorphins play in creating a "feel good" sensation.

Hippocrates, the Father of Medicine, reportedly used exercise to treat people suffering from depression. The ancient Greek idea was to treat a problem with its opposite. Consequently, for depression and its accompanying lethargy the remedy was activity.

Several theories have been developed to explain why the reaction to stress is reduced following exercise:

- The "time out" theory suggests that time spent away from the stressor reduces the body's reaction to them,
- The "opponent's process theory" supports the idea that the physical stress of exercise produces an "opposing response" to stressors thereby reducing their effects.
- The "sympathetic toughness concept" implies that repeated bouts of exercise and physical stress (exercise) may train the body to be less affected by psychological stress.

*Yoga*

Regardless of the theory, people have been found to display both lower reactivity to stress and improved ability to return to their pre-stress level.

## T'ai Chi and Yoga

Many of the positive outcomes of regular exercise are not outwardly visible. Physical activity has been shown to affect mental and emotional processes both during and after the exercise. Two such activity practices that have mind-body benefits are T'ai Chi and Yoga.

# THE ACTIVITY PYRAMID

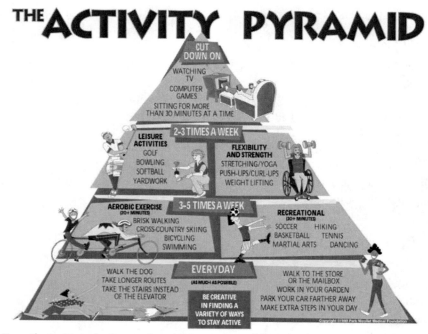

*From the Institute for Research and Education, HealthSystem Minnesota, © 1996. Reprinted by permission.*

For thousands of years T'ai Chi and Yoga have been accepted as an ideal exercise for lifelong well-being. These ancient arts have great potential for widespread use for all ages.

T'ai Chi combines slow graceful movements called forms into what has been described as moving meditation. T'ai Chi is based on the belief that good health results from balanced "chi" or life force.

## Exercise: A Matter of Choice

The decisions to be made in life are limitless and by no means easy. Decisions must often be made today that may not show their true impact for weeks, months, or even years to come. Making a choice regarding the inclusion of exercise in one's life is such a decision. The quality and quantity of life ahead very much depends on habits that are begun in the present: If you could omit *heredity, the two factors that would influence your well-being the most are exercise and diet.*

Lack of exercise and resulting low levels of fitness are very important risk factors in disease and early death. Large volumes of exercise are not necessary to produce significant improvement in health status; in fact, moderate exercise and fitness levels seem to offer considerable health benefit. Children and adults in America may be at risk because of low activity and fitness. This constitutes a public health problem of major proportions.

Including exercise as a life-style habit can make a substantial impact on both immediate and lifelong health status. The choice and commitment is up to each individual.

## Summary

The human body has a physiological need for exercise, which serves to enhance functional capacity to optimal levels. This, in turn, can affect one's health status and the tendency to resist the effects of degenerative diseases so prevalent in our sedentary society. This list of benefits that can be derived from exercise and resulting increased fitness seem to transcend the physical and begin to enhance mental and emotional factors as well.

Research supports several significant conclusions:

- Low levels of exercise and fitness are important risk factors for disease and early death.
- Relatively low levels of exercise produce definitive benefit: A little exercise is better than no exercise.
- The basic beliefs about exercise and its benefit rest on solid scientific foundation.
- Moderate exercise goals requires moderate exercise.

## A Look at Our Health Status

- More than 60 million people are overweight to the extent that it is dangerous.
- 8 million people have type 2 diabetes.
- 13.5 million people have CAD (coronary artery disease)
- 1.5 million people have a heart attack each year

- 50 million people have high blood pressure
- 250,000 people experience a hip fracture each year (due to osteoporosis)
- 95,000 are diagnosed with colon cancer each year.

Exercise has been shown to have a positive influence in combating the occurrence, rehabilitation and severity of these health related issues.

## Check Out These Websites

www.netsweat.com - Has been called the Grandmother of all the fitness links. Very user-friendly site that is dedicated to providing links for the various topics under health and fitness.

thriveonline.com - This site offers information on fitness, nutrition, weight, serenity, and much more! Offers expert advice, sample workouts, fitness strategies, and more!

primusweb.com/fitnesspartner - Gives practical info on how to overcome fitness plateaus, and ways to spice up your fitness routine to prevent boredom. Also has a large fitness library covering everything related to a fit, healthy lifestyle.

# Exercise: A Health Habit

Scientific study of the responses of the body to exercise began early in this century and has expanded since the 1950s. When the results of these studies are examined, there is strong evidence that regular exercise is an important health habit. Generally, it is revealed that sedentary lifestyles and low levels of physical fitness are associated with higher rates of morbidity and mortality. Recently, a study directed by Dr. Steven Blair at the Institute for Aerobics Research involving 10,224 men and 3,120 women covering a period of eight years was completed. In this study fitness was assessed via a treadmill stress test and participants were grouped in fitness categories based on results: low fitness level (bottom 20%); moderate fitness level (middle 40%); and high fitness level (upper 40%). When the data was analyzed, it was determined that men and women in the low fitness category were more than twice as likely to die from cancer, cardiovascular disease, and from all causes combined than those in the moderate fitness group. The lowest death rates from all causes were found in the high fitness group. When factors such as cigarette smoking, high cholesterol, family history of heart disease, high blood sugar levels, and high body mass index (overweight and obesity) were statistically adjusted for cause of death, it was found that low fitness level is just as important as other risk factors in early mortality; that is, low physical fitness is an independent risk factor for early death.

# Review Questions

1. What are "degenerative diseases?" Give three examples and tell how they relate to "exercise as medicine."

2. What "law of biology" illustrates the relationship between exercise and general body function? How would a broken leg be an example?

3. Review the year 2000 objectives. What do these indicate about the understanding, practice and importance of exercise for health?

CHAPTER ACTIVITY

# Exercise Knowledge Tally

## Purpose

To critically respond to statements about exercise and therefore gain a better understanding of facts that support or refute the statement.

## Procedure

Since this is not a test and no grade is involved, you can be honest in your responses; there is no penalty for guessing. Read each statement carefully and select your response by placing a checkmark or X in the appropriate blank space.

| Statement | Definitely False | Probably False | Not Sure | Probably True | Definitely True | Reference |
|---|---|---|---|---|---|---|
| 1. A lack of exercise as well as no exercise may cause tight shortened muscles | _____ | _____ | _____ | _____ | _____ | Chap 6 |
| 2. All exercise produces the same benefits | _____ | _____ | _____ | _____ | _____ | Chap 7 |
| 3. Regular exercise may help prevent and cure low back pain | _____ | _____ | _____ | _____ | _____ | Chap 8 |
| 4. Regular exercise can make bones stronger | _____ | _____ | _____ | _____ | _____ | Chap 2 |

| Statement | Definitely False | Probably False | Not Sure | Probably True | Definitely True | Reference |
|---|---|---|---|---|---|---|
| 5. For cardiovascular benefit to last, only a single exercise session is necessary | _____ | _____ | _____ | _____ | _____ | Chap 6 |
| 6. Regular exercise tends to raise someone's resting blood pressure | _____ | _____ | _____ | _____ | _____ | Chap 2 |
| 7. People who have fit muscular systems also have fit cardiovascular systems | _____ | _____ | _____ | _____ | _____ | Chap 7 |
| 8. Exercise can turn fat into muscle | _____ | _____ | _____ | _____ | _____ | Chap 8 |
| 9. Most problems of excess weight result from hormone problems | _____ | _____ | _____ | _____ | _____ | Chap 3 |
| 10. Static stretching is the best way to improve flexibility | _____ | _____ | _____ | _____ | _____ | Chap 8 |
| 11. Exercising a specific body part or place removes fat from the spot | _____ | _____ | _____ | _____ | _____ | Chap 3 |
| 12. Problems like depression, hypertension, and ulcer may partly be caused by a lack of exercise | _____ | _____ | _____ | _____ | _____ | Chap 2 |
| 13. Walking, running, tennis, and racquetball are all aerobic exercise | _____ | _____ | _____ | _____ | _____ | Chap 7 |
| 14. A regular program need not involve a great deal of time | _____ | _____ | _____ | _____ | _____ | Chap 7 |
| 15. All exercise burns the same number of calories | _____ | _____ | _____ | _____ | _____ | Chap 6 |

| Statement | Definitely False | Probably False | Not Sure | Probably True | Definitely True | Reference |
|---|---|---|---|---|---|---|
| 16. Intensity of exercise is measured by how much you sweat | _____ | _____ | _____ | _____ | _____ | Chap 6 |
| 17. Warm-up has little benefit and should only be performed by those in poor condition | _____ | _____ | _____ | _____ | _____ | Chap 6 |
| 18. Aerobic exercise must be performed at least three times per week for optimal benefit | _____ | _____ | _____ | _____ | _____ | Chap 7 |
| 19. For benefit, target heart rate must be 90% of your maximum | _____ | _____ | _____ | _____ | _____ | Chap 6 |
| 20. Calories don't count, only the type of food is important | _____ | _____ | _____ | _____ | _____ | Chap 3 |
| 21. Low-calorie diets produce the best weight and fat losses | _____ | _____ | _____ | _____ | _____ | Chap 3 |
| 22. Duration, frequency, and intensity are all forms of overload | _____ | _____ | _____ | _____ | _____ | Chap 6 |
| 23. Regular exercise can slow down the aging process | _____ | _____ | _____ | _____ | _____ | Chap 2 |
| 24. Active people are less likely to have heart attacks | _____ | _____ | _____ | _____ | _____ | Chap 5 |
| 25. Research has not shown any relationship of fitness to job performance | _____ | _____ | _____ | _____ | _____ | Chap 2 |
| 26. Exercise needs remain the same throughout one's life | _____ | _____ | _____ | _____ | _____ | Chap 6 |

| Statement | Definitely False | Probably False | Not Sure | Probably True | Definitely True | Reference |
|---|---|---|---|---|---|---|
| 27. The best way to burn fat is to exercise very hard—"no pain, no gain" | _____ | _____ | _____ | _____ | _____ | Chap 3 |
| 28. Using resistance (weight, etc.) is the best way to improve muscle strength | _____ | _____ | _____ | _____ | _____ | Chap 6,7 |
| 29. Anyone who exercises needs vitamin supplements and extra protein to build muscle | _____ | _____ | _____ | _____ | _____ | Chap 4 |
| 30. If you have an injury you should "work through it" | _____ | _____ | _____ | _____ | _____ | Chap 9 |

CHAPTER ACTIVITY

# Dealing with Stress

In today's complex and rapidly advancing technology, the physical effort required for daily living has been decreased significantly. Due to this ever-increasing pace of life, the human organism is being forced to adapt at a phenomenal rate. People are continually exposed to innumerable visual, auditory, and psychological stimuli to which they must make a variety of responses.

The attempt to deal successfully with these changing situations produces wear and tear on the body called stress. Prolonged stress, unless dealt with effectively, can elicit physiological, psychological, and emotional deterioration. However, when individuals learn to recognize stress the overall effect on the body can be diminished.

Researchers have determined that the body reacts to stress situations in a number of different patterns. It has also been shown that certain individuals exhibit different kinds of "stress symptoms." Stress symptoms that most commonly display themselves include the following: increased heart rate (HR), increased blood pressure (BP), increased respiration rate (RR), increased eye blink rate (EBR), pupil dilation, decreases in hand steadiness, and an increase in muscle tension.

## Part A—Measuring Stress

Dr. Thomas Holmes has published his "Social Readjustment Scale," which is a means of quantifying the stresses over a period of time. To determine the amount of stress that has occurred in your life during the last 12 months, simply check the appropriate events on the list provided and total your score. This score can be used to *predict* your chances of suffering illness within the next two years. *It merely gives an indication not a guarantee.*

# Stress Test

## The Social Readjustment Scale
*Developed by Dr. Thomas Holmes and Dr. Richard Rahe*

| Points | Rank | Event |
|--------|------|-------|
| 100 | _____ | 1. Death of Spouse |
| 73 | _____ | 2. Divorce |
| 65 | _____ | 3. Marital Separation |
| 63 | _____ | 4. Jail Term |
| 63 | _____ | 5. Death of Family Member |
| 53 | _____ | 6. Personal Injury |
| 50 | _____ | 7. Marriage |
| 47 | _____ | 8. Fired From Work |
| 45 | _____ | 9. Marital Reconciliation |
| 45 | _____ | 10. Retirement |
| 44 | _____ | 11. Change in Health of Family Member |
| 40 | _____ | 12. Pregnancy |
| 39 | _____ | 13. Sex Difficulties |
| 39 | _____ | 14. Gain New Family Member |
| 39 | _____ | 15. Business Readjustment |
| 39 | _____ | 16. Financial Change |
| 37 | _____ | 17. Death of Close Friend |
| 36 | _____ | 18. Change to New Line of Work |
| 35 | _____ | 19. Change amount of Arguments with Spouse |
| 33 | _____ | 20. Large Mortgage |
| 29 | _____ | 21. Child Leaves Home |
| 29 | _____ | 22. Trouble with In-laws |
| 28 | _____ | 23. Personal Achievement |
| 26 | _____ | 24. Wife Begin/End Work |
| 26 | _____ | 25. Begin/End Work |
| 25 | _____ | 26. Change Living Conditions |
| 24 | _____ | 27. Revise Personal Habits |
| 23 | _____ | 28. Trouble with Boss |
| 20 | _____ | 29. Change Work Hours or Conditions |
| 20 | _____ | 30. Change in Residence |
| 20 | _____ | 31. Change in School |
| 19 | _____ | 32. Change in Recreation |
| 19 | _____ | 33. Change in Church Activity |
| 18 | _____ | 34. Change in Social Activity |

## Stress Test—*Continued*

| Points | Rank | Event |
|--------|------|-------|
| 17 | _____ | 35. Small Mortgage Loan |
| 16 | _____ | 36. Change in Sleep Habits |
| 15 | _____ | 37. Change in Number of Family Get-Togethers |
| 15 | _____ | 38. Change in Eating Habits |
| 13 | _____ | 39. Vacation |
| 12 | _____ | 40. Christmas |
| 11 | _____ | 41. Minor Law violation |

(Total Points _____)

Total points of 50–100 show a Low-stress life. Over 100 to 200, a moderate-stress life. Over 200 to 300, a high-stress life. Over 300 indicates an extremely high-stress life.

## Daily Distress Test

| Behavior statement | Daily Frequency Rating | | |
|---|---|---|---|
| | Usually (2 points) | Sometimes (1 point) | Infrequently (0 points) |
| I am not able to find the time to relax. | _____ | _____ | _____ |
| When I do find the time, it is difficult to relax. | _____ | _____ | _____ |
| I have difficulty maintaining my concentration because of worrying or negative thoughts | _____ | _____ | _____ |
| At the end of the workday I have difficulty turning work off enough to start the next day. | _____ | _____ | _____ |
| I have tension, headaches, sleep disturbances, neck or shoulder pain, or lower back pain. | _____ | _____ | _____ |
| I feel muscle tension or have a nervous stomach or irritable bowel. | _____ | _____ | _____ |
| I use food, alcohol, or tobacco in response to distress. | _____ | _____ | _____ |
| I take any kind of drug to relax. | _____ | _____ | _____ |
| People in my immediate life, home, or workplace cause me to feel distressed. | _____ | _____ | _____ |
| I feel anxiety or a general emotional heaviness. | _____ | _____ | _____ |

From TCC Friends for Life Bulletin. Copyright by Tulane Cancer Center. Reprinted by permission.

**How did you score?**

0 to 5      You very rarely experience unhealthy stress and are at low risk.

6 to 12     You are at medium risk for experiencing unhealthy stress and may want to make a few changes in your daily habits.

13 to 20    You are at high risk for compromising your health because of daily stresses and you should seriously consider making some changes in your daily habits.

**What relieves stress?**

Deep breathing, aerobic activity (walking, running, cycling, hiking, swimming, etc.), doing a kind act for someone else, getting a massage, reading for enjoyment, strength training, stretching or yoga or meditation, taking a break, taking a long hot bath.

# Part C—Dealing with Stress

One of the greatest problems is the inability to relax—physically, mentally, and emotionally. If one can learn to relax physically, the simultaneous relaxation effects begin to be achieved emotionally and mentally.

This ability to consciously control body function forms the basis of relaxation techniques like yoga, biofeedback, and transcendental meditation (TM) as well as those developed by Jacobson, Rathbene, and Schade dealing with progressive muscle relaxation.

Dr. Herbert Benson of Harvard Medical School has developed a procedure that produces the same physiological changes as TM.

1. Sit comfortably in a quiet place.
2. Close eyes and relax all muscles.
3. Breathe easily and naturally through your nose. Inhale, then as you exhale say in your mind the word "one." Repeat "one" to yourself each time you breathe out.
4. "One" is a mantra, a mental device to anchor your thoughts. Your thoughts may wander to problems, events, or desires. Try to replace these thoughts with the word "one," and your steady breathing rhythm.

"Meditate" for 10 to 20 minutes, twice daily. Given time and practice the technique will work.

## *Questions*

1. Do you believe it is possible to have "psychological stress" without physiological involvement? How does this relate to "psychosomatic?"

2. Explain briefly the statement "one person's stress may be another person's pleasure."

3. How does exercise work as a stress management technique?

# CHAPTER 2

# Fitness as an Important Dimension of Human Health

## What Is Physical Fitness?

Physical fitness is a term often used but little understood by many people, because fitness is very difficult to define. A widely accepted concept of fitness involves a condition of living that characterizes the degree to which a person is able to function efficiently in daily life. Doctors may indicate that fitness could substitute for health; athletes may indicate that fitness is synonymous with skill, speed, power, and models may indicate that fitness requires a slim, shapely figure. In essence, each is correct by describing one part of what fitness includes. It must be remembered that fitness does not come in a "have" or "have not" package. Everyone possesses those qualities described by the doctor, athlete, and model. Those qualities and many others all describe fitness as a quality of life, with only the amount or degree showing variation from person to person. As described previously, some parts of fitness directly affect health status whereas others primarily affect performance or skill-related fitness (sports/athletics).

Each person should possess those qualities of fitness which support health and well-being. These qualities are:

- **Cardiorespiratory Efficiency**—The optimal functional capacity of the heart, lungs, and blood vessels.
- **Body Weight—Body Composition Measures**—optimal total body weight and lean/fat proportions.
- **Musculoskeletal Efficiency** (strength, endurance, and flexibility)—Optimal levels of muscular function accompanied by optimal ranges of motion and integrity of body segments.

# Health-Related Fitness

Since these components of fitness have direct bearing on health status, they become the focus in the pursuit of optimal physical fitness. This is the most favorable health which is needed for the enthusiastic undertaking of daily responsibilities and tasks as well as recreational and exercise activities. It is optimal physical fitness that aids in creating a life-style experience that the unfit cannot enjoy or understand. People who possess optimal physical fitness tend to *look better, feel better, and experience good health, which all contribute to the quality of life.*

Optimal cardiorespiratory function, musculoskeletal efficiency, and body composition are the most important **components of fitness for health**.

**Strength** is probably the most familiar component of fitness. It is defined as the maximum amount of force that can be produced by muscle. Strength is important to all sports and daily activities. Whether one is exercising or carrying groceries, muscular strength supports the activity. Strength training (weight training) results in some enlargement (hypertrophy) of muscle and a resulting increase in the ability to produce force.

Research has established a relationship between muscular strength and bone density. The stronger the muscle, the greater the bone density. Thus, this may have significant impact on osteoporosis.

**Muscular endurance** is the ability of muscle to produce repetitive movement over extended periods of time. The ability to do sit-ups, pushups, shovel snow, wash windows, and paint are all examples of when muscular endurance becomes very important.

**Flexibility** is the ability to move the joints of the body. Bending, stretching, twisting all involve the use of muscle to move a skeletal joint throughout a range of motion. Maintenance of flexibility at optimal levels is important so that the activities of daily living (ADL) can be accomplished without difficulty.

**Body composition** is the component of fitness that relates to total body weight and its parts—fat and lean body weight. The amounts of fat and lean tissue, like muscle and bone, form a proportion that is more important than total body weight. The relative amounts of lean body weight and fat weight are very much related to health and fitness.

**Cardiorespiratory efficiency** is the most important fitness component. The ability of the body to supply and deliver oxygen is the key to life. All activities depend on muscle function, which in turn is determined by adequate oxygen supply. Efficient functioning of the heart and lungs is a basic requirement for the enjoyment of activities that support fitness, as well as health.

# Why Exercise?

Why then, is fitness, the result of exercise important? Surveys would produce a listing of hundreds of reasons. Basically, there are only two:

1. **To Create a Physical Change**—to lose weight/fat; to reduce blood pressure; to reduce the effects of stress; to reduce a diabetic condition; to reduce osteoporosis; to reduce cholesterol; to increase strength; to increase endurance; to reduce the effects of smoking; to decrease fatigue; to reduce low back pain; and to feel better.

### Disease Dangers

Research has found the lack of physical activity to be a direct cause of numerous harmful diseases.

**Percentage of disease attributable to physical inactivity**

| | |
|---|---|
| Stroke | 24% |
| Osteoporosis | 24 |
| Type 2 diabetes | 21 |
| Coronary-artery disease | 19 |
| Colon cancer | 18 |
| Hypertension | 14 |
| Breast Cancer | 14 |

Source: *Newsweek*, March 26, 2007

2. **To Prevent a Physical Change**—to prevent weight gain/fat gain; to prevent increases in blood pressure; to prevent the deterioration related to stress; to prevent adult diabetes; to prevent osteoporosis; to prevent increases in cholesterol; to prevent losses of strength/endurance; to prevent low back pain; and to prevent feeling lousy.

**Long-Term (Training) Effects:** Changes that occur in the body after regular exercise. The time span will vary but usually consists of exercise programs done regularly (3-5 times per week) for a period of several weeks.

The beneficial changes will depend on the specificity of the exercise program in determining *the training effect*. These changes include:

- Increased size of the heart: The heart, as any muscle, will increase in overall size in response to exercise. The walls will become thicker and stronger allowing for greater efficiency and increased work capacity.
- Increased stroke volume: All chambers of the heart will become capable of pumping increased amounts of blood each time they contract. This amount of blood pumped with each contraction of the heart is called the stroke volume. The heart muscle can get more blood to the body with each beat as the left ventricle forces more blood out of the heart with each contraction (called a systole).

## Weighty Woman

A 2002 study found that unfit women, whatever their weight, had a higher risk of death compared with fit women.

**Relative risk of death in fit and unfit women.**

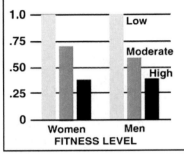

Source: *Newsweek*, March 26, 2007

## Age and Activity

Exercise is particularly vital to older people, who are often more susceptible to health problems.

**Relative risk of death in people 60 and older**

Source: *Newsweek*, March 26, 2007

- Decreased resting pulse rate: The body's need for blood will be satisfied by fewer beats per minute as each beat represents greater stroke volume. The heart is capable of supplying enough blood by performing less work. This increased efficiency can be noticed by a decrease in the number of beats per minute.

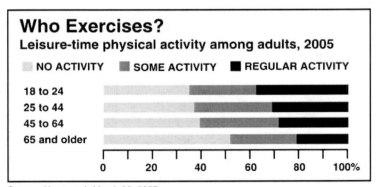

## Who Exercises?

**Leisure-time physical activity among adults, 2005**

NO ACTIVITY    SOME ACTIVITY    REGULAR ACTIVITY

18 to 24
25 to 44
45 to 64
65 and older

0    20    40    60    80    100%

Source: *Newsweek*, March 26, 2007

- Decreased exercise pulse rate: The maximum heart rate will decrease with age, but conditioned people will have lower exercise pulse rates regardless of age. The efficiency of the heart is reflected during exercise by having to beat at a lower rate.
- Faster pulse rate recovery: The exercised person will have a faster return to normal pulse rate after an exercise bout. The increased pulse rate recovery occurs because you are capable of providing the cells with more oxygenated blood and removing fatigue products after exercise. The cell needs will be satisfied more quickly than in the deconditioned individual.
- Faster oxygen debt recovery: The respiratory system is capable of an increased ability to exchange air with an increased ability to absorb oxygen from the air. The body will be provided with enough oxygen for the need to be satisfied.
- Increased ability to sustain activity for long periods of time: An increase in the length of exercise time will be readily apparent due to increased physiological efficiency in the production of energy, supply of oxygen, and removal of fatigue products.
- A decrease in the amount of body fat: Exercise that uses entire body movement will place significantly greater demands on energy expenditure. Consequently the body must supply more energy, which is achieved through various metabolic processes. A strenuous exercise program could burn off as much as 10 times the calories needed at rest. Exercise, in conjunction with proper diet, would aid in reducing body fat because the additional energy would be supplied from stored fat.
- Increased size of muscle fibers: The muscle fibers will increase in size, providing greater tone and muscle definition. The amount of increase will depend on the intensity of the exercise and will be subject to the anatomical differences between individuals and between the sexes.
- Increased muscular strength: Exercise programs that place increasing stress on the musculature will produce impressive strength gains in the muscle or muscle groups being exercised. Skeletal bone density will also increase, therefore helping to prevent osteoporosis.
- Increased muscular endurance: Exercise programs that increase the number of repetitions a muscle or muscle group performs will produce an increased capacity of the muscles to continue in the particular exercise before muscle fatigue occurs.

| A Summary of the Adaptation Effects of Endurance Training after Several Weeks | |
|---|---|
| **Measure** | **Change** |
| Myocardial size and weight | Increase |
| Muscle capillarization | Increase |
| Percentage of body fat | Decrease |
| Hemoglobin (carries oxygen) | Increase |
| Vital Capacity (lung capacity) | Increase |
| Serum Cholesterol | No change/or decrease |
| HDL Cholesterol | Increase |
| LDL Cholesterol | Decrease |
| Triglycerides | Decrease |
| Total Blood Volume | Increase |
| Systolic Blood Pressure | Decrease/no change |
| Diastolic Blood Pressure | Decrease/no change |
| Heart rate (Resting) | Decrease |
| Stroke volume | Increase |

• Reduced emotional stress: Regular, continuous exercise provides an outlet for stress and enables you to have a satisfying psychological experience while gaining physical benefit as well.

Moderate goals require moderate exercise. Not everyone needs or wants the same amount of exercise. Some people choose to run marathons; others choose to take a nice walk. Research supports the need for physical activity—just moving, thusly requiring muscular effort—and its benefits. Exercise can be considered "formalized physical activity" performed in a certain manner, effort level and length of time on a regular basis. Merely becoming more physically active produces benefits—not equal to high level conditioning (exercise)—but benefits just the same.

# Fitness: Interest and Action

Eighty percent of American adults say that they are either "somewhat satisfied" or "very satisfied" with their physical condition, according to a recent survey completed by the University of Michigan, Ann Arbor. The director of the study, Dr. Christine L. Brooks, finds these responses alarming because the vast majority of these individuals never did any form of physical activity that would even begin to challenge their cardiovascular systems. The most frequent activity indicated was walking. This study was supported by findings reported by the National Center for Health Statistics Survey of 1979 which indicated that 58 percent of adults do not exercise regularly, but 80 percent consider themselves to be as active or more active than others of the same age group.

Additionally, relative to understanding exercise, most Americans are not knowledgeable about the scientific recommendations for frequency, intensity, and duration of exercise. The University of Michigan study raises significant questions about the popularity of exercise; the participation rate by adults; and the scientific understanding of exercise.

# Exercise Lite—Exercise Heavy

It is important to remember that for whatever reason one chooses to exercise, it is never necessary to do so at "all out effort levels." However, some effort is necessary. Someone must do more than take a bath, pull the plug, and fight the current!

A new recommendation from the Centers of Disease Control and the American College of Sports Medicine regarding physical activity can be regarded as *exercise lite*—accumulating 30 minutes of moderate physical activity most days of the week. Almost everything from working in the yard to doing household chores would qualify as physical activity. The support of exercise lite lies in the research which has indicated that if you take a totally inactive person and have that person do something, the effects will have a relatively measurable impact. However, the true benefit relative to the effect on quality of life is very questionable. Doing something is better than doing nothing.

Since exercise-lite does not have significant benefit for aerobic fitness (heart/lung), muscular fitness, flexibility, body composition/weight control and overall health status perhaps we should *exercise-heavy.* This effort takes many forms and would subscribe to the guidelines set forth which create an exercise prescription (see Chapter 7). An exercise prescription formalizes what will be done, how hard, how long and how often. As a result the benefits are very predictable and significant which will impact on looking better, feeling better and functioning better.

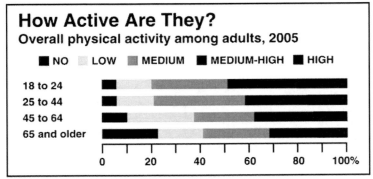

Source: *Newsweek,* March 26, 2007

# Summary

Physical fitness characterizes the degree to which a person is able to function efficiently. Each person has different fitness needs depending on his or her individual life-style. The components usually needed for good fitness are muscular strength, muscular endurance, flexibility, cardiovascular endurance. The long-term effects of exercise programs done at least three times a week for several weeks include an increase in heart size, increased stroke volume, decreased resting pulse rate, faster recovery rate of the heart, increased ability to sustain the heart for long periods of time, increased caloric burn off, increased muscle tone, increased muscle strength, and increased muscle endurance.

Most of us have learned some commonsense "health rules" from our parents, grandparents, aunts, uncles, and teachers, ranging from "smoking is bad for you" and "breakfast is the most important meal of the day" to "don't get fat." Research from all areas of the medical and physiological areas implicates many health habits as factors in creating a wide range of major disease problems. One such health habit is exercise/physical activity.

When consideration is made relative to the result of exercise/physical activity, fitness, it is reasonable to expect improved health and longevity. An editorial in the Journal of the American Medical Association in 1978 supported the concept that the most promising factor for improving public health rests with what people can be motivated to do for themselves.

*"There is more to health than just feeling good-GET FIT"*
David E. Jenkins, Physical Education Teacher
Ridgewood Public Schools, New Jersey

# Check Out These Websites

www.bodyisland.com - One of the few websites updated daily to provide the latest nutrition, health and fitness news, along with links and advice. Very informational site!

www.healthanswers.com - This very informational site is focused on overall health, not just fitness and exercise. It includes information on every health topic from asthma to sleep disorders to weight control. A must see!

exercise.about.com - Features many common exercise topics to help the beginner through advanced reach their goals. Includes topics such as: cycling, nutrition, running, yoga, and much more!

# Review Questions

1. Why doesn't fitness come in a "have or have not" package, and what qualities are part of health related fitness?

2. What does "health-related" fitness mean and why are the components important?

3. List five long term benefits of exercise. Why may these be important?

4. Explain the concept: Moderate goals require moderate exercise.

5. How does prevention and rehabilitation relate to the two reasons presented for exercising?

# CHAPTER 3

# Body Composition—
# Your Look
# Present and Future

In addition to being of major importance to physiological efficiency, psychological well-being, and self-image, weight control is probably the most abused aspect of self-maintenance. This is due to basic misunderstanding about the causes of physical change, which is why obesity continues to be a major medical and personal fitness problem. Almost half of all Americans think they need to lose weight. A third actually do.

Diet fads, gimmicks, and quackery gross more than $100 million each year. The public has indicated its gullibility by spending some $500 million each year on short-term cure-all gadgets for fitness and fat control.

Since obesity ranks as such a major problem—mentally, emotionally, and physically—some consideration should be given to what causes the onset of this condition. Obesity probably has no one single cause but rather is caused by an interplay of a number of factors. From this standpoint it may be said that there are various causes in various people, but these factors acting alone or in any combination have one final manifestation—increased fat storage leading toward obesity.

Presently, four principal factors appear to control weight gain and potential obesity. When considered as an *obesity syndrome*, these factors work together to produce one inevitable result: increased fatness. These factors are:

- *Genetic influences*—those inherited tendencies toward obesity which include physical and biochemical markers.
- *Sedentary life-style*—inactivity that starts early in the childhood years and has lifelong consequences affecting caloric expenditure and body composition.

39

- *Overeating*—insensitivity to the energy equation, which involves calories consumed relative to calories expended.
- *Psychological inducements*—those associations made with food, that is, love, security, comfort, socializing, the use of food as a stress escape mechanism, and the constant barrage of advertisements which encourage eating.

The cause of extreme obesity appears to be more genetic than previously believed. Researchers have discovered an obesity gene that appears to predispose someone to heavy weight and excess fat. This genetic tendency would affect all of the biochemical, physiological, and neurological factors that play a role in obesity. While the precise implications of this finding are yet to be determined, it must be concluded that the cause of obesity reflects a complicated mix of environmental and genetic factors.

Earlier this year a report by the Centers for Disease Control confirmed a suspicion that most experts held, that is, obesity is caused by eating too much relative to the energy expended.

- Adult women are now eating 335 calories more than they did in 1971;
- Adult men are now eating 168 calories more than they did in 1971;
- Adults ate 1775 pounds of food in the year 2000 which is an increase from 1497 pounds in 1970;
- Most of the increase in calories comes from carbohydrates (refined, processed)
- Twice as many Americans are obese compared to thirty years ago, enough that the CDC has declared this problem an epidemic;
- 15 percent of children and teenagers are overweight which is three times the number compared to 1980.

# The Set-Point Theory

A great deal of research over recent years supports the belief that there is a **set-point** for body weight and fatness that is automatically maintained by all our biochemical physiology. The theory is that without external influences the body strives to create and maintain a certain genetically determined weight and fatness. Some persons have a high setting or larger capacity for fat storage, whereas others have a low setting or smaller capacity for fat storage. Obviously, variations exist between the two extremes. The

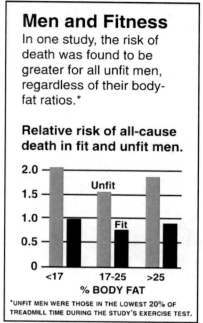

**Fat America**

Being overweight or obese greatlyincreases the likeli-hood of developing several diseases, including CAD.

**Percentage of people who are overweight or obese**

1976-80 · 88-94 · 99-00 · 01-02 · 03-04

Source: *Newsweek*, March 26, 2007

**Men and Fitness**

In one study, the risk of death was found to be greater for all unfit men, regardless of their body-fat ratios.*

**Relative risk of all-cause death in fit and unfit men.**

% BODY FAT

*UNFIT MEN WERE THOSE IN THE LOWEST 20% OF TREADMILL TIME DURING THE STUDY'S EXERCISE TEST.

Source: *Newsweek*, March 26, 2007

center for this set-point appears to be a section in the brain called the hypo-thalamus.

The set-points in animals and humans seem to change in response to two external factors: what you do (exercise) and what you eat. Sweet and fatty foods appear to drive the set-point higher. If the set-point theory is at all correct, exercise appears to be the best, if not the only, method for controlling a high set-point.

# Physical Appearance

We are all products of **heredity** and **environment.** These two factors in life have determined everything that we have been, what we are now, and will determine what we will be; in other words, what we get from parents and what we do with what we get.

Since the problem of weight control seems to focus on physical appear-ance, it is important to understand why you appear as you do.

# Somatotyping

Your physical appearance is called a **somatotype** (body build). There are three classifications of somatotypes—**endomorph**, **mesomorph**, and **ectomorph**. Each has specific characteristics based on the relative predominance of bone, fat, and muscle. Some of the general characteristics that apply more commonly to these body builds are:

**Endomorph**—A large soft bulging body, a "pear-shaped"' appearance, short arms and legs, most of the body weight centered around the hips and abdomen, lack of bony angularity, and heavy fat pad distribution. The endomorph's response to conditioning is slow, but great improvements are possible. See page **43** for illustration.

**Mesomorph**—Solid, muscular, large-boned physique, most of the body weight is away from the abdominal area, wide shoulders, narrow hips, and well-muscled throughout. Mesomorphs respond very well to conditioning. See page **43** for illustration.

**Ectomorph**—Slender bodies and a slight build, very little body fat, light musculature, long arms and legs, bony in appearance, narrow chest and hips, and generally linear in appearance. Ectomorphs' response to conditioning may be slow with greater success in endurance activities and those involving support of the body weight and little body contact. See page **43** for illustration.

# Assessing Body Build

It should be obvious that most people have some characteristics of each body type because everyone has certain amounts of bone, fat, and muscle. Dr. William Sheldon, M.D., developed the most comprehensive system of somatotyping, that is, classifying physical appearances. His system is based on the use of a number scale (1-7) indicating to what degree characteristics from each category are present in an individual's appearance. Using the scale, the number 1 would indicate the lowest degree and the number 7 would indicate the highest degree of represented characteristics. Therefore, a somatotype is represented by three numbers: The first always indicates endomorphy, the middle number always indicates mesomorphy, and the third number always indicates ectomorphy. For example, if you were to give a somatotype to Santa Claus, the first number may be 7—indicating maximum "roundness"; the middle number may be 3—indicating "muscularity"; and the third number may be 1—indicating "linearity." So the somatotype becomes 7-3-1, a numerical picture of a physical appearance. The body type named depends on where the highest number is found. Santa Claus would be called an endomorph, since the highest number is in the first category.

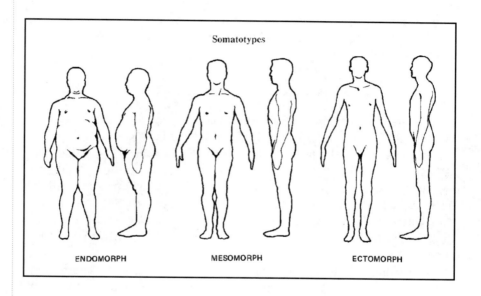

Somatotypes

ENDOMORPH          MESOMORPH          ECTOMORPH

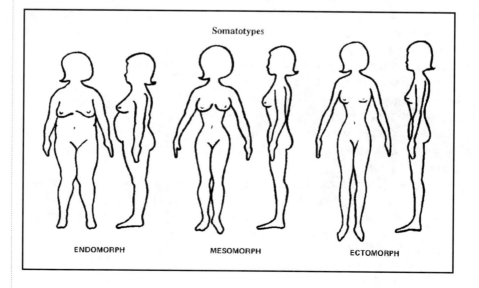

Somatotypes

ENDOMORPH          MESOMORPH          ECTOMORPH

# Body Weight and Body Composition

Your **total body weight (TBW)** will generally be related to your somatotype due to the predominance of fat, muscle, or bone. If you are like most
Americans your weight will receive considerable attention during your lifetime, and well it should. Most people rely on a bathroom scale and a
height-weight chart to determine if they are underweight, proper weight, or
overweight. Although this method is easy and certainly accessible, it may
also be very misleading.

## Overweight and Overfat

When using a scale and height-weight charts you are finding only total
body weight (TBW), not how much of that weight is bone, fat, and muscle.
This becomes important because the so-called ideal weight on a chart may
vary as much as twenty pounds. The important consideration is not only
body weight but also how much of the total is lean body weight and how
much of the total is fat (adipose). **Lean body weight (LBW)** is composed
of essentially four elements: bone, muscle, viscera (internal organs), and
fluids. The other component of total weight is **fat weight (FW)**, called
adipose tissue.

When using height-weight charts a general guideline for determining
overweight is to follow a "**10% rule**." If you exceed a recommended weight
by more than 10% you are considered to be **overweight**. However, it does
not reveal whether this "excess weight" is due predominantly to lean body
weight or too much fat.

A "**20% rule**" exists as well in relation to body weight and weight charts.
If you exceed a recommended weight by more than 20%, you are considered to be **obese**.

Although the terms overweight and overfat (obese) are used inter-
changeably, they are not necessarily synonymous. Overweight reflects only
total body weight, not what composes that total. Overfat reflects an aspect
of body composition that represents the presence of too much adipose as
part of the total.

Many individuals may be overweight but not overfat. Some individuals,
like professional football players, for example, may be 20 to 30 lb or more
above a recommended weight (height-weight table). Technically they are
overweight, but most of that weight is lean body weight with just a small
percentage of fat. Consequently, these individuals would not be classified
as overfat.

# Determining How Much Fat and Lean

How does one determine the composition of their total body weight, that is, how much lean weight and how much fat weight? There are a number of methods, which vary in sophistication. Probably, the most simple method is to stand in front of a mirror with minimal or no clothes on. Mirrors tend to tell the truth.

Other relatively common methods include the following:

1. **Hydrostatic Weighing**—comparison of your weight while you are under water to your scale weight. This is considered the best method but it is not very practical.
2. **Skinfold Measurement**—a caliper is used to measure the thickness of skin and subcutaneous (under skin) fat. The thickness is measured at

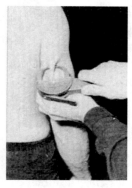

*Triceps skinfold*

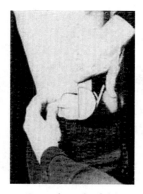

*Suprailiac skinfold*

*Subscapular skinfold*

*Biceps skinfold*

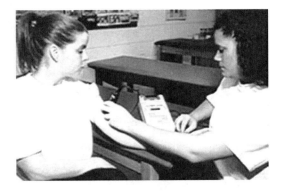

various points on the body and results yield an estimate of total fat. This method is very practical and is considered good because most of your fat is subcutaneous, about 60%.

3. **Ultrasound, Light Wave**, and **Electrical Impedance**—all are results of "high-tech" advancements and involve sophisticated equipment. The amount of fat is determined by the speed of sound, light, or electricity through fat and muscle, which have different densities.

4. **Body Mass Index** and **Ponderal Index**—are mathematical methods based on height and weight. These are very easy to do but do not allow for differences in somatotype.

## How Much Body Fat?

As indicated in a previous section, a certain amount of body fat is always present in each individual. Body fat is classified as either essential fat or storage fat. The **essential fat** is that located in various organs of the body such as the heart, lungs, liver, spleen, kidneys, intestines, and brain. **Storage fat** accumulates in adipose tissue found surrounding internal organs and subcutaneously. A certain amount of fat is both necessary and valuable to adequate physiological function. However, a point does exist at which an individual can possess too much fat.

Generally recomended body fat levels for adults:
- Men: 15% to 20% of total body weight
- Women: 25% to 30% of total body weight

The relative standards for both sexes reflecting overfatness would be above 20% for men and above 30% for women. The disparity between the two standards for obesity exists due to a greater amount of essential fat that is found in the female. A high percentage of body fat may occur at any total body weight and has a significant effect on normal physiological function and health.

It must be remembered that although guidelines exist for both weight and fatness, *adjustments must be made on an individual basis* that reflects body build or somatotype. For example, a person who is an endomorph is genetically destined to have higher amounts of fat than other body types and should not be expected to be able to create or maintain a very low percentage of fat. Also, a mesomorph would probably be heavier (TBW) than other body builds due to higher levels of lean body mass.

## Consequences of Obesity

When total percent body fat exceeds what is considered average or optimal, the amount of fat begins to have deleterious effects on health. **Since about 40% of our population can be considered obese, it is easy to understand why obesity is considered a medical problem in and of itself, in addition to causing or contributing to others.**

The list of dangers of being obese includes:

- diabetes
- hypertension
- heart disease
- stroke
- respiratory ailments
- kidney disease
- gall stones
- surgical risk
- pregnancy problems
- less resistance to infection
- longevity
- social discrimination
- psychological-emotional problems

In addition, where you are carrying excess body fat, as your *genetic fat pattern*, is significant. Scientific research has revealed two classic fat distribution patterns: **android** and **gynoid**, referring to male and female, respectively. The android pattern resembles an "apple shape," with the largest portion of weight around the middle. The gynoid pattern resembles a "pear shape," with most of the weight in the lower half. The apple shape is not restricted to males and the pear shape is not restricted to females. These fat storage tendencies are genetic.

Research studies have found that apple-shaped fat storage is accompanied by increased risk for high cholesterol, glucose intolerance (diabetes), and high blood pressure. This cluster of factors in the android fat pattern is called **syndome X or metabolic syndrome**. For pear-shaped fat storage, the most difficult problem may be the nonresponsiveness of these fat cells to diet and exercise. These fat cells cling to their fat content more tenaciously, therefore making diet and exercise efforts very frustrating. The risks of heart disease, diabetes, and hypertension do not appear to exist at the same level as with the apple shape fat storage pattern.

A *waist-to-hip* ratio is a method of assessing health risk relative to fat-pattern distribution. To compute this ratio, measure your waist (on skin, no clothing) and your hips (around the buttocks). Then divide the waist measurement by the hip measurement.

## Causes of Obesity

As mentioned previously, there is probably no one cause of obesity, but rather it is caused by an interaction of many factors.

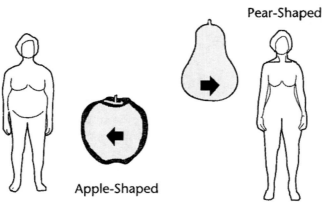

### Taking Shape

Scientists have learned that the male pattern of obesity--that is, gaining weight in the abdomen--puts women at higher risk of having a heart attack. Recent findings have emphasized this, reporting that even thinner women who are apple-shaped are at higher risk than obese but pear-shaped women who carry weight in their hips and thighs.

Pear-Shaped

Apple-Shaped

The major factor in developing obesity revolves around the food you eat, that is, the number of calories you consume. A **calorie** is an energy value of food. Different foods and varying amounts of food will enable the body to produce energy through a process called **metabolism**. Each individual requires a certain amount of calories (energy) just to live. This is called your **resting metabolic rate (RMR)**. The basal metabolic rate is the amount of energy the body needs to carry on all its internal (basic) body functions. The mature adult needs approximately 11 calories/lb to support the basal metabolism of the body. Thus, a person with greater mass requires more calories for basal metabolism than a lighter individual. If you consume more calories than you expend, it will result in the storage of unused calories as fat.

For some individuals, who may have both a genetic predisposition for obesity and a metabolic function that allows for greater fat storage, the number of calories they eat may not matter, since they will always store more as fat. Early determination of such a tendency is critical as is the need for dietary control and exercise.

When fat is stored in the body it is done so in **adipose tissue** in cells called **adipocytes**. Fat cells can enlarge (**hypertrophy**) as they store more fat. The storage form of fat is called **triglyceride**. Research indicates that a fat cell can reach a point of hypertrophy where it then will divide or undergo **hyperplasia** resulting in more fat cells. Once a fat cell is formed it is permanent. Diet, exercise or diet and exercise will not affect the number of fat cells but will affect the size of existing fat cells. Surgical removal of fat called **liposuction** is the only way to rid the body of fat cells.

In spite of hundreds of diets and diet plans such as Atkins, Stillman, the water diet, the peanut butter diet, the drinking mans diet, NutriSystem, Jenny Craig, and Weight Watchers as well as gadgets and gimmicks such as spot reducing creams, pro-collagen anti-cellulite body complex and calorie blocking pills. The key to weight management is to regulate calorie intake relative to calorie expenditure.

By regulating the energy equation, body weight and fatness can be better controlled over many years. The Center for Disease Control now recognizes successful weight loss as losing more than 5% of one's total body weight **and** maintaining that loss for at least one year. The key for long lasting results emphasizes exercise.

Attempts should be made to avoid continuous loss and regain of body weight called **the yo-yo syndrome**. Evidence indicates that each time weight loss is attempted it is more difficult and takes longer. Each time weight is regained it occurs faster and usually results in greater weight and fatness.

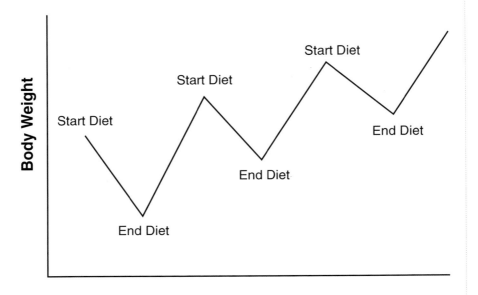

## The Role of Exercise

Weight control is a matter of controlling energy. It involves manipulating the variables that affect the energy equation. The two related sides of this equation involve the energy we consume in food (calories) and the energy we expend throughout the day largely for two purposes, resting metabolic requirements (RMR) and activity. When these two sides of the equation are equal, that is, calories in equal calories out, an isocaloric balance is created.

Energy expenditure includes several factors. The single largest expenditure of energy is the RMR (sometimes referred to as BMR, Basal Metabolic Requirements). This includes the energy used to maintain bodily functions in a resting state and is affected by body size (especially lean body mass), gender, and age.

Physical activity and exercise during the day also increase energy expenditure. The total caloric expenditure is determined by the length of time of activity/exercise and the effort required during that period of time.

Another factor that impacts the RMR is the energy required for the digestion, absorption, and transportation of nutrients after eating. This is referred to as the **thermic effect of eating** (TEE) or **dietary-induced thermogenesis** (DIT). The ingestion of food (eating) increases the energy expenditure by the body. Some food types contribute significantly to this process. Complex carbohydrates produce a high DIT compared to fats, which have a much lower effect (see chapter 4 for further discussion).

There are probably as many ways of dealing with weight control as there are people who are involved in that endeavor. Unfortunately, not enough people use exercise as one of those methods. Most use diet after diet after diet. Research over the years has shown a 95% failure rate with the "diet only" approach; that is, people just don't keep the weight off for more than a few months. This repeated cycle of weight loss followed by the regaining of weight is referred to as the "Yo-Yo syndrome." Each time the attempt is made to lose weight, it takes longer and less weight is lost and then the regain is faster with more of the weight being fat.

Interestingly, research completed over the past 10 years supports the fact that *the one factor that is most influential in preventing, reducing, and controlling obesity is exercise.*

The most effective weight loss is one that occurs over an extended period of time and involves a loss of about *1 lb per week.* This approach allows for a long-lasting modification of eating and activity habits. Exercise can make a significant contribution to the loss of body fat, especially when combined with a prudent choice of foods.

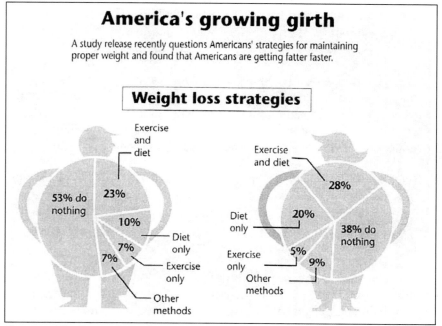

# America's growing girth

A study release recently questions Americans' strategies for maintaining proper weight and found that Americans are getting fatter faster.

## Weight loss strategies

Exercise and diet

53% do nothing   23%
10%
Diet only
7%
7%   Exercise only
Other methods

Exercise and diet
28%
Diet only   20%
38% do nothing
Exercise only   5%
9%
Other methods

*Courtesy: The Bergen Record.*

One lb of fat equals about 3,500 calories. Therefore, to lose 1 lb of fat you must perform enough activity to expend that much energy. This involves an unbelievable amount of physical exertion. However, when regular exercise is combined with caloric reduction, benefits are virtually guaranteed. For example, Golding and Zuti conducted a study in which three groups of women, all 20 to 40 lb overweight, were placed on a 500-calorie-per-day deficit for 16 weeks. One group was using a caloric restriction only approach, another group used an exercise only approach, and the third group combined caloric restriction plus increased activity. The results were as follows: The diet group loss was an average of 11.7 lb (9.3 lb fat and 2.4 lb lean body weight); the exercise group loss was an average of 10.6 lb (12.6 lb fat loss but a gain of 2 lb of lean body weight); and the combination group loss was an average of 12 lb (13 lb of fat and a 1 lb gain in lean body weight).

"The benefits of exercise in weight control extend far beyond the number of calories burned during the activity. In addition to raising the BMR for up to 15 hours afterward, exercise has been shown to have an appetite-suppressing effect, to enhance self-image and to reduce feelings of tension, anxiety and depression that prompt many people to overeat. Any kind of exercise is helpful that involves prolonged movement of the body's long muscles, as does walking, running, stair-climbing, swimming, cycling, skiing and skating."

In a study in California, 34 obese persons who had failed to maintain a weight loss on diet alone were started on a daily exercise program while consuming an unrestricted diet. All 11 who persisted for a year or more, most of them walking at least half an hour a day, lost weight—22 lb on the average—without dieting.

Exercise is also crucial to maintaining muscle tissue during a weight-loss program. A Chicago study among 32 college women who were 20% or more overweight showed that those who jogged three times a week and followed a reduced calorie diet lost more body fat and less lean muscle tissue than those who simply dieted.

However, Dr. Barry A. Franklin of Sinai Hospital in Detroit cautioned that passive exercise devices that "do the work for you" and spot-reducing gadgets are ineffective in producing weight loss or loss of selected fat deposits. "Unfortunately, the primary reduction often occurs in the exerciser's wallet," he said.

Permanent and long-lasting "cures" for obesity have yet to be discovered. The combination of exercise and diet appears to be the most effective approach to taking off pounds and keeping them off. To lose fat you must expend more calories than you consume. A moderate reduction in calories is the key when accompanied by the best exercise for fat burning, which is aerobic. By using large muscle movements that elevate heart rate and the supply, delivery, and use of oxygen, aerobic exercise triggers muscle to burn more fat as fuel. This occurs predominately at lower levels of effort (intensity) and longer time periods (duration) of exercise, with 30 to 45 minutes being optimal. At higher levels of intensity (70% HR max and up), the energy being supplied for the exercise is produced in part anaerobically and more glycogen (sugar) and less fat is being burned.

When aerobic exercise is combined with strength training, the result seems to be more effective than with aerobic exercise alone. Running, cycling, swimming, dance exercise, and so on, do burn many calories, but when these are coupled with strength exercise, better body composition ratios are the result.

For example, in a recent study directed by Dr. Wayne Wescott at South Shore YMCA in Quincy, Massachusetts, the effects of two different exercise regimens were realized on body composition. Two groups of men and women used a recommended diet of 60% carbohydrates, 20% protein, and 20% fats. Both groups exercised 30 minutes each day, three days per week. However, one group performed 30 minutes of cycling on stationary bicycles while the other performed 15 minutes of cycling and 15 minutes of strength training. After eight weeks the aerobic exercisers lost an average of 3 lb of fat and a half pound of muscle. The aerobic/strength exercisers lost an average of 10 lb of fat and gained 2 lb of muscle for a 12-lb improvement.

The supportive evidence on behalf of exercise is incontrovertible. Not only is it the best way to guarantee that lost weight stays lost, it also yields other benefits as well. In one study of 21,000 men, exercisers had 40 percent less adult onset diabetes than nonexercisers. In another, a 25 year study of 13,000 people, moderate exercisers had a death rate of at least 50 percent lower than those who were sedentary.

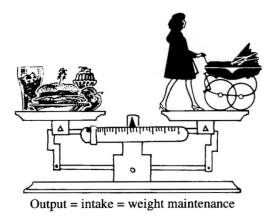

Output = intake = weight maintenance

# The Energy Equation

When the number of calories that you consume is equal to the number of calories expended for RMR and activity an **isocaloric balance** exists. Therefore, body weight should remain constant.

A **positive calorie balance exists** when more calories are consumed than are expended. This situation is further complicated by the interaction of three major factors that cause creeping obesity: a reduction in basal metabolic rate as age increases; a tendency to decrease activity; and a tendency to maintain eating habits that are formed early in life. This combination has one end result—an increase in the amount of body fat and a usual increase in total body weight.

Out put ≤ intake = weight gain

### Days Required to Lose 5 to 25 Lb by Walking* and Lowering Daily Calorie Intake

| Minutes of Walking | + Reduction of Calories per Day (in kcal) | Days to Lose 5 Lb | Days to Lose 10 Lb | Days to Lose 15 Lb | Days to Lose 20 Lb | Days to Lose 25 Lb |
|---|---|---|---|---|---|---|
| 30 | 400 | 27 | 54 | 81 | 108 | 135 |
| 30 | 600 | 20 | 40 | 60 | 80 | 100 |
| 30 | 800 | 16 | 32 | 48 | 64 | 80 |
| 30 | 1,000 | 13 | 26 | 39 | 52 | 65 |
| 45 | 400 | 23 | 46 | 69 | 92 | 115 |
| 45 | 600 | 18 | 36 | 54 | 72 | 90 |
| 45 | 800 | 14 | 28 | 42 | 56 | 70 |
| 45 | 1,000 | 12 | 24 | 36 | 48 | 60 |
| 60 | 400 | 21 | 42 | 63 | 84 | 105 |
| 60 | 600 | 16 | 32 | 48 | 64 | 80 |
| 60 | 800 | 13 | 26 | 39 | 52 | 65 |
| 60 | 1,000 | 11 | 22 | 33 | 44 | 55 |

*Walking briskly (3.5–4.0 mph), calculated at 5.2 Cal/minute.

### Days Required to Lose 5 to 25 Lb by Bicycling* and Lowering Daily Calorie Intake

| Minutes of Bicycling | + Reduction of Calories per Day (in kcal) | Days to Lose 5 Lb | Days to Lose 10 Lb | Days to Lose 15 Lb | Days to Lose 20 Lb | Days to Lose 25 Lb |
|---|---|---|---|---|---|---|
| 30 | 400 | 25 | 50 | 75 | 100 | 125 |
| 30 | 600 | 19 | 38 | 57 | 76 | 95 |
| 30 | 800 | 17 | 34 | 51 | 58 | 85 |
| 30 | 1,000 | 13 | 26 | 39 | 52 | 65 |
| 45 | 400 | 22 | 44 | 66 | 88 | 110 |
| 45 | 600 | 17 | 34 | 51 | 68 | 85 |
| 45 | 800 | 14 | 28 | 42 | 56 | 70 |
| 45 | 1,000 | 12 | 24 | 36 | 48 | 60 |
| 60 | 400 | 19 | 38 | 57 | 76 | 95 |
| 60 | 600 | 15 | 30 | 45 | 60 | 75 |
| 60 | 800 | 13 | 26 | 39 | 52 | 65 |
| 60 | 1,000 | 11 | 22 | 33 | 44 | 55 |

*Bicycling calculated at 6.5 Cal/minute, at approximately 7 mph.

## Days Required to Lose 5 to 25 Lb by Swimming* and Lowering Daily Calorie Intake

| Minutes of Swimming | + Reduction of Calories per Day (in kcal) | Days to Lose 5 Lb | Days to Lose 10 Lb | Days to Lose 15 Lb | Days to Lose 20 Lb | Days to Lose 25 Lb |
|---|---|---|---|---|---|---|
| 30 | 400 | 23 | 46 | 69 | 92 | 115 |
| 30 | 600 | 18 | 36 | 52 | 72 | 90 |
| 30 | 800 | 14 | 28 | 42 | 56 | 70 |
| 30 | 1,000 | 12 | 24 | 36 | 48 | 60 |
| 45 | 400 | 19 | 38 | 57 | 76 | 95 |
| 45 | 600 | 15 | 30 | 45 | 60 | 75 |
| 45 | 800 | 13 | 26 | 39 | 52 | 65 |
| 45 | 1,000 | 11 | 22 | 33 | 44 | 55 |
| 60 | 400 | 16 | 32 | 48 | 64 | 80 |
| 60 | 600 | 14 | 28 | 42 | 56 | 70 |
| 60 | 800 | 11 | 22 | 33 | 44 | 55 |
| 60 | 1,000 | 10 | 20 | 30 | 40 | 50 |

*Swimming at about 30 yards/minute calculated at 8.5 Cal/minute.

## Days Required to Lose 5 to 25 Lb by Stepping* and Lowering Daily Calorie Intake

| Minutes of Stepping | + Reduction of Calories per Day (in kcal) | Days to Lose 5 Lb | Days to Lose 10 Lb | Days to Lose 15 Lb | Days to Lose 20 Lb | Days to Lose 25 Lb |
|---|---|---|---|---|---|---|
| 30 | 400 | 24 | 48 | 72 | 96 | 120 |
| 30 | 600 | 18 | 36 | 54 | 72 | 90 |
| 30 | 800 | 15 | 30 | 45 | 60 | 75 |
| 30 | 1,000 | 12 | 24 | 36 | 48 | 60 |
| 45 | 400 | 20 | 40 | 60 | 80 | 100 |
| 45 | 600 | 16 | 32 | 48 | 64 | 80 |
| 45 | 800 | 13 | 26 | 39 | 52 | 65 |
| 45 | 1,000 | 11 | 22 | 33 | 44 | 55 |
| 60 | 400 | 18 | 36 | 54 | 72 | 90 |
| 60 | 600 | 14 | 28 | 42 | 56 | 70 |
| 60 | 800 | 12 | 24 | 36 | 48 | 60 |
| 60 | 1,000 | 10 | 20 | 30 | 40 | 50 |

*Stepping up and down on a regular 7" step at 25 steps/minute, calculated at 7.5 Cal/minute.

| Days Required to Lose 5 to 25 Lb by Jogging* and Lowering Daily Calorie Intake | | | | | | |
|---|---|---|---|---|---|---|
| Minutes of Jogging | + Reduction of Calories per Day (in kcal) | Days to Lose 5 Lb | Days to Lose 10 Lb | Days to Lose 15 Lb | Days to Lose 20 Lb | Days to Lose 25 Lb |
| 30 | 400 | 21 | 42 | 63 | 84 | 105 |
| 30 | 600 | 17 | 34 | 51 | 68 | 85 |
| 30 | 800 | 14 | 28 | 42 | 56 | 70 |
| 30 | 1,000 | 12 | 24 | 36 | 48 | 60 |
| 45 | 400 | 18 | 36 | 54 | 72 | 90 |
| 45 | 600 | 14 | 28 | 42 | 56 | 70 |
| 45 | 800 | 12 | 24 | 36 | 48 | 60 |
| 45 | 1,000 | 10 | 20 | 30 | 40 | 50 |
| 60 | 400 | 15 | 30 | 45 | 60 | 75 |
| 60 | 600 | 12 | 24 | 36 | 48 | 60 |
| 60 | 800 | 11 | 22 | 33 | 44 | 55 |
| 60 | 1,000 | 9 | 18 | 27 | 36 | 45 |

*Jogging—Alternate jogging and walking, calculated at 10.0 Cal/minute.

# A Lifelong Solution

To achieve permanent long-lasting weight control you must *integrate exercise into your life in such a manner as to effect a consistent body composition and weight throughout life.* This procedure requires a great deal of self-discipline and ever-constant awareness of change. At the same time exercise is infinitely more important to your well-being than falling victim to sporadic diets that will not produce the desired results.

See Chapter 8 for "Burning Fat Workouts."

From *Exercise Equivalents of Foods: A Practical Guide for the Overweight* by Frank Konishi, 1973, Southern Illinois University Press.

# Fat-Burning Guidelines

- Set reasonable and attainable goals—be realistic.
- Exercise aerobically at lower-intensity levels for 30 minutes or more at least three times per week.
- Consider resistance training as an adjunct to the aerobic exercise.
- Eat sensibly: adequate calories with emphasis on complex carbohydrate and less fat and sugar.
- Chart your progress with a caliper and tape measure rather than the bathroom scale.

# Summary

Somatotyping is a subjective evaluation of body build. There are three general classifications of body builds: endomorphs (stocky), mesomorphs (muscular), and ectomorphs (thin). Most people are mixtures of all three classifications with one classification usually dominant. Endomorphs are prone to obesity. Obesity is a significant problem to the general population. Height and weight charts may not be the best way to determine if you carry too much weight. The percentage of fat (overfat) may be a better way of determining excess weight, because body weight alone may indicate a high level of muscle development rather than fat. Obesity can contribute to a number of maladies, including high blood pressure, stroke, diabetes, and heart attack, as well as a reduced self-image.

- Obesity can best be controlled by a combination of diet and exercise.
- "Spot reducing" does not occur in response to exercising specific areas, such as sit-ups for the abdomen or leg lifts for the thighs.
- Exercise may alter body composition with little, if any, change in total body weight.
- One of the benefits of aerobic exercise is that it improves the ability to use fat as fuel; fit people are better fat burners.
- Body build (somatotype) and the distribution of body fat are more important than overall fat in relation to morbidity and mortality.
- Exercise tends to build muscles. Muscle is very metabolically active, burning more calories in resting metabolism than fat cells.

- Risks are associated with weight loss and with repeated diet failures— the yo-yo syndrome. Maintaining optimal body composition and weight is the key.
- Exercise does not automatically increase appetite and may decrease appetite for some people.

## Check Out These Websites

www.shapeup.org/bmi/index.html - a comprehensive site dealing with body measurements from Shape Up, America.

www.worldguide.com/Fitness/med.html - features body fat myths and truths, body fat ranges, body composition and somatotyping.

www.healthcentral.com/cooltools/CT_Fitness/bodyfat1.cfm - features body fat calculation; questions about weight, age and gender; information about body composition from Covert Bailey, a noted expert.

www.eatright.org/nuresources.html - Very helpful site geared towards someone just beginning an exercise program. Provides daily fitness tips, food pyramid guides, a rate your plate quiz, and more!

www.onhealth.com - Excellent overall health website. Features sections for: mind and body, staying well, and medicine. Also includes many references, chats with experts, an interactive calorie counter, and more!

www.phys.com - This very helpful website covers many aspects of the fitness and health spectrum. Offers information on: fitness, health, nutrition, weight loss, exercise, diet, and more. Check it out!

# Diets: A Losing Effort

Not surprisingly, one of the most common four letter words in our society is DIET. Estimates reveal that as many as 25% of men and 50% of women are on a diet at any given time. The term "diet" has come to imply that in some way attempts are being made to lose weight by manipulating food consumption. Approximately $44 billion dollars was spent in 1991 on diets. Unfortunately, most people did not get their money's worth.

At best, the benefits of dieting are short term. At worst, research indicates that for the long term—dieting simply doesn't work. The most important reason why diets don't work for long-term weight loss lies in the fact that muscle is lost. Dieting actually worsens the most critical concern involved in weight gain—muscle loss—and this can result in weight gain as fat.

Typically, as we progress through our 20s, about one-half pound of muscle tissue is lost each year. Less muscle means a decrease in resting metabolic rate because muscle is very active tissue, even at rest. If this effect on metabolic rate is compounded by the effect of very low calorie dieting (VLCD) it is easy to see why the long-term effects can be disastrous. Even if we made no changes in the amount of calories we eat, weight will be gained because the caloric intake begins to exceed the body's caloric use. The result is a gain of a pound or more of fat each year.

The solution? Well, there is no cure but science has revealed the best control—exercise. With appropriate exercise, fat can be lost and lean weight (muscle) can be gained, allowing for optimal body composition values to be controlled for future years of life. Aerobic exercise combined with strength training produces the most favorable control. When you combine resistance training with aerobic exercise and sensible eating habits the result is increased lean body weight, decreases in fat weight, and improved fitness—you'll look better, feel better, function better.

# Review Questions

1. What factors are included in the obesity syndrome? Which one seems to be most important?

2. What are the three somatotype classifications? Can you name one characteristic of each?

3. What are the two composition parts of your total body weight? Can you name two methods of determining the amount of fat and lean weight?

4. What is RMR?; TEE or DIT?

5. What are three benefits of using exercise as a weight control practice? and what kind appears to work best?

CHAPTER ACTIVITY

# Somatotype and Body Composition

## Purpose

To explore the interrelationships of body type, metabolism, and weight control so that students can make judgments concerning their own weight control problems, if any.

## Procedure

Place all results on sheet provided at end of this laboratory.

## Part A—Subjective Evaluation of Body Type

Researchers have determined that body type is a function of body weight. These same researchers have also identified three basic body types. These are endomorphic, mesomorphic, and ectomorphic. In the extremes, the endomorph is characterized by a soft, rounded body possessing large amounts of adipose tissue, particularly in the abdominal region, the mesomorph by a highly solid muscular physique, and the ectomorph by a slender, delicate physique. Although most individuals fall somewhere between classifications, somatotyping can serve a useful purpose in helping individuals determine a desirable body weight for their body type.

Using the somatotype continuum scale below, rate your own somatotype based on Sheldon's system. Circle the number you believe expresses the degree of endomorphy, mesomorphy, and ectomorphy, remembering that a low number indicates very little of those characteristics while a high number indicates a great deal. It might be interesting to have a friend give a rating of your somatotype for comparison. Record your estimates on the results sheet.

| | Somatotype Continuum | | |
|---|---|---|---|
| *Raters:* | 1 2 3 4 5 6 7 | 1 2 3 4 5 6 7 | 1 2 3 4 5 6 7 |
| Self | Endomorph | Mesomorph | Ectomorph |
| Classmate | 1 2 3 4 5 6 7 | 1 2 3 4 5 6 7 | 1 2 3 4 5 6 7 |
| | Endomorph | Mesomorph | Ectomorph |

**Sample Rating.** John Doe might receive a 2 in endomorphic characteristics, a 3 in mesomorphic characteristics and a 1 in ectomorphic characteristics which means his body type, though having some endomorphic characteristics, is more clearly mesomorphic or meso-endomorphic.

# Part B—Determining a Desirable Weight

Table 1 indicates a range of weights based on a variance in body type for the heights listed.

| Table I Desirable Weights for Adults | | |
|---|---|---|
| | Weight (lb) | |
| Height (inches) | Men | Women |
| 60 | | 109 + or − 9 |
| 62 | | 115 + or − 9 |
| 64 | 133 + or − 11 | 122 + or − 10 |
| 66 | 142 + or − 12 | 129 + or − 10 |
| 68 | 151 + or − 14 | 136 + or − 10 |
| 70 | 159 + or − 14 | 144 + or − 11 |
| 72 | 167 + or − 15 | 152 + or − 12 |
| 74 | 175 + or − 15 | |
| 76 | 183 + or − 15 | |

*Heights and weights are determined without shoes or clothing.

*Source: Food and Nutritional Board. National Research Council.

Determine if your weight is appropriate when compared to accepted standards.

1. List your height: _____ in.

2. List your weight: _____ lb.

3. My allowable weight range for height and body type from Table 1: from _____ lb to _____ lb.

4. I am within this allowable weight range: _____

   I am above this allowable weight range: _____

   I am below this allowable weight range: _____

# Part C—Body Fat Level: Ponderal Index

The above exercise might be sufficient to assess your desirable body weight, but it does not identify your degree of obesity, since obesity does not correlate exactly with being over-weight.

To assess one's percentage of body fat a simplified procedure involves a mathematical formula designed to yield a "ponderal index." The ponderal index is a ratio of height to weight. This is calculated by dividing your height in inches by the cube root of your weight in pounds. The accuracy of the method varies, since it comes closest with individuals of average bone structure and proportions. It is least accurate for extremes in body build. This method will, however, yield a "ball park" estimate of body composition.

A chart of cube roots for various weights is indicated below (divide the appropriate one into your height in inches).

| | | |
|---|---|---|
| 91 lbs. = 4.5 | 149 lbs. = 5.3 | 226 lbs. = 6.1 |
| 97 lbs. = 4.6 | 157 lbs. = 5.4 | 238 lbs. = 6.2 |
| 104 lbs. = 4.7 | 166 lbs. = 5.5 | 250 lbs. = 6.3 |
| 111 lbs. = 4.8 | 175 lbs. = 5.6 | 262 lbs. = 6.4 |
| 118 lbs. = 4.9 | 185 lbs. = 5.7 | 274 lbs. = 6.5 |
| 125 lbs. = 5.0 | 195 lbs. = 5.8 | 287 lbs. = 6.6 |
| 133 lbs. = 5.1 | 205 lbs. = 5.9 | 300 lbs. = 6.7 |
| 141 lbs. = 5.2 | 216 lbs. = 6.0 | |

Once you have calculated your ponderal index, find it on the vertical axis of the following graph.

Next draw a line from your ponderal index so that it intersects with the diagonal line on the graph.

From this point of intersection draw a line down so that it intersects with the horizontal axis labeled percent body fat. This will be an approximation of the percentage of your total body weight that is fat.

The example shown on the graph is with a ponderal index of 13 and a resultant percent body fat of 14.

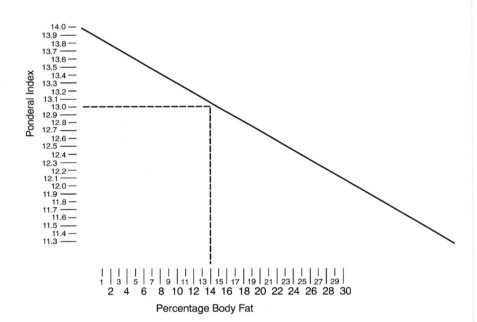

# Part D—Determination of Body Composition Via Skinfold Measurement

As explained in the related chapter on body composition, it is not unusual for an individual to fall within the normal range for body weight but actually have excess body fat.

To arrive at an accurate estimate of percent body fat, various skinfold measurements must be taken. To do this, skinfold calipers are used. These measure skinfold thickness in millimeters. Skinfold thicknesses will be measured using the following procedure:

1. The calipers should be held in the right hand with the thumb on the "trigger," which controls the pincers.
2. A skinfold is pinched up at the appropriate site with the thumb and index finger of the left hand. The skinfold should be pinched up along the natural line of the body; for example, with the triceps skinfold, the natural line would produce a vertical skinfold. (All skinfolds taken on dominant side.)
3. After the skinfold has been pinched up, open the pincers of the caliper and place them approximately one centimeter (1 cm) below the thumb and index finger. Let the pincers close on the fold slowly, completely releasing the trigger.
4. After the trigger has been released, count two seconds before reading the meter. This is done because the tissue will compress to some degree.
5. Read the meter to the nearest millimeter and record the findings.

The sites of skinfold measurement: Men take 4; Women take 2.

## For Men and Women

1. **The Triceps** (back of the arm): arms at your side; your partner will grasp a skinfold on the back of the arm halfway between the shoulder and elbow. It will be a vertical skinfold. (See appropriate picture.)
2. **The Suprailiac** (hip): halfway between the lower rib and the hip bone (about an inch above the hip) the skinfold should be taken so that it runs horizontally (parallel to the beltline). (See appropriate picture.)
3. **The Subscapular** (base of shoulder blade): along the lower edge of the shoulder blade at a slight angle. (See appropriate picture.)
4. **The Biceps** (front of upper arm): at the point of greatest curvature of the muscle, measured vertically. (See appropriate picture.)

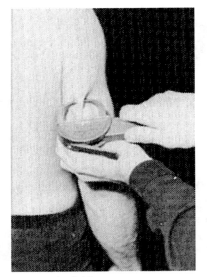

*Triceps skinfold*

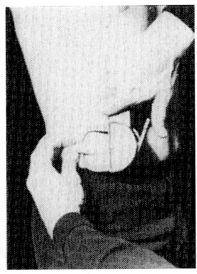

*Suprailiac skinfold*

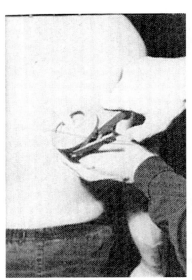

*Subscapular skinfold*

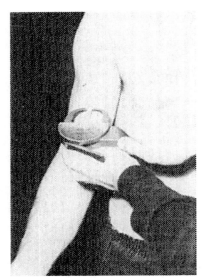

*Biceps skinfold*

## Table 2

| Women | | Men | |
|---|---|---|---|
| Total mm Skinfold | % Fat | Total mm Skinfold | % Fat |
| 8 | 13 | 15 | 5 |
| 12 | 14 | 20 | 9 |
| 14 | 15 | 25 | 11 |
| 18 | 16 | 30 | 13 |
| 20 | 17 | 35 | 15 |
| 24 | 18 | 40 | 17 |
| 26 | 19 | 45 | 18 |
| 30 | 20 | 50 | 20 |
| 32 | 21 | 55 | 21 |
| 34 | 22 | 60 | 22 |
| 38 | 23 | 65 | 23 |
| 40 | 24 | 70 | 24 |
| 42 | 25 | 75 | 25 |
| 44 | 26 | 80 | 26 |
| 48 | 27 | 90 | 27 |
| 50 | 28 | 100 | 28 |
| 52 | 29 | 110 | 29 |
| 56 | 30 | 120 | 30 |
| 58 | 31 | 130 | 31 |
| 62 | 32 | 140 | 32 |
| 64 | 33 | 150 | 33 |
| 68 | 34 | 160 | 34 |
| 70 | 35 | 175 | 35 |
| 76 | 37 | 190 | 36 |
| 80 | 38 | 205 | 37 |
| 82 | 39 | 220 | 38 |
| 86 | 40 | 235 | 39 |
| 88 | 41 | 255 | 40 |
| 90 | 42 | 275 | 41 |
| | | 295 | 42 |

From *Activities*, by Charles T. Kuntzleman.

# Laboratory 3 Results Sheet

## Part A—Somatotype

1. My Somatotype is: _____ — _____ — _____

2. Body type is called a (an): _____

## Part B—Skinfold Results

1. Women:    Triceps Skinfold _____ mm

                 Suprailiac Skinfold _____ mm

                 Total _____ mm

2. Men:      Triceps Skinfold _____ mm

                 Suprailiac Skinfold _____ mm

                 Biceps Skinfold _____ mm

                 Subscapular Skinfold _____ mm

                     Total _____ mm

3. Percent Fat (see table 2) _____ %

4. Weight of Fat in Pounds

$$\underbrace{\text{_____}}_{\textbf{TBW}} \times \underbrace{\text{_____}}_{\textbf{\% FAT}} = \underbrace{\text{_____}}_{\substack{\textbf{FW} \\ \text{(pounds of fat in body)}}}$$

5. Weight of Lean Body Mass (**LBM**): _____

$$\underbrace{\text{_____}}_{\textbf{TBW}} - \underbrace{\text{_____}}_{\textbf{FW}} = \underbrace{\text{_____}}_{\substack{\textbf{LBM} \\ \text{(in pounds)}}}$$

6. Determining optimal body weight (this mathematical adjustment will be most reliable if the percent fat exceeds recommended values, i.e., 30% for women; 20% for men.

    Optimal body weight = your lean body mass divided by the difference between 100% and the percent fat you would like to be (example: 100% − 15% = 8% or .85)

a. Subtract the percent fat you would like to be from 100%:

100% (1.00) – _____%(.           ) = %(_____)

b. Divide the result into your Lean Body Mass (LBM) determined in number 5.

_____ _____

c. The result is your optimal body weight, which is _____ lb.

7. Required **fat** loss = Present TBW – Optimal body weight

Required **fat** loss = _____ – _____

Required **fat** loss = _____ pounds

CHAPTER ACTIVITY

# Apples and Pears—
# Waist to Hip Ratio

## Purpose

To determine relative health risk based on fat pattern and distribution by creating a waist to hip measurement ration (WHR).

## Procedure

1. Measure your waist at the level of your umbilicus (belly button) in inches. Preferably this measure is done on bare skin.
2. Measure your hips at the level of the buttocks, in inches. Preferably this measure is done on bare skin.
3. Divide the waist measurement by the hip measurement to yield a ratio.

_____ waist measurement

_____ = (WHR)

_____ hip measurement

## Rating

- less than .80 is good
- .81 to .90 is not so good
- over .91 is considered unhealthy relative to the heart.

## Question

1. What are the two most important controllable factors in changing or maintaining this ratio?

CHAPTER ACTIVITY

# Body Mass Index: (BMI)

## Part A

### Purpose

To determine the health risk of your height relative to body weight. BMI is a ratio of height and weight that can be used as an indicatior of existing or potential health problems.

### Procedure

Use the following chart to determine your BMI. Locate your height in the column on the left; read to the right to locate your weight; then look to the top line to find your BMI.

| BMI | 19 | 20 | 21 | 22 | 23 | 24 | 25 | 26 | 27 | 28 | 29 | 30 | 35 | 40 |
|------|-----|-----|-----|-----|-----|-----|-----|-----|-----|-----|-----|-----|-----|-----|
| 4'10" | 91 | 96 | 100 | 105 | 110 | 115 | 119 | 124 | 129 | 134 | 138 | 143 | 167 | 191 |
| 4'11" | 94 | 99 | 104 | 109 | 114 | 119 | 124 | 128 | 133 | 138 | 143 | 148 | 173 | 198 |
| 5'0" | 97 | 102 | 107 | 112 | 118 | 123 | 128 | 133 | 138 | 143 | 148 | 153 | 179 | 204 |
| 5'1" | 100 | 106 | 111 | 116 | 122 | 127 | 132 | 137 | 143 | 148 | 153 | 158 | 185 | 211 |
| 5'2" | 104 | 109 | 115 | 120 | 126 | 131 | 136 | 142 | 147 | 153 | 158 | 164 | 191 | 218 |
| 5'3" | 107 | 113 | 118 | 124 | 130 | 135 | 141 | 146 | 152 | 158 | 163 | 169 | 197 | 225 |
| 5'4" | 110 | 116 | 122 | 128 | 134 | 140 | 145 | 151 | 157 | 163 | 169 | 174 | 204 | 232 |
| 5'5" | 114 | 120 | 126 | 132 | 138 | 144 | 150 | 156 | 162 | 168 | 174 | 180 | 210 | 240 |
| 5'6" | 118 | 124 | 130 | 136 | 142 | 148 | 155 | 161 | 167 | 173 | 179 | 186 | 216 | 247 |
| 5'7" | 121 | 127 | 134 | 140 | 146 | 153 | 159 | 166 | 172 | 178 | 185 | 191 | 223 | 255 |
| 5'8" | 125 | 131 | 138 | 144 | 151 | 158 | 164 | 171 | 177 | 184 | 190 | 197 | 230 | 262 |
| 5'9" | 128 | 135 | 142 | 149 | 155 | 162 | 169 | 176 | 182 | 189 | 196 | 203 | 236 | 270 |
| 5'10" | 132 | 139 | 146 | 153 | 160 | 167 | 174 | 181 | 188 | 195 | 202 | 207 | 243 | 278 |
| 5'11" | 136 | 143 | 150 | 157 | 165 | 172 | 179 | 186 | 193 | 200 | 208 | 215 | 250 | 286 |
| 6'0" | 140 | 147 | 154 | 162 | 169 | 177 | 184 | 191 | 199 | 206 | 213 | 221 | 258 | 294 |
| 6'1" | 144 | 151 | 159 | 166 | 174 | 182 | 189 | 197 | 204 | 212 | 219 | 227 | 265 | 302 |
| 6'2" | 148 | 155 | 163 | 171 | 179 | 186 | 194 | 202 | 210 | 218 | 225 | 233 | 272 | 311 |
| 6'3" | 152 | 160 | 168 | 176 | 184 | 192 | 200 | 208 | 216 | 224 | 232 | 240 | 279 | 319 |
| 6'4" | 156 | 164 | 172 | 180 | 189 | 197 | 205 | 213 | 221 | 230 | 238 | 246 | 287 | 328 |

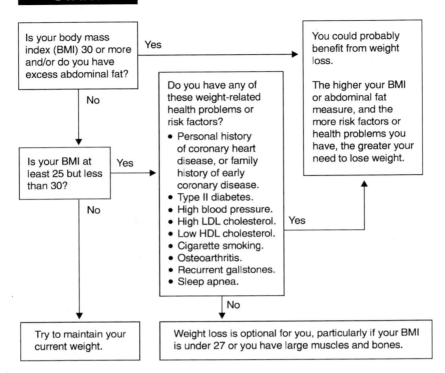

**START**

Is your body mass index (BMI) 30 or more and/or do you have excess abdominal fat?

— Yes → You could probably benefit from weight loss.

No ↓

Is your BMI at least 25 but less than 30?

— Yes →

Do you have any of these weight-related health problems or risk factors?

- Personal history of coronary heart disease, or family history of early coronary disease.
- Type II diabetes.
- High blood pressure.
- High LDL cholesterol.
- Low HDL cholesterol.
- Cigarette smoking.
- Osteoarthritis.
- Recurrent gallstones.
- Sleep apnea.

Yes →

The higher your BMI or abdominal fat measure, and the more risk factors or health problems you have, the greater your need to lose weight.

No ↓

No ↓

Try to maintain your current weight.

Weight loss is optional for you, particularly if your BMI is under 27 or you have large muscles and bones.

# CHAPTER 4

# Elements of Good Nutrition

Throughout history the link between good nutrition and personal health has been scientifically connected. Diet and nutrition play key roles in weight management as well as the development and progression of certain diseases. Coronary heart disease, artherosclerosis, hypertension, obesity, osteoporosis and a variety of cancers have all been associated with nutrition. Nutrition can be overdone (too much of some nutrient) and underdone (too little of some nutrient) resulting in notable effects on health status. It appears that the problems related to nutrition do not result from insufficient food consumption but rather from overconsumption of food. Our "**supersize**" mentality has created a plethora of health problems. Diseases of nutrition excesses and imbalances are among the leading causes of death in America.

Although the American lifestyle provides availability of the most abundant and diverse food supply in the world, much remains to be done regarding control of this situation. Good dietary practices provide all essential nutrients (chemicals that the body uses) for growth and repair of tissue and sufficient energy to carry out daily activities thus maintaining optimal health status.

There are six classes of nutrients with only three providing energy (calories). These three are **proteins**, **carbohydrates** and **fats**. The other three are **vitamins**, **minerals** and **water** (the most crucial nutrient). Additionally, some experts include **fiber** as a seventh class because of its importance in the diet. Proteins, carbohydrates and fats are referred to as **macronutrients** because they are required in relatively large amounts when compared to vitamins, minerals (**micronutrients**) which are required in only small amounts.

Foods that provide energy (calories) in addition to a variety of nutrients can be referred to as **nutrient dense**. Foods that provide energy but contain very few nutrients can be referred to as **calorie dense**. Processed and refined foods typically contain calories but provide very few nutrients. Whereas fresh fruits and vegetables contain calories in addition to a wide variety of nutrients called **phytochemicals** (plant chemicals) that have been shown to have a profound effect on health and well-being.

These phytochemicals (see following chart) are referred to as **neutriceuticals** because they provide distinct medical and health benefits.

| Some antioxidant nutrients and phytochemicals with common food sources | |
| --- | --- |
| **Antioxidant nutrients** | **Common plant sources** |
| Vitamin C | Citrus fruits |
| | Potatoes |
| | Strawberries |
| Vitamin E | Dark-green leafy vegetables |
| | Margarine |
| | Vegetable oils |
| | Wheat germ |
| | Whole grains |
| **Phytochemicals** | **Common plant sources** |
| Allium sulfides | Garlic |
| Organosulfides | Onions |
| | Scallions |
| Capsaicin | Hot peppers |
| Carotenoids | Carrots |
|   Beta-carotene | Dark-green leafy vegetables |
|   Lycopene | Sweet potatoes |
|   Lutein | Tomatoes |
| Flavonoids | Citrus fruits |
|   Quercetin | Broccoli |
| Indoles | Cruciferous vegetables |
| |   Broccoli |
| |   Brussels sprouts |
| |   Cabbage |
| |   Cauliflower |
| |   Kale |

| Some antioxidant nutrients and phytochemicals with common food sources (cont.) | |
| --- | --- |
| **Phytochemicals** | **Common plant sources** |
| Isoflavones | Soybeans |
|   Phytoestrogens | Peanuts |
|   Genistein | Soy milk |
| Isothiocyanates | Cruciferous vegetables |
|   Sulforaphane |   Broccoli |
| |   Brussels sprouts |
| |   Cabbage |
| |   Cauliflower |
| |   Kale |
| Phenolic acids | Carrots |
| | Citrus fruits |
| | Tomatoes |
| | Whole grains |
| Polyphenols | Grapes |
|   Resveratol | Green tea |
| | Wine |
| Saponins | Beans |
| | Legumes |
| Terperenes | Cherries |
|   Limonene | Citrus fruits |

The concept of a *Food Pyramid* has become the contemporary replacement for the basic four food groups. It portrays a fifth group—fats, oils, sweets—which appears at the top of the pyramid. The pyramid illustrates the relative amounts of the food groups that should form a sensible diet; most foods should come from the grain group and the fewest foods from the fat group.

The Food Guide Pyramid was released by the United States Department of Agriculture (USDA) in 1992 emphasizing foods from the five major food groups shown in the three lower levels of the Pyramid. Each of these food groups provides some but not all of the nutrients needed to maintain a balanced diet.

The Food Guide Pyramid shows that foods from the grain group along with vegetables and fruits are the basis of healthful diets. You should plan

*Figure 4.1    Food Guide Pyramid: A Guide to Daily Food Choices*    Each of these
*food groups provides some, but not all, of the nutrients you need. No one food group
is more important than another—for good health, you need them all. Go easy on fats,
oils, and sweets, the foods at the tip of the pyramid.*

Source: U.S. Department of Agriculture and U.S Department of Health and
Human Services.

meals that are low in total fat, saturated fat and cholesterol; using sodium
and sugar in moderation.

Some foods fit into more than one group. Starchy vegetables such as
white potatoes, sweet potatoes and corn, can be counted as servings in the
grain products group or in the vegetable group. Dry beans, peas and lentils
are in the meat group but they can alternatively be counted as serving of
vegetables. These crossover foods can be counted as servings from either
one or the other group, but not both.

Notice that a range of servings is given for each food group. The lower
limit is for people who consume about 1,600 calories a day. While the
upper limit is for people who consume about 2,800 calories per day.

# Proteins

**Proteins** have always been considered the most important nutrient. They
are needed for essential growth during youth and adolescence and are important for needed body repair by mature individuals. A lack of protein
during the formative stages of life will result in diminished growth and
vigor. It also leads to poor hair and skin condition and a slower healing

process. Proteins contain twenty amino acids, which are broken down and used for the growth and repair process. Protein foods are classified as complete and incomplete. This refers to the number and proportions of amino acids present in a particular food. A protein such as egg whites and most red meats are complete proteins because of the presence of all necessary amino acids and the appropriate proportion of each. Vegetables, such as beans, provide some protein but are classified as incomplete protein. That is, the vegetable will not have all amino acids, and the amino acids would not be present in appropriate proportions. Most often, complete and incomplete proteins are included in the diet to satisfy needs. This would be different for a strict vegetarian and would present some distinct concerns relative to protein sources. Protein is not normally used as an energy source by cells except if carbohydrate and fat supplies are at low levels, a VLCD for example.

Typically, the American diet contains approximately 15% of all calories as protein. This appears to be adequate except perhaps for women who are pregnant, athletes who are trying to gain lean body mass (muscle), and adolescents who are pursuing athletics. The protein needs of these groups may be somewhat higher.

Protein does provide energy for cellular growth and repair. Its caloric content is 4 calories per gram (1/30 of an ounce).

# Carbohydrates

**Carbohydrates** are our major sources of energy. They are usually available in abundance throughout the world and are often pleasant tasting "sweet" foodstuffs. Carbohydrates are classified as either simple (sugars) or complex. Sugar is the major source of sweet taste but carbohydrates are also found in starches present in many vegetables. The refining of carbohydrates causes a lower nutritive value. Refined carbohydrates, such as white table sugar (sucrose), have had the vitamins and minerals removed. Processed carbohydrate foods, such as flour for baking, are high in calories but low in vitamins and minerals.

Most of our carbohydrates are used on a daily basis but some is stored in the liver in the form of glycogen. The glycogen is secreted when the blood sugar is low and the muscles need additional energy. Carbohydrates are found in the bread and cereals group as well as in some fruits and vegetables. The major sources are sugar, bread, potatoes, pasta, and other white and yellow vegetables. The American diet contains about 50% carbohydrate intake and the figure is higher in some other cultures. The caloric yield of carbohydrates is, surprisingly, 4 calories per gram—the same as protein.

## Bread, Cereal, Rice and Pasta Group

6-11 servings per day

### What Counts as a Serving?

1 slice of bread
1 ounce of ready to eat cereal; ½ cup of cooked cereal
1 cup of rice or pasta

Notice that for this food group 6-11 servings are recommended. The lower limit (6) is for people who consume about 1,600 calories a day. While the upper limit (11) is for people who consume about 2,800 calories a day.

## Vegetable Group

3-5 servings per day

### What Counts as a Serving?

1 cup of raw leafy vegetables
½ cup of cooked vegetables
¾ cup of vegetable juice

Notice that for this food group 3-5 servings are recommended. The lower limit (3) is for people who consume about 1,600 calories a day. While the upper limit (5) is for people who consume about 2,800 calories a day.

## Fruit Group

2-4 servings per day

### What Counts as a Serving?

1 medium piece of fresh fruit
½ cup of chopped, cooked, or canned fruit
¾ cup of fruit juice

Notice that for this food group 2-4 servings are recommended. The lower limit (2) is for people who consume about 1,600 calories a day. While the upper limit (4) is for people who consume about 2,800 calories a day.

# Fats

**Fat**, or **lipids** are a key ingredient in the human diet. They serve as a source of energy and, when stored as adipose, cushion the major organs of the body. Almost half of all the fat in the body is a layer of fat beneath the skin to protect the body from extreme fluctuations in temperature. Fat provides protective padding beneath the kidneys as well as other vital organs. Fats slow down digestion, prompting the stomach to empty at a slower pace, which diminishes feelings of hunger. Fats often provide energy when the daily carbohydrate yield cannot provide needed energy. The primary source of fat is the milk and milk product group and meat and meat products. Foods such as butter, oils, whole milk, fatty meats, and ice cream are major sources of fat. Fats have a much higher yield of calories than proteins and carbohydrates (9 calories per gram) and are most easily stored as body fat if intake is excessive. The typical American diet includes about 40% of all calories from fat sources. The use of alcohol, with high calorie yield and little nutritive value, is also a contributor, although not a fat food. There also appears to be a relationship between excessive fat intake and high levels of cholesterol in the blood. High cholesterol levels have been identified as one of the major predisposing factors to heart disease and our diets should minimize foods that elevate cholesterol. Remember, *the fat you eat is the fat you wear*—in two places: in your arteries and under your skin.

Lipids (fats) are classified as either saturated or unsaturated (includes polyunsaturated and monounsaturated) based on the chemical formation. Saturated fats are solid at room temperature and are derived from animal sources: beef, lamb, pork, and butter, for example. There are only two saturated fat sources found in the plant kingdom: coconut and palm. These are very often used in commercial baking. Unsaturated fats are found in the plant kingdom. Sources would include corn oil, olive oil, safflower oil, cannola oil, and peanut oil. Although these contain the same number of calories per gram they are much less damaging to the cardiovascular system. These fats do not promote atherosclerosis and in addition to fatty oils found in fish (omega-3 oils) may help to reduce cholesterol.

There is little, if any, difference in the way normal weight subjects and obese subjects metabolize carbohydrates. The actual difference is the fat content of the diet. Virtually all fat calories are stored in fat cells waiting to be called on for use as energy. Fats have a very low *dietary-induced thermogenesis (DIT),* so it is easy for the body to store them as fat. The bottom line is that simply reducing the total fat in a diet while continuing the same level of caloric intake can mean a slow weight loss. Combining the reduction of dietary fat with appropriate exercise provides the best control.

## Some Dietary Sources of Fat

| Animal sources | Approximate percent of Fat |
|---|---|
| Pork | 32 |
| Butter | 80 |
| Ham | 25 |
| Beef | 25 |
| Ground Beef, lean | 20 |
| Veal | 15 |
| Salmon Steak | 15 |
| Fish, white | 3 |
| Tuna, in water | 3 |

| Plant sources | Approximate percent of Fat |
|---|---|
| Corn Oil | 100 |
| Soybean Oil | 100 |
| Olive Oil | 100 |
| Canola Oil | 100 |
| Peanut butter | 50 |
| Butter | 100 |
| Margarine | 80 |
| Nuts | 50 |

## *Milk, Yogurt and Cheese Group*

2-3 servings per day

### What Counts as a Serving?

1 cup of milk or yogurt
1½ ounces of natural cheese
2 ounces of processed cheese

Notice that for this food group 2-3 servings are recommended. The lower limit (2) is for people who consume about 1,600 calories a day. While the upper limit (3) is for people who consume about 2,800 calories a day.

## *Meat, Poultry, Fish, Dry Beans, Eggs, and Nuts Group*

2-3 servings per day

### What Counts as a Serving?

2-3 ounces of cooked lean meat, poultry, or fish
½ cup of cooked dry beans or 1 egg or 2 tablespoons of peanut butter count as 1 ounce of lean meat.

Notice that for this food group 2-3 servings are recommended. The lower limit (2) is for people who consume about 1,600 calories a day. While the upper limit (3) is for people who consume about 2,800 calories a day.

## Calorie Counter

| Meat, Fish, Eggs | Size of Portion | Calories |
|---|---|---|
| Meat, fish, poultry lean-to-medium fat, averaged | 1 serving (3 oz. cooked) | 230 |
| Liver | 1 serving (3 oz. cooked) | 180 |
| Frankfurter | 1 medium | 125 |
| Luncheon meat | 2 medium slices (2oz.) | 165 |
| Ham, boiled or baked | 1 thin slice, 5 x 4" (1 oz.) | 85 |
| Tuna or salmon, canned | ⅜ cup (2 oz.) | 105 |
| Bacon, crisp | 2 long slices (½ oz.) | 100 |
| Eggs | 1 medium | 75 |

| Vegetables | Size of Portion | Calories |
|---|---|---|
| Green beans | ½ cup, cooked | 15 |
| Carrots | ½ cup, cooked | 20 |
| Beets | ½ cup, cooked | 35 |
| Peas | ½ cup, cooked | 65 |
| Lima beans | ½ cup, cooked | 75 |
| Corn | ½ cup, cooked | 70 |
| Potatoes, white | 1 small potato, cooked | 80 |
| Potatoes, Mashed | ½ cup | 120 |
| Potatoes, French Fried | 6 pieces, ½ x ½ x 2" | 120 |
| Potatoes, sweet | ½ medium potato, cooked | 90 |
| Raw carrot, tomato | 1 small to medium | 25 |
| Celery | 2 small stalks | 5 |
| Lettuce | ¼ medium head | 10 |
| Tossed salad, mixed vegetable | ¾ cup, without dressing | 30 |

## Calorie Counter—*Continued*

| Dairy Foods | Size of Portion | Calories |
|---|---|---|
| Milk, whole | I glass (8 oz.) | 170 |
| Milk, skim or buttermilk | I glass (8 oz.) | 85 |
| Cheese, American or Swiss | I" cube or medium slice (I oz.) | 110 |
| Cheese, cottage creamed | 2 tablespoons (I oz.) | 30 |
| Butter | I teaspoon or small pat | 35 |
| Cream, light, table | 2 tablespoons | 60 |
| Half and Half | ¼ cup | 80 |
| Ice cream, vanilla | ¼ pint (½ cup) | 150 |
| Sherbet | ½ cup | 146 |

| Bread and Cereals | Size of Portion | Calories |
|---|---|---|
| Bread, whole-grain or enriched | I medium slice (⅘ oz.) | 60 |
| Cereal, cooked, whole-grain or enriched | ½ cup | 70 |
| Cereal, ready-to-eat, whole-grained or enriched | ½ cup | 50 |
| Rice or spaghetti | ½ cup, cooked | 105 |
| Noodles | ½ cup, cooked | 55 |
| Rolls, plain | I small (I oz.) | 85 |
| Rolls, sweet | I medium (2 oz.) | 180 |
| Waffle | I medium 4½ x 5½ x ½ | 215 |
| Pancake | I thin 4" diameter | 60 |
| Crackers, plain or graham | 2 medium | 50 |

| Pastries and Puddings | Size of Portion | Calories |
|---|---|---|
| Cookies, plain | 2 small or I large | 100 |
| Cupcakes, iced | I medium I ¾" diameter | 130 |
| Cake, layer, plain icing | Med. piece, ⅙ 6" cake | 250–400 |
| Cake, angel food or sponge | Small piece | 115 |
| Doughnut | I medium | 135 |
| Pie, fruit | ⅐ medium-size pie | 300-350 |
| Pie, custard type | ⅐ medium-size pie | 250-300 |

All excess calories have the potential to be stored as body fat. From a quantity standpoint "a calorie is a calorie is a calorie." Calories from fat sources are most easily converted to body fat.

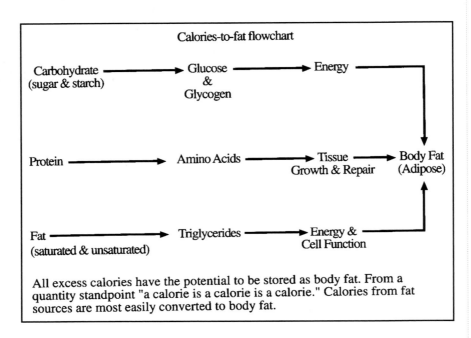

Calories-to-fat flowchart

All excess calories have the potential to be stored as body fat. From a quantity standpoint "a calorie is a calorie is a calorie." Calories from fat sources are most easily converted to body fat.

# Vitamins

Vitamins are essential to body function. Each vitamin possesses unique chemical structure which determines a particular function in the body. Vitamins are classified as either **water soluble** or **fat soluble** (see following chart). They act as **catalysts** in the body which means they help a particular chemical process to occur. The body does not make most vitamins so they must be obtained in various foods. The water soluble vitamins are not stored so must be replaced on a continuous basis. The fat soluble vitamins can be storied in the body. Some vitamins act as **antioxidants (A, C, and E)** which combine with what are called **free radicals**. Free radicals are molecules that result from metabolism (oxidation) and can do damage to cells. The antioxidant vitamins help to prevent this damage. These free radicals are implicated in a variety of diseases (cancer) and the aging process. The chief source of vitamins is plants but some are available in meats. Vitamins are available as **supplements** and many people consume them just to "cover their bases." It appears that vitamins occurring in fruits, vegetables and meats are better absorbed than pills and capsules. Since processing and cooking can destroy vitamin content, the emphasis on fresh, raw fruits and vegetables make sense.

## Water Soluble Vitamins

| Vitamin | Sources | Function |
|---------|---------|----------|
| $B_1$ (Thiamine) | Meat, milk, whole grain cereals, legumes | All metabolism |
| $B_2$ (Riboflavin) | Milk, meat, eggs, fish, green vegetables | All metabolism |
| $B_6$ (Pyridoxine) | Whole grain cereals, meat, spinach, beans, bananas | Metabolism of amino acids |
| $B_{12}$ (Cobalamin) | Animal products | Metabolism; Red blood cell production |
| Folic Acid | Green vegetables, legumes, grains, orange juice | Metabolism; normal growth |
| Niacin | Meat, nuts, grains | All metabolism |
| C (Ascorbic Acid) | Citrus fruits, broccoli, green pepper, strawberries | Antioxidant; tissue formation |
| Pantothenic acid | Grains, meats, vegetables | All metabolism |
| Biotin | Cereals, legumes, meats, egg yolk | All metabolism |

## Fat Soluble Vitamins

| Vitamin | Sources | Function |
|---------|---------|----------|
| A | Fortified dairy products, liver, colored vegetables | Antioxidant |
| D | Fortified dairy products, egg yolk, sunlight | Promotes calcium absorption |
| E | Vegetable oils, greens, nuts | Antioxidant—prevents cell damage |
| K | Green vegetables, meats | Blood clotting |

# How to Read the New Food Labels

**Serving Size**
Is your serving the same size as the one on the label? If you eat double the serving size listed, you need to double the nutrient and calorie values. If you eat one-half the serving size shown here, cut the nutrient and calorie values in half.

**Calories**
Are you overweight? Cut back a little on calories! Look here to see how a serving of the food adds to your daily total. A 5'4", 138-lb. active woman needs about 2,200 calories each day. A 5'10", 174-lb. active man needs about 2,900. How about you?

**Total Carbohydrate**
When you cut down on fat, you can eat more carbohydrates. Carbohydrates are in foods like bread, potatoes, fruits and vegetables. Choose these often! They give you more nutrients than sugars like soda pop and candy.

**Dietary Fiber**
Grandmother called it "roughage," but her advice to eat more is still up-to-date! That goes for both soluble and insoluble kinds of dietary fiber. Fruits, vegetables, whole-grain foods, beans and peas are all good sources and can help reduce the risk of heart disease and cancer.

**Protein**
Most Americans get more protein than they need. Where there is animal protein, there is also fat and cholesterol. Eat small servings of lean meat, fish and poultry. Use skim or low-fat milk, yogurt and cheese. Try vegetable proteins like beans, grains and cereals.

**Vitamins & Minerals**
Your goal here is 100% of each for the day. Don't count on one food to do it all. Let a combination of foods add up to a winning score.

## Nutrition Facts

Serving Size ½ cup (114g)
Servings Per Container 4

**Amount Per Serving**

| **Calories** 90 | Calories from Fat 30 |
|---|---|

| | **% Daily Value\*** |
|---|---|
| **Total Fat** 3g | **5%** |
| Saturated Fat 0g | **0%** |
| **Cholesterol** 0mg | **0%** |
| **Sodium** 300mg | **13%** |
| **Total Carbohydrate** 13g | **4%** |
| Dietary Fiber 3g | **12%** |
| Sugars 3g | |
| **Protein** 3g | |

| Vitamin A | 80% | • | Vitamin C | 60% |
|---|---|---|---|---|
| Calcium | 4% | • | Iron | 4% |

*Percent Daily Values are based on a 2000 calorie diet. Your daily values may be higher or lower depending on your calorie needs:

| | Calories | 2000 | 2500 |
|---|---|---|---|
| Total Fat | Less than | 65g | 80g |
| Sat Fat | Less than | 20g | 25g |
| Cholesterol | Less than | 300mg | 300mg |
| Sodium | Less than | 2400mg | 2400mg |
| Total Carbohydrate | | 300g | 375g |
| Fiber | | 25g | 30g |

Calories per gram:
Fat 9 • Carbohydrates 4 • Protein 4

*More nutrients may be listed on some labels.*

g = grams (About 28 g = 1 ounce)
mg = milligrams (1,000 mg = 1 g)

**Total Fat**
Aim low: Most people need to cut back on fat! Too much fat may contribute to heart disease and cancer. Try to limit your **calories from fat.** For a healthy heart, choose foods with a big difference between the total number of calories and the number of calories from fat.

**Saturated Fat**
A new kind of fat? No — saturated fat is part of the total fat in food. It is listed separately because it's the key player in raising blood cholesterol and your risk of heart disease. Eat less!

**Cholesterol**
Too much cholesterol — a second cousin to fat — can lead to heart disease. Challenge yourself to eat less than 300 mg each day.

**Sodium**
You call it "salt," the label calls it "sodium." Either way, it may add up to high blood pressure in some people. So, keep your sodium intake low — 2,400 to 3,000 mg or less each day.\*

\* The AHA recommends no more than 3,000 mg sodium per day for healthy adults.

**Daily Value**
Feel like you're drowning in numbers? Let the Daily Value be your guide. Daily Values are listed for people who eat 2,000 or 2,500 calories each day. If you eat more, your personal daily value may be higher than what's listed on the label. If you eat less, your personal daily value may be lower.

For fat, saturated fat, cholesterol and sodium, choose foods with a low **% Daily Value.** For total carbohydrate, dietary fiber, vitamins and minerals, your daily value goal is to reach 100% of each.

# Minerals

**Minerals** are also important for well-being. Calcium helps to build and maintain healthy teeth and bones and is found in milk and dairy products. Fluoride aids in strengthening bones and teeth. Seafoods and fluorinated water are its best source. Iodine, found in seafood and iodized salt, is necessary for the proper function of the thyroid gland (goiter prevention). Iron is stressed in most diets and is critical for the production of hemoglobin, which is the oxygen-carrying element in the blood. A lack of iron leads to anemia, characterized by a lack of vigor. Lean meats are the major source of iron. Potassium has received much concern in recent time. The daily banana as well as green, leafy vegetables promotes healthy skin and general well-being. Sodium regulates water in the body as well as blood pressure. An excess of sodium, particularly through salt intake, is thought to produce elevated blood pressure and excess weight through water retention.

# Fiber

Found only in plants, **fiber** is the indigestible cellulose component which provides bulk in the diet. Since it is indigestible it provides no calories but is recognized as a very important part of a diet. According to some experts the typical diet of an American is too low in its fiber content. This may be linked to a variety of health consequences such as constipation, diverticulitis, and cancer of the gastrointestinal system. Higher fiber intake, which would accompany increased consumption of grains, fruits and vegetables may aid in regulating blood sugar levels and blood cholesterol levels.

# Fast-Foods Calorie Counter

The trouble with a scoop of Rocky Road ice cream is that it's a particularly rocky road to travel if you're on a strict diet. Still, the calorie count (204) might not be quite as high as you suspected—and it looks almost dietetic compared with the count for McDonald's Big Mac. These and other fast-food calorie counts (approximate) below may or may not confirm your worst suspicions.

## Baskin-Robbins® Ice Cream (serving size = ½ cup)

| | Calories | Carbohydrate (gm) | Protein (gm) | Total Fat (gm) | Saturated Fat (gm) | Cholesterol (mg) | Sodium (mg) | Dietary Fiber (gm) | Total Carb Exchange | Suggested Exchange Value |
|---|---|---|---|---|---|---|---|---|---|---|
| Banana Strawberry | 130 | 17 | 2 | 7 | 5 | 25 | 40 | 0 | 1 | 1 other carb. 1 fat |
| Baseball Nut | 160 | 16 | 2 | 9 | 5 | 30 | 55 | 0 | 1 | 1 other carb. 2 fat |
| Black Walnut | 160 | 13 | 3 | 11 | 5 | 30 | 45 | 1 | 1 | 1 other carb. 2 fat |
| Cherries Jubilee | 140 | 16 | 2 | 7 | 5 | 30 | 40 | 0 | 1 | 1 other carb. 1 fat |
| Chocolate | 150 | 16 | 2 | 9 | 6 | 30 | 60 | 0 | 1 | 1 other carb. 2 fat |
| Chocolate Almond | 180 | 17 | 3 | 11 | 5 | 30 | 55 | 1 | 1 | 1 other carb. 2 fat |
| Chocolate Chip | 150 | 15 | 2 | 10 | 6 | 35 | 45 | 0 | 1 | 1 other carb. 2 fat |
| Chocolate Chip Cookie Dough | 170 | 20 | 2 | 9 | 6 | 35 | 70 | 0 | 1 | 1 other carb. 2 fat |
| Chocolate Raspberry Truffle | 180 | 23 | 3 | 9 | 6 | 30 | 60 | 0 | 1½ | 1½ other carb. 2 fat |
| Cookies 'N Cream | 170 | 16 | 2 | 11 | 7 | 30 | 80 | 0 | 1 | 1 other carb. 2 fat |
| French Vanilla | 160 | 14 | 2 | 10 | 6 | 70 | 45 | 0 | 1 | 1 other carb. 2 fat |
| Fudge Brownie | 170 | 19 | 3 | 11 | 6 | 25 | 75 | 1 | 1 | 1 other carb. 2 fat |
| German Chocolate Cake | 160 | 20 | 3 | 10 | 6 | 25 | 75 | 0 | 1 | 1 other carb. 2 fat |
| Jamoca | 140 | 14 | 2 | 9 | 5 | 35 | 45 | 0 | 1 | 1 other carb. 2 fat |
| Jamoca Almond Fudge | 160 | 17 | 3 | 9 | 5 | 25 | 40 | 0 | 1 | 1 other carb. 2 fat |
| Mint Chocolate Chip | 150 | 15 | 3 | 10 | 6 | 35 | 45 | 0 | 1 | 1 other carb. 2 fat |
| Old-Fashioned Butter Pecan | 160 | 13 | 2 | 11 | 6 | 35 | 50 | 0 | 1 | 1 other carb. 2 fat |
| Oregon Blackberry | 140 | 16 | 2 | 8 | 5 | 30 | 50 | 0 | 1 | 1 other carb. 2 fat |
| Peanut Butter 'N Chocolate | 180 | 16 | 3 | 12 | 6 | 30 | 95 | 1 | 1 | 1 other carb. 2 fat |
| Pistachio Almond | 170 | 13 | 3 | 12 | 5 | 30 | 45 | 1 | 1 | 1 other carb. 2 fat |

## Baskin-Robbins® Ice Cream—*Continued* (serving size = ½ cup)

| | Calories | Carbohydrate (gm) | Protein (gm) | Total Fat (gm) | Saturated Fat (gm) | Cholesterol (mg) | Sodium (mg) | Dietary Fiber (gm) | Total Carb Exchange | Suggested Exchange Value |
|---|---|---|---|---|---|---|---|---|---|---|
| Prailines 'N Cream | 160 | 19 | 2 | 9 | 5 | 30 | 85 | 0 | 1 | 1 other carb. 2 fat |
| Quarterback Crunch | 160 | 18 | 2 | 10 | 7 | 30 | 75 | 0 | 1 | 1 other carb. 2 fat |
| Reeses® Peanut Butter Cup | 160 | 17 | 3 | 11 | 6 | 30 | 70 | 0 | 1 | 1 other carb. 2 fat |
| Rocky Road | 170 | 19 | 3 | 10 | 5 | 30 | 60 | 0 | 1 | 1 other carb. 2 fat |
| Vanilla | 140 | 14 | 3 | 8 | 5 | 40 | 40 | 0 | 1 | 1 other carb. 2 fat |
| Very Berry Strawberry | 130 | 16 | 1 | 7 | 4 | 25 | 40 | 0 | 1 | 1 other carb. 2 fat |
| Winter White Chocolate | 150 | 16 | 2 | 9 | 6 | 25 | 50 | 0 | 1 | 1 other carb. 2 fat |
| **Low Fat Ice Cream** | | | | | | | | | | |
| Caramel Apple ala Mode | 100 | 20 | 3 | 2 | 1 | 5 | 75 | 0 | 1 | 1 other carb. |
| Devine Cherry Cheesecake | 110 | 20 | 3 | 3 | 2 | 5 | 70 | 0 | 1 | 1 other carb. 1 fat |
| Espresso 'N Cream | 100 | 18 | 3 | 3 | 1 | 5 | 60 | 1 | 1 | 1 other carb. 1 fat |
| **Non-Fat Ice Cream** | | | | | | | | | | |
| Berry Innocent Cheesecake | 110 | 24 | 3 | 0 | 0 | 0 | 100 | 0 | 1½ | 1½ other carb. |
| Check-It-Out Cherry | 100 | 22 | 3 | 0 | 0 | 0 | 90 | 0 | 1½ | 1½ other carb. |
| Chocolate Vanilla Twist | 100 | 21 | 4 | 0 | 0 | 5 | 100 | 0 | 1 | 1 other carb. |
| Jamoca Swirl | 110 | 23 | 3 | 0 | 0 | 5 | 105 | 0 | 1½ | 1½ other carb. |
| **Non-Fat Frozen Yogurt** | | | | | | | | | | |
| Chocolate | 100 | 23 | 4 | 0 | 0 | 0 | 60 | 1 | 1½ | 1½ other carb. |
| Vanilla | 80 | 16 | 4 | 0 | 0 | 5 | 80 | 1 | 1 | 1 other carb. |
| Other Assorted Flavors | 100 | 22 | 3 | 0 | 0 | 0 | 55 | 0 | 1½ | 1½ other carb. |

## Baskin-Robbins® Ice Cream—*Continued* (serving size = ½ cup)

| | Calories | Carbohydrate (gm) | Protein (gm) | Total Fat (gm) | Saturated Fat (gm) | Cholesterol (mg) | Sodium (mg) | Dietary Fiber (gm) | Total Carb Exchange | Suggested Exchange Value |
|---|---|---|---|---|---|---|---|---|---|---|
| **Truly Free™ Frozen Yogurt** (Fat Free/Reduced Sugar) | | | | | | | | | | |
| Chocolate | 80 | 15 | 5 | 0 | 0 | 0 | 80 | 1 | 1 | 1 other carb. |
| Vanilla | 90 | 18 | 4 | 0 | 0 | 5 | 80 | 1 | 1 | 1 other carb. |
| Other Assorted Flavors | 90 | 17 | 4 | 0 | 0 | 5 | 80 | 1 | 1 | 1 other carb. |
| **Ices** | | | | | | | | | | |
| Assorted Flavors | 110 | 28 | 0 | 0 | 0 | 0 | 10 | 0 | 2 | 2 other carb. |
| **Sherbet** | | | | | | | | | | |
| Assorted Flavors | 120 | 26 | 1 | 2 | 1 | 5 | 25 | 0 | 2 | 2 other carb. |
| **Sorbet** | | | | | | | | | | |
| Mixed Berry Lemonade | 110 | 28 | 0 | 0 | 0 | 0 | 10 | 0 | 2 | 2 other carb. |
| Pink Raspberry Lemonade | 120 | 29 | 0 | 0 | 0 | 0 | 10 | 0 | 2 | 2 other carb. |
| Red Rasberry | 120 | 30 | 0 | 0 | 0 | 0 | 10 | 0 | 2 | 2 other carb. |

## Nathan's® Famous

### Platters

| | Calories | Carbohydrate (gm) | Protein (gm) | Total Fat (gm) | Saturated Fat (gm) | Cholesterol (mg) | Sodium (mg) | Dietary Fiber (gm) | Total Carb Exchange | Suggested Exchange Value |
|---|---|---|---|---|---|---|---|---|---|---|
| Chicken Platter<br>Serving: 2-piece meal | 1096 | 72 | 54 | 66 | 14 | 212 | 1413 | N/A | 5 | 5 starch<br>6 med. fat meat<br>7 fat |
| Chicken Platter<br>Serving: 4-piece meal | 1788 | 99 | 102 | 109 | 23 | 425 | 2369 | N/A | 6½ | 6½ starch<br>12 med. fat meat<br>10 fat |
| Fillet of Fish Platter<br>Serving: 1 meal | 1455 | 137 | 61 | 74 | 10 | 147 | 1837 | N/A | 9 | 9 starch<br>5 med. fat meat<br>10 fat |
| Fried Clam Platter<br>Serving: 2-piece meal | 1024 | 119 | 23 | 51 | 7 | 49 | 1826 | N/A | 8 | 8 starch<br>10 fat |

## Nathan's® Famous—*Continued*

### Platters—*Continued*

| | Calories | Carbohydrate (gm) | Protein (gm) | Total Fat (gm) | Saturated Fat (gm) | Cholesterol (mg) | Sodium (mg) | Dietary Fiber (gm) | Total Carb Exchange | Suggested Exchange Value |
|---|---|---|---|---|---|---|---|---|---|---|
| Fried Shrimp Platter<br>Serving: 1 meal | 796 | 100 | 23 | 34 | 5 | 83 | 1436 | N/A | 6½ | 6½ starch<br>1 med. fat meat<br>6 fat |

### Burgers/Sandwiches

| | Calories | Carbohydrate (gm) | Protein (gm) | Total Fat (gm) | Saturated Fat (gm) | Cholesterol (mg) | Sodium (mg) | Dietary Fiber (gm) | Total Carb Exchange | Suggested Exchange Value |
|---|---|---|---|---|---|---|---|---|---|---|
| Hamburger<br>Serving: 1 | 434 | 32 | 25 | 23 | 10 | 77 | 281 | N/A | 2 | 2 starch<br>3 med. fat meat<br>2 fat |
| Double Burger<br>Serving: 1 | 671 | 32 | 44 | 41 | 18 | 154 | 460 | N/A | 2 | 2 starch<br>5 med. fat meat<br>3 fat |
| Super Burger<br>Serving: 1 | 533 | 34 | 27 | 32 | 9 | 86 | 525 | N/A | 2 | 2 starch<br>3 med. fat meat<br>3 fat |
| Breaded Chicken Sandwich<br>Serving: 1 | 510 | 48 | 23 | 25 | 4 | 56 | 927 | N/A | 3 | 3 starch<br>2 med. fat meat<br>3 fat |
| Charbroiled Chicken Sandwich<br>Serving: 1 | 288 | 35 | 24 | 6 | 1 | 53 | 861 | N/A | 2 | 2 starch<br>3 lean meat |
| Chicken Salad<br>Serving: 1 | 154 | 9 | 20 | 4 | 1 | 49 | 345 | N/A | ½ | ½ starch<br>3 very lean meat |
| Cheese Steak Sandwich<br>Serving: 1 | 485 | 37 | 26 | 26 | 10 | 73 | 579 | N/A | 2½ | 2½ starch<br>3 med. fat meat<br>2 fat |
| Filet of Fish Sandwich<br>Serving: 1 | 403 | 46 | 20 | 15 | 2 | 32 | 714 | N/A | 3 | 3 starch<br>2 med. fat meat<br>1 fat |
| Frank Nuggets<br>Serving: 7-piece | 357 | 25 | 9 | 24 | 6 | 46 | 744 | N/A | 1½ | 1½ starch<br>1 med. fat meat<br>4 fat |
| Frankfurter<br>Serving: 1 | 310 | 22 | 13 | 19 | 8 | 45 | 820 | N/A | 1½ | 1½ starch<br>1 med. fat meat<br>3 fat |
| Pastrami Sandwich<br>Serving: 1 | 325 | 34 | 21 | 12 | 4 | 48 | 1013 | N/A | 2 | 2 starch<br>2 med. fat meat |

## Nathan's® Famous—*Continued*

| | Calories | Carbohydrate (gm) | Protein (gm) | Total Fat (gm) | Saturated Fat (gm) | Cholesterol (mg) | Sodium (mg) | Dietary Fiber (gm) | Total Carb Exchange | Suggested Exchange Value |
|---|---|---|---|---|---|---|---|---|---|---|
| **Burgers/Sandwiches—*Continued*** | | | | | | | | | | |
| Turkey Sandwich<br>Serving: 1 | 270 | 34 | 28 | 2 | 0 | 27 | 1458 | N/A | 2 | 2 starch<br>3 very lean meat |

## Wendy's®

### Sandwiches (serving size = 1)

| | Calories | Carbohydrate (gm) | Protein (gm) | Total Fat (gm) | Saturated Fat (gm) | Cholesterol (mg) | Sodium (mg) | Dietary Fiber (gm) | Total Carb Exchange | Suggested Exchange Value |
|---|---|---|---|---|---|---|---|---|---|---|
| Plain Single | 360 | 31 | 24 | 16 | 6 | 65 | 580 | 2 | 2 | 2 starch<br>3 med. fat meat |
| Single w/Everything | 420 | 37 | 25 | 20 | 7 | 70 | 920 | 3 | 2 | 2 starch<br>3 med. fat meat<br>1 fat |
| Big Bacon Classic | 580 | 46 | 34 | 30 | 12 | 100 | 1460 | 3 | 3 | 3 starch<br>4 med. fat meat<br>2 fat |
| Jr. Hamburger | 270 | 34 | 15 | 10 | 4 | 30 | 610 | 2 | 2 | 2 starch<br>1 med. fat meat<br>1 fat |
| Jr. Cheeseburger | 320 | 34 | 17 | 13 | 6 | 45 | 830 | 2 | 2 | 2 starch<br>2 med. fat meat |
| Jr. Bacon Cheeseburger | 380 | 34 | 20 | 19 | 7 | 60 | 850 | 2 | 2 | 2 starch<br>2 med. fat meat<br>2 fat |
| Jr. Cheeseburger Deluxe | 360 | 36 | 18 | 17 | 6 | 50 | 890 | 3 | 2 | 2 starch<br>2 med. fat meat<br>1 fat |
| Hamburger (Kid's Meal) | 270 | 33 | 15 | 10 | 4 | 30 | 610 | 2 | 2 | 2 starch<br>1 med. fat meat<br>1 fat |
| Cheeseburger (Kid's Meal) | 320 | 33 | 17 | 13 | 6 | 45 | 830 | 2 | 2 | 2 starch<br>2 med. fat meat |
| Grilled Chicken Sandwich | 310 | 35 | 27 | 8 | 2 | 65 | 790 | 2 | 2 | 2 starch<br>3 very lean meat<br>1 fat |
| Breaded Chicken Sandwich | 440 | 44 | 28 | 18 | 4 | 60 | 840 | 2 | 3 | 3 starch<br>3 med. fat meat<br>1 fat |

## Wendy's®—*Continued*

| | Calories | Carbohydrate (gm) | Protein (gm) | Total Fat (gm) | Saturated Fat (gm) | Cholesterol (mg) | Sodium (mg) | Dietary Fiber (gm) | Total Carb Exchange | Suggested Exchange Value |
|---|---|---|---|---|---|---|---|---|---|---|
| **Sandwiches—*Continued* (serving size = 1)** | | | | | | | | | | |
| Chicken Club Sandwich | 470 | 44 | 31 | 20 | 4 | 70 | 970 | 2 | 3 | 3 starch<br>3 med. fat meat<br>1 fat |
| Spicy Chicken Sandwich | 410 | 43 | 28 | 15 | 3 | 65 | 1280 | 2 | 3 | 3 starch<br>3 med. fat meat |
| **Baked Potatoes** | | | | | | | | | | |
| Plain<br>Serving: 1 | 310 | 71 | 7 | 0 | 0 | 0 | 25 | 7 | 5 | 5 starch |
| Bacon & Cheese<br>Serving: 1 | 530 | 78 | 17 | 18 | 4 | 20 | 1390 | 7 | 5 | 5 starch<br>1 high fat meat<br>2 fat |
| Broccoli & Cheese<br>Serving: 1 | 470 | 80 | 9 | 14 | 3 | 5 | 470 | 9 | 5 | 5 starch<br>1 vegetable<br>3 fat |
| Cheese<br>Serving: 1 | 570 | 78 | 14 | 23 | 8 | 30 | 640 | 7 | 5 | 5 starch<br>1 high fat meat<br>3 fat |
| Chili & Cheese<br>Serving: 1 | 630 | 83 | 20 | 24 | 9 | 40 | 770 | 9 | 5½ | 5½ starch<br>1 med. fat meat<br>4 fat |
| Sour Cream & Chives<br>Serving: 1 | 380 | 74 | 8 | 6 | 4 | 15 | 40 | 8 | 5 | 5 starch<br>1 fat |
| Sour Cream<br>Serving: 1 oz. pkt. | 60 | 1 | 1 | 6 | 4 | 10 | 15 | 0 | 0 | 1 fat |
| Whipped Margarine<br>Serving: ½ oz. pkt. | 60 | 0 | 0 | 7 | 2 | 0 | 115 | 0 | 0 | 1 fat |
| **French Fries/Chili/Nuggets** | | | | | | | | | | |
| French Fries<br>Serving: small | 270 | 35 | 4 | 13 | 2 | 0 | 85 | 3 | 2 | 2 starch<br>3 fat |
| Biggie Fries<br>Serving: 1 order | 470 | 61 | 7 | 23 | 4 | 0 | 150 | 6 | 4 | 4 starch<br>5 fat |
| Great Biggie Fries<br>Serving: 1 order | 570 | 73 | 8 | 27 | 4 | 0 | 180 | 7 | 5 | 5 starch<br>5 fat |

## Wendy's®—*Continued*

| | Calories | Carbohydrate (gm) | Protein (gm) | Total Fat (gm) | Saturated Fat (gm) | Cholesterol (mg) | Sodium (mg) | Dietary Fiber (gm) | Total Carb Exchange | Suggested Exchange Value |
|---|---|---|---|---|---|---|---|---|---|---|
| **French Fries/Chili/Nuggets—*Continued*** | | | | | | | | | | |
| Chicken Nuggets Serving: 5-piece | 230 | 11 | 11 | 16 | 3 | 30 | 470 | 0 | 1 | 1 starch 1 med. fat meat 2 fat |
| Chicken Nugget's Child's Portion Serving: 4-piece | 190 | 9 | 9 | 13 | 3 | 25 | 380 | 0 | ½ | ½ starch 1 med. fat meat 2 fat |
| Barbecue Sauce Serving: 1 oz. pkt. | 45 | 10 | 1 | 0 | 0 | 0 | 160 | 0 | ½ | ½ other carb. |
| Honey Mustard Serving: 1 oz. pkt. | 130 | 6 | 0 | 12 | 2 | 10 | 220 | 0 | ½ | ½ other carb. 2 fat |
| Sweet & Sour Sauce Serving: 1 oz. pkt. | 50 | 12 | 0 | 0 | 0 | 0 | 120 | 0 | 1 | 1 other carb. |
| Small Chili Serving: 8 oz. | 210 | 21 | 15 | 7 | 3 | 30 | 800 | 5 | 1½ | 1½ starch 2 med. fat meat |
| Large Chili Serving: 12 oz. | 310 | 32 | 23 | 10 | 4 | 45 | 1190 | 7 | 2 | 2 starch 2 med. fat meat |
| Cheddar Cheese Serving: 2 tbsp. | 70 | 1 | 4 | 6 | 4 | 15 | 110 | 0 | 0 | 1 high fat meat |

## KFC®

### Tender Roast® Chicken (serving size = 1)

| | Calories | Carbohydrate (gm) | Protein (gm) | Total Fat (gm) | Saturated Fat (gm) | Cholesterol (mg) | Sodium (mg) | Dietary Fiber (gm) | Total Carb Exchange | Suggested Exchange Value |
|---|---|---|---|---|---|---|---|---|---|---|
| Breast w/skin | 251 | 1 | 37 | 11 | 3 | 151 | 830 | 0 | 0 | 5 lean meat |
| Breast w/o skin | 169 | 1 | 31 | 4 | 1 | 112 | 797 | 0 | 0 | 4 very lean meat |
| Leg w/skin | 97 | <1 | 15 | 4 | 1 | 85 | 271 | 0 | 0 | 2 med. fat meat |
| Leg w/o skin | 67 | <1 | 11 | 2 | <1 | 63 | 259 | 0 | 0 | 2 very lean meat |
| Thigh w/skin | 207 | 2 | 18 | 12 | 4 | 120 | 504 | 0 | 0 | 3 med. fat meat |
| Thigh w/o skin | 106 | <1 | 13 | 6 | 2 | 84 | 312 | 0 | 0 | 2 lean meat |
| Wing w/skin | 121 | 1 | 12 | 8 | 2 | 74 | 331 | 0 | 0 | 2 med. fat meat |

### Original Recipe® Chicken (serving size = 1)

| | Calories | Carbohydrate (gm) | Protein (gm) | Total Fat (gm) | Saturated Fat (gm) | Cholesterol (mg) | Sodium (mg) | Dietary Fiber (gm) | Total Carb Exchange | Suggested Exchange Value |
|---|---|---|---|---|---|---|---|---|---|---|
| Breast | 400 | 16 | 29 | 24 | 6 | 135 | 1116 | 1 | 1 | 1 starch 4 med. fat meat 1 fat |

## KFC®—*Continued*

| | Calories | Carbohydrate (gm) | Protein (gm) | Total Fat (gm) | Saturated Fat (gm) | Cholesterol (mg) | Sodium (mg) | Dietary Fiber (gm) | Total Carb Exchange | Suggested Exchange Value |
|---|---|---|---|---|---|---|---|---|---|---|
| **Original Recipe® Chicken—*Continued* (serving size = 1)** | | | | | | | | | | |
| Leg | 140 | 4 | 13 | 9 | 2 | 75 | 422 | 0 | 0 | 2 med. fat meat |
| Thigh | 250 | 6 | 16 | 18 | 5 | 95 | 747 | 1 | ½ | ½ starch |
| | | | | | | | | | | 2 med. fat meat |
| | | | | | | | | | | 2 fat |
| Whole Wing | 140 | 5 | 9 | 10 | 3 | 55 | 414 | 0 | 0 | 1 med. fat meat |
| | | | | | | | | | | 1 fat |
| **Extra Crispy™ Chicken (serving size = 1)** | | | | | | | | | | |
| Breast | 470 | 25 | 31 | 28 | 7 | 80 | 930 | 1 | 1½ | 1½ starch |
| | | | | | | | | | | 4 med. fat meat |
| | | | | | | | | | | 2 fat |
| Leg | 190 | 8 | 13 | 11 | 3 | 60 | 260 | <1 | ½ | ½ starch |
| | | | | | | | | | | 2 med. fat meat |
| Thigh | 370 | 18 | 19 | 25 | 6 | 70 | 540 | 2 | 1 | 1 starch |
| | | | | | | | | | | 2 med. fat meat |
| | | | | | | | | | | 3 fat |
| Whole Wing | 200 | 10 | 10 | 13 | 4 | 45 | 290 | <1 | ½ | ½ starch |
| | | | | | | | | | | 1 med. fat meat |
| | | | | | | | | | | 2 fat |
| **Hot & Spicy Chicken (serving size = 1)** | | | | | | | | | | |
| Breast | 530 | 23 | 32 | 35 | 8 | 110 | 1110 | 2 | 1½ | 1½ starch |
| | | | | | | | | | | 4 med. fat meat |
| | | | | | | | | | | 3 fat |
| Leg | 190 | 10 | 13 | 11 | 3 | 50 | 300 | <1 | ½ | ½ starch |
| | | | | | | | | | | 2 med. fat meat |
| Thigh | 370 | 13 | 18 | 27 | 7 | 90 | 570 | 1 | 1 | 1 starch |
| | | | | | | | | | | 2 med. fat meat |
| | | | | | | | | | | 3 fat |
| Whole Wing | 210 | 9 | 10 | 15 | 4 | 50 | 340 | <1 | ½ | ½ starch |
| | | | | | | | | | | 1 med. fat meat |
| | | | | | | | | | | 2 fat |

## KFC®—*Continued*

| | Calories | Carbohydrate (gm) | Protein (gm) | Total Fat (gm) | Saturated Fat (gm) | Cholesterol (mg) | Sodium (mg) | Dietary Fiber (gm) | Total Carb Exchange | Suggested Exchange Value |
|---|---|---|---|---|---|---|---|---|---|---|
| **Other Entrees** | | | | | | | | | | |
| Crispy Strips® <br> Serving: 3-piece | 261 | 10 | 20 | 16 | 4 | 40 | 658 | 3 | ½ | ½ starch <br> 3 med. fat meat |
| Spicy Buffalo Crispy Strips™ <br> Serving: 3-piece | 350 | 22 | 22 | 19 | 4 | 35 | 1110 | 2 | 1½ | 1½ starch <br> 3 med. fat meat <br> 1 fat |
| Chunky Chicken Pot Pie <br> Serving: 1 | 770 | 69 | 29 | 42 | 13 | 70 | 2160 | 5 | 4½ | 4½ starch <br> 2 med. fat meat <br> 6 fat |
| Hot Wings™ <br> Serving: 6-piece | 471 | 18 | 27 | 33 | 8 | 150 | 1230 | 2 | 1 | 1 starch <br> 3 med. fat meat <br> 4 fat |
| Original Recipe® Chicken Sandwich <br> Serving: 1 | 497 | 46 | 29 | 22 | 5 | 52 | 1213 | 3 | 3 | 3 starch <br> 3 med. fat meat <br> 1 fat |
| Value BBQ Flavored Chicken Sandwich <br> Serving: 1 | 256 | 28 | 17 | 8 | 1 | 57 | 782 | 2 | 2 | 2 starch <br> 2 med. fat meat |
| Kentucky Nuggets® <br> Serving: 6-piece | 284 | 15 | 16 | 18 | 4 | 66 | 865 | <1 | 1 | 1 starch <br> 2 med. fat meat <br> 2 fat |
| **Side Choices** (serving size = 1) | | | | | | | | | | |
| BBQ Baked Beans | 190 | 33 | 6 | 3 | 1 | 5 | 760 | 6 | 2 | 2 starch <br> 1 fat |
| Biscuit | 180 | 20 | 4 | 10 | 3 | 0 | 560 | <1 | 1 | 1 starch <br> 2 fat |
| Cole Slaw | 180 | 21 | 2 | 9 | 2 | 5 | 280 | 3 | 1 | 1 other carb. <br> 1 vegetable <br> 2 fat |
| Corn on the Cob | 150 | 35 | 5 | 2 | 0 | 0 | 20 | 2 | 2 | 2 starch |
| Cornbread | 228 | 25 | 3 | 13 | 2 | 42 | 194 | 1 | 1½ | 1½ starch <br> 3 fat |
| Green Beans | 45 | 7 | 1 | 2 | <1 | 5 | 730 | 3 | 0 | 1 vegetable |
| Macaroni & Cheese | 180 | 21 | 7 | 8 | 3 | 10 | 860 | 2 | 1½ | 1½ starch <br> 2 fat |

## KFC®—*Continued*

| | Calories | Carbohydrate (gm) | Protein (gm) | Total Fat (gm) | Saturated Fat (gm) | Cholesterol (mg) | Sodium (mg) | Dietary Fiber (gm) | Total Carb Exchange | Suggested Exchange Value |
|---|---|---|---|---|---|---|---|---|---|---|
| **Side Choices—*Continued* (serving size = 1)** | | | | | | | | | | |
| Mean Greens™ | 70 | 11 | 4 | 3 | 1 | 10 | 650 | 5 | 0 | 2 vegetable<br>1 fat |
| Potato Salad | 230 | 23 | 4 | 14 | 2 | 15 | 540 | 3 | 1½ | 1½ starch<br>3 fat |
| Potatoes w/Gravy | 120 | 17 | 1 | 6 | 1 | <1 | 440 | 2 | 1 | 1 starch<br>1 fat |
| Potato Wedges | 280 | 28 | 5 | 13 | 4 | 5 | 750 | 5 | 2 | 2 starch<br>3 fat |

## McDonald's®

| | Calories | Carbohydrate (gm) | Protein (gm) | Total Fat (gm) | Saturated Fat (gm) | Cholesterol (mg) | Sodium (mg) | Dietary Fiber (gm) | Total Carb Exchange | Suggested Exchange Value |
|---|---|---|---|---|---|---|---|---|---|---|
| **Sandwiches (serving size = 1)** | | | | | | | | | | |
| Hamburger | 260 | 34 | 13 | 9 | 4 | 30 | 580 | 2 | 2 | 2 starch<br>1 med. fat meat<br>1 fat |
| Cheeseburger | 320 | 35 | 15 | 13 | 6 | 40 | 820 | 2 | 2 | 2 starch<br>1 med. fat meat<br>2 fat |
| Quarter Pounder® | 420 | 37 | 23 | 21 | 8 | 70 | 820 | 2 | 2½ | 2½ starch<br>2 med. fat meat<br>2 fat |
| Quarter Pounder®<br>w/Cheese | 530 | 38 | 28 | 30 | 13 | 95 | 1290 | 2 | 2½ | 2½ starch<br>3 med. fat meat<br>3 fat |
| Big Mac® | 560 | 45 | 26 | 31 | 10 | 85 | 1070 | 3 | 3 | 3 starch<br>2 med. fat meat<br>4 fat |
| Arch Deluxe® | 550 | 39 | 28 | 31 | 11 | 90 | 1010 | 4 | 2½ | 2½ starch<br>3 med. fat meat<br>3 fat |
| Arch Deluxe®<br>w/Bacon | 590 | 39 | 32 | 34 | 12 | 100 | 1150 | 4 | 2½ | 2½ starch<br>4 med. fat meat<br>3 fat |
| Crispy Chicken<br>Deluxe™ | 500 | 43 | 26 | 25 | 4 | 55 | 1100 | 4 | 3 | 3 starch<br>2 med. fat meat<br>3 fat |

## McDonald's®—*Continued*

| | Calories | Carbohydrate (gm) | Protein (gm) | Total Fat (gm) | Saturated Fat (gm) | Cholesterol (mg) | Sodium (mg) | Dietary Fiber (gm) | Total Carb Exchange | Suggested Exchange Value |
|---|---|---|---|---|---|---|---|---|---|---|
| **Sandwiches—*Continued* (serving size = 1)** | | | | | | | | | | |
| Fish Filet Deluxe™ | 560 | 54 | 23 | 28 | 6 | 60 | 1060 | 4 | 3½ | 3½ starch<br>2 med. fat meat<br>4 fat |
| Filet-O-Fish® | 450 | 42 | 16 | 25 | 5 | 50 | 870 | 2 | 3 | 3 starch<br>1 med. fat meat<br>4 fat |
| Grilled Chicken Deluxe™ | 440 | 38 | 27 | 20 | 3 | 60 | 1040 | 4 | 2½ | 2½ starch<br>3 lean meat<br>3 fat |
| Grilled Chicken Deluxe™ w/o mayonnaise | 300 | 38 | 27 | 5 | 1 | 50 | 930 | 4 | 2½ | 2½ starch<br>3 lean meat |
| **French Fries** | | | | | | | | | | |
| French Fries<br>Serving: small | 210 | 26 | 3 | 10 | 2 | 0 | 135 | 2 | 2 | 2 starch<br>2 fat |
| French Fries<br>Serving: large | 450 | 57 | 6 | 22 | 4 | 0 | 290 | 5 | 4 | 4 starch<br>4 fat |
| French Fries<br>Serving: super size® | 540 | 68 | 8 | 26 | 5 | 0 | 350 | 6 | 4½ | 4½ starch<br>5 fat |
| **Chicken McNuggets®/Sauces** | | | | | | | | | | |
| Chicken McNuggets®<br>Serving: 4-piece | 190 | 10 | 12 | 11 | 3 | 40 | 340 | 0 | ½ | ½ starch<br>2 med. fat meat |
| Chicken McNuggets®<br>Serving: 6-piece | 290 | 15 | 18 | 17 | 4 | 60 | 510 | 0 | 1 | 1 starch<br>2 med. fat meat<br>1 fat |
| Chicken McNuggets®<br>Serving: 9-piece | 430 | 23 | 27 | 26 | 5 | 90 | 770 | 0 | 1½ | 1½ starch<br>3 med. fat meat<br>2 fat |
| Hot Mustard Sauce<br>Serving: 1 oz. pkt. | 60 | 7 | 1 | 4 | 0 | 5 | 240 | <1 | ½ | ½ other carb.<br>1 fat |
| Barbeque Sauce<br>Serving: 1 oz. pkt. | 45 | 10 | 0 | 0 | 0 | 0 | 250 | 0 | ½ | ½ other carb. |

## McDonald's®—*Continued*

| | Calories | Carbohydrate (gm) | Protein (gm) | Total Fat (gm) | Saturated Fat (gm) | Cholesterol (mg) | Sodium (mg) | Dietary Fiber (gm) | Total Carb Exchange | Suggested Exchange Value |
|---|---|---|---|---|---|---|---|---|---|---|
| **Chicken McNuggets®—*Continued*** | | | | | | | | | | |
| Sweet 'N Sour Sauce | 50 | 11 | 0 | 0 | 0 | 0 | 140 | 0 | 1 | 1 other carb. |
| Serving: 1 oz. pkt. | | | | | | | | | | |
| Honey | 45 | 12 | 0 | 0 | 0 | 0 | 0 | 0 | 1 | 1 other carb. |
| Serving: 1 oz. pkt. | | | | | | | | | | |
| Honey Mustard | 50 | 3 | 0 | 5 | <1 | 10 | 85 | 0 | 0 | 1 fat |
| Serving: 1 oz. pkt. | | | | | | | | | | |
| Light Mayonnaise | 40 | 1 | 0 | 4 | <1 | 5 | 85 | 0 | 0 | 1 fat |
| **Salads/Salad Dressings** | | | | | | | | | | |
| Garden Salad+ | 35 | 7 | 2 | 0 | 0 | 0 | 20 | 3 | 0 | 1 vegetable |
| Serving: 1 | | | | | | | | | | |
| Grilled Chicken Salad Deluxe+ | 120 | 7 | 21 | 2 | 0 | 45 | 240 | 3 | 0 | 1 vegetable 3 very lean meat |
| Serving: 1 | | | | | | | | | | |
| Ceasar | 160 | 7 | 2 | 14 | 3 | 20 | 450 | 0 | ½ | ½ other carb. 3 fat |
| Serving: 2 oz. pkt. | | | | | | | | | | |
| Red French (Red. Cal.) | 160 | 23 | 0 | 8 | 1 | 0 | 490 | 0 | 1½ | 1½ other carb. 2 fat |
| Serving: 2 oz. pkt. | | | | | | | | | | |
| Ranch | 230 | 10 | 1 | 21 | 3 | 20 | 550 | 0 | ½ | ½ other carb. 4 fat |
| Serving: 2 oz. pkt. | | | | | | | | | | |
| Herb Vinaigrette | 50 | 11 | 0 | 0 | 0 | 0 | 330 | 0 | 1 | 1 other carb. |
| Serving: 2 oz. pkt. | | | | | | | | | | |
| **Breakfast (serving size = 1)** | | | | | | | | | | |
| English Muffin | 140 | 25 | 4 | 2 | 0 | 0 | 210 | 1 | 2 | 2 starch |
| Egg McMuffin® | 290 | 27 | 17 | 12 | 5 | 235 | 790 | 1 | 2 | 2 starch 2 med. fat meat |
| Sausage McMuffin® | 360 | 26 | 13 | 23 | 8 | 45 | 740 | 1 | 2 | 2 starch 1 high fat meat 3 fat |
| Sausage McMuffin® w/Egg | 440 | 27 | 19 | 28 | 10 | 255 | 890 | 1 | 2 | 2 starch 2 med. fat meat 4 fat |

## McDonald's®—*Continued*

| | Calories | Carbohydrate (gm) | Protein (gm) | Total Fat (gm) | Saturated Fat (gm) | Cholesterol (mg) | Sodium (mg) | Dietary Fiber (gm) | Total Carb Exchange | Suggested Exchange Value |
|---|---|---|---|---|---|---|---|---|---|---|
| **Breakfast—*Continued* (serving size = 1)** | | | | | | | | | | |
| Biscuit | 290 | 34 | 5 | 15 | 3 | 0 | 780 | 1 | 2 | 2 starch<br>3 fat |
| Sausage Biscuit | 470 | 35 | 11 | 31 | 9 | 35 | 1080 | 1 | 2 | 2 starch<br>1 high fat meat<br>5 fat |
| Sausage Biscuit w/Egg | 550 | 35 | 18 | 37 | 10 | 245 | 1160 | 1 | 2 | 2 starch<br>2 med. fat meat<br>5 fat |
| Bacon, Egg & Cheese Biscuit | 470 | 36 | 18 | 28 | 8 | 235 | 1250 | 1 | 2 | 2 starch<br>2 med. fat meat<br>4 fat |
| Sausage | 170 | 0 | 6 | 16 | 5 | 35 | 290 | 0 | 0 | 1 high fat meat<br>2 fat |
| Scrambled Eggs | 160 | 1 | 13 | 11 | 4 | 425 | 170 | 0 | 0 | 2 med. fat meat |
| Hash Browns | 130 | 14 | 1 | 8 | 2 | 0 | 330 | 1 | 1 | 1 starch<br>2 fat |
| Hot Cakes (plain) | 340 | 58 | 9 | 9 | 2 | 25 | 540 | 2 | 4 | 4 starch<br>2 fat |
| Hot Cakes w/syrup & margarine | 610 | 104 | 9 | 18 | 4 | 25 | 680 | 2 | 7 | 4 starch<br>3 other carb.<br>3 fat |
| Breakfast Burrito | 320 | 23 | 13 | 20 | 7 | 195 | 600 | 2 | 1½ | 1½ starch<br>1 med. fat meat<br>3 fat |

### Desserts/Shakes

| | Calories | Carbohydrate (gm) | Protein (gm) | Total Fat (gm) | Saturated Fat (gm) | Cholesterol (mg) | Sodium (mg) | Dietary Fiber (gm) | Total Carb Exchange | Suggested Exchange Value |
|---|---|---|---|---|---|---|---|---|---|---|
| Vanilla Cone<br>Serving: 1 | 150 | 23 | 4 | 5 | 3 | 20 | 75 | 0 | 1½ | 1½ other carb.<br>1 fat |
| Strawberry Sundae<br>Serving: 1 | 290 | 50 | 7 | 7 | 5 | 30 | 95 | <1 | 3 | 3 other carb.<br>1 fat |
| Hot Caramel Sundae<br>Serving: 1 | 360 | 61 | 7 | 10 | 6 | 35 | 180 | 0 | 4 | 4 other carb.<br>2 fat |
| Hot Fudge Sundae<br>Serving: 1 | 340 | 52 | 8 | 12 | 9 | 30 | 170 | 1 | 3½ | 3½ other carb.<br>2 fat |
| Nut Topping<br>Serving: ¼ oz. | 40 | 2 | 2 | 4 | 0 | 0 | 55 | <1 | 0 | 1 fat |

## McDonald's®—*Continued*

| | Calories | Carbohydrate (gm) | Protein (gm) | Total Fat (gm) | Saturated Fat (gm) | Cholesterol (mg) | Sodium (mg) | Dietary Fiber (gm) | Total Carb Exchange | Suggested Exchange Value |
|---|---|---|---|---|---|---|---|---|---|---|
| **Desserts/Shakes—*Continued*** | | | | | | | | | | |
| Butterfinger® McFlurry™ Serving: 1 | 620 | 90 | 16 | 22 | 14 | 70 | 260 | <1 | 6 | 6 other carb. 4 fat |
| M&M® McFlurry™ Serving: 1 | 630 | 90 | 16 | 23 | 15 | 75 | 210 | 1 | 6 | 6 other carb. 5 fat |
| Nestle Crunch® McFlurry™ Serving: 1 | 630 | 89 | 16 | 24 | 16 | 75 | 230 | <1 | 6 | 6 other carb. 5 fat |
| Oreo® McFlurry™ Serving: 1 | 570 | 82 | 15 | 20 | 12 | 70 | 280 | <1 | 5 | 5 other carb. 4 fat |
| Baked Apple Pie Serving: 1 slice | 260 | 34 | 3 | 13 | 4 | 0 | 200 | <1 | 2 | 2 other carb. 3 fat |
| Chocolate Chip Cookie Serving: 1 | 170 | 22 | 2 | 10 | 6 | 20 | 120 | 1 | 1½ | 1½ other carb. 2 fat |
| McDonaldland® Cookies Serving: 1 pkg. | 180 | 32 | 3 | 5 | 1 | 0 | 190 | 1 | 2 | 2 other carb. 1 fat |
| Chocolate Shake Serving: small | 360 | 60 | 11 | 9 | 6 | 40 | 250 | 1 | 4 | 4 other carb. 2 fat |
| Strawberry Shake Serving: small | 360 | 60 | 11 | 9 | 6 | 40 | 180 | 0 | 4 | 4 other carb. 2 fat |
| Vanilla Shake Serving: small | 360 | 59 | 11 | 9 | 6 | 40 | 250 | 0 | 4 | 4 other carb. 2 fat |

## Burger King®

### Breakfast

| | Calories | Carbohydrate (gm) | Protein (gm) | Total Fat (gm) | Saturated Fat (gm) | Cholesterol (mg) | Sodium (mg) | Dietary Fiber (gm) | Total Carb Exchange | Suggested Exchange Value |
|---|---|---|---|---|---|---|---|---|---|---|
| Croissan'wich® w/Sausage, Egg & Cheese Serving: 1 | 530 | 23 | 18 | 41 | 13 | 185 | 1120 | 1 | 1½ | 1½ starch 2 med. fat meat 6 fat |
| Croissan'wich® w/Sausage & Cheese Serving: 1 | 450 | 21 | 13 | 35 | 12 | 45 | 940 | 1 | 1½ | 1½ starch 2 high fat meat 4 fat |

## Burger King®—*Continued*

### Breakfast—*Continued*

| | Calories | Carbohydrate (gm) | Protein (gm) | Total Fat (gm) | Saturated Fat (gm) | Cholesterol (mg) | Sodium (mg) | Dietary Fiber (gm) | Total Carb Exchange | Suggested Exchange Value |
|---|---|---|---|---|---|---|---|---|---|---|
| Biscuit | 300 | 35 | 6 | 15 | 3 | 0 | 830 | 1 | 2 | 2 starch |
| Serving: 1 | | | | | | | | | | 3 fat |
| Biscuit w/Egg | 380 | 37 | 11 | 21 | 5 | 140 | 1010 | 1 | 2 | 2 starch |
| Serving: 1 | | | | | | | | | | 1 med. fat meat |
| | | | | | | | | | | 3 fat |
| Biscuit w/Sausage | 490 | 36 | 13 | 33 | 10 | 35 | 1240 | 1 | 2 | 2 starch |
| Serving: 1 | | | | | | | | | | 1 high fat meat |
| | | | | | | | | | | 5 fat |
| Biscuit w/Sausage, | 620 | 37 | 20 | 43 | 14 | 185 | 1650 | 1 | 2 | 2 starch |
| Egg & Cheese | | | | | | | | | | 2 med. fat meat |
| Serving: 1 | | | | | | | | | | 7 fat |
| French Toast Sticks | 440 | 51 | 7 | 23 | 5 | 2 | 490 | 3 | 3 | 3 starch |
| Serving: order of 5 | | | | | | | | | | 5 fat |
| Cini-Minis w/o Icing | 440 | 51 | 6 | 23 | 6 | 25 | 710 | 1 | 3 | 3 other carb. |
| Serving: order of 4 | | | | | | | | | | 4 fat |
| Vanilla Icing | 110 | 20 | 0 | 3 | <1 | 0 | 40 | 0 | 1 | 1 other carb. |
| Serving: 1 oz. pkt. | | | | | | | | | | |
| Hash Brown Rounds | 240 | 25 | 2 | 15 | 6 | 0 | 440 | 2 | 1½ | 1½ starch |
| Serving: small | | | | | | | | | | 3 fat |
| Hash Brown Rounds | 410 | 42 | 3 | 26 | 10 | 0 | 750 | 4 | 3 | 3 starch |
| Serving: large | | | | | | | | | | 5 fat |
| Bacon | 40 | 0 | 3 | 3 | 1 | 10 | 170 | 0 | 0 | 1 fat |
| Serving: 3-piece | | | | | | | | | | |
| Ham | 35 | 0 | 6 | 1 | 0 | 15 | 770 | 0 | 0 | 1 lean meat |
| Serving: 1 slice | | | | | | | | | | |
| A.M. Express® Dip | 80 | 21 | 0 | 0 | 0 | 0 | 20 | 0 | 1½ | 1½ other carb. |
| Serving: 1 oz. pkt. | | | | | | | | | | |
| A.M. Express® | 30 | 7 | 0 | 0 | 0 | 0 | 0 | 0 | ½ | ½ other carb. |
| Grape Jam | | | | | | | | | | |
| Serving: ½ oz. pkt. | | | | | | | | | | |
| A. M. Express® | 30 | 8 | 0 | 0 | 0 | 0 | 0 | 0 | ½ | ½ other carb. |
| Strawberry Jam | | | | | | | | | | |
| Serving: ½ oz. pkt. | | | | | | | | | | |
| Land O'Lakes® | 65 | 0 | 0 | 7 | 1 | 0 | 75 | 0 | 0 | 1 fat |
| Classic Blend | | | | | | | | | | |
| Serving: ⅓ oz. pkt. | | | | | | | | | | |

## Burger King®—*Continued*

| | Calories | Carbohydrate (gm) | Protein (gm) | Total Fat (gm) | Saturated Fat (gm) | Cholesterol (mg) | Sodium (mg) | Dietary Fiber (gm) | Total Carb Exchange | Suggested Exchange Value |
|---|---|---|---|---|---|---|---|---|---|---|
| **Burgers** (serving size = 1) | | | | | | | | | | |
| Whopper® Sandwich | 660 | 47 | 29 | 40 | 12 | 85 | 900 | 3 | 3 | 3 starch<br>3 med. fat meat<br>5 fat |
| Whopper® w/Cheese | 760 | 47 | 35 | 48 | 17 | 110 | 1380 | 3 | 3 | 3 starch<br>4 med. fat meat<br>5 fat |
| Double Whopper® | 920 | 47 | 49 | 59 | 21 | 155 | 980 | 3 | 3 | 3 starch<br>6 med. fat meat<br>6 fat |
| Double Whopper® w/Cheese | 1010 | 47 | 55 | 67 | 26 | 180 | 1460 | 3 | 3 | 3 starch<br>7 med. fat meat<br>6 fat |
| Whopper Jr.® Sandwich | 400 | 28 | 19 | 24 | 8 | 55 | 530 | 2 | 2 | 2 starch<br>2 med. fat meat<br>3 fat |
| Whopper Jr.® w/Cheese | 450 | 28 | 22 | 28 | 10 | 65 | 770 | 2 | 2 | 2 starch<br>2 med. fat meat<br>4 fat |
| Big King™ Sandwich | 640 | 28 | 38 | 42 | 18 | 125 | 980 | 1 | 2 | 2 starch<br>5 med. fat meat<br>3 fat |
| Hamburger | 320 | 27 | 19 | 15 | 6 | 50 | 520 | 1 | 2 | 2 starch<br>2 med. fat meat<br>1 fat |
| Cheeseburger | 360 | 27 | 21 | 19 | 9 | 60 | 760 | 1 | 2 | 2 starch<br>2 med. fat meat<br>2 fat |
| Bacon Cheeseburger | 400 | 27 | 24 | 22 | 10 | 70 | 940 | 1 | 2 | 2 starch<br>3 med. fat meat<br>1 fat |
| Double Cheeseburger | 580 | 27 | 38 | 36 | 17 | 120 | 1060 | 1 | 2 | 2 starch<br>4 med. fat meat<br>3 fat |
| Bacon Double Cheeseburger | 620 | 28 | 41 | 38 | 18 | 125 | 1230 | 1 | 2 | 2 starch<br>5 med. fat meat<br>3 fat |

## Burger King®—*Continued*

| | Calories | Carbohydrate (gm) | Protein (gm) | Total Fat (gm) | Saturated Fat (gm) | Cholesterol (mg) | Sodium (mg) | Dietary Fiber (gm) | Total Carb Exchange | Suggested Exchange Value |
|---|---|---|---|---|---|---|---|---|---|---|
| **Sandwiches/Side Items** | | | | | | | | | | |
| BK Big Fish® Sandwich<br>Serving: 1 | 720 | 59 | 23 | 43 | 9 | 80 | 1180 | 3 | 4 | 4 starch<br>2 med. fat meat<br>6 fat |
| BK Broiler® Chicken Sandwich<br>Serving: 1 | 530 | 45 | 29 | 26 | 5 | 105 | 1060 | 2 | 3 | 3 starch<br>3 very lean meat<br>4 fat |
| Chicken Sandwich<br>Serving: 1 | 710 | 54 | 26 | 43 | 9 | 60 | 1400 | 2 | 3 | 3 starch<br>2 med. fat meat<br>7 fat |
| Chick 'N Crisp<br>Serving: 1 | 460 | 37 | 16 | 27 | 6 | 35 | 890 | 3 | 2½ | 2½ starch<br>1 med. fat meat<br>4 fat |
| Chicken Tenders®<br>Serving: 4-piece | 180 | 9 | 11 | 11 | 3 | 30 | 470 | 0 | ½ | ½ starch<br>1 med. fat meat<br>1 fat |
| Chicken Tenders®<br>Serving: 5-piece | 230 | 11 | 14 | 14 | 4 | 40 | 590 | <1 | ½ | ½ starch<br>2 med. fat meat<br>1 fat |
| Chicken Tenders®<br>Serving: 8-piece | 350 | 17 | 22 | 22 | 7 | 65 | 940 | 1 | 1 | 1 starch<br>3 med. fat meat<br>1 fat |
| French Fries (salted)<br>Serving: small | 250 | 32 | 2 | 13 | 5 | 0 | 550 | 2 | 2 | 2 starch<br>3 fat |
| French Fries (salted)<br>Serving: medium | 400 | 50 | 3 | 21 | 8 | 0 | 820 | 4 | 3 | 3 starch<br>4 fat |
| French Fries (salted)<br>Serving: king-size | 590 | 74 | 5 | 30 | 12 | 0 | 1180 | 5 | 5 | 5 starch<br>6 fat |
| Onion Rings<br>Serving: medium | 380 | 46 | 5 | 19 | 4 | 2 | 550 | 4 | 3 | 3 starch<br>4 fat |
| Onion Rings<br>Serving: king-size | 600 | 74 | 8 | 30 | 7 | 4 | 880 | 6 | 5 | 5 starch<br>6 fat |
| Dutch Apple Pie<br>Serving: 1 | 300 | 39 | 3 | 15 | 3 | 0 | 230 | 2 | 2½ | 2½ other carb.<br>3 fat |

## Burger King®—*Continued*

| | Calories | Carbohydrate (gm) | Protein (gm) | Total Fat (gm) | Saturated Fat (gm) | Cholesterol (mg) | Sodium (mg) | Dietary Fiber (gm) | Total Carb Exchange | Suggested Exchange Value |
|---|---|---|---|---|---|---|---|---|---|---|
| **Shakes** | | | | | | | | | | |
| Chocolate Shake | 440 | 75 | 12 | 10 | 6 | 30 | 330 | 4 | 5 | 5 other carb. |
| Serving: 14 fl. oz. | | | | | | | | | | 2 fat |
| Chocolate Shake | 570 | 105 | 14 | 10 | 6 | 30 | 520 | 3 | 7 | 7 other carb. |
| w/syrup added | | | | | | | | | | 2 fat |
| Serving: 16 fl. oz. | | | | | | | | | | |
| Strawberry Shake | 550 | 104 | 13 | 9 | 5 | 30 | 350 | 2 | 7 | 7 other carb. |
| w/syrup added | | | | | | | | | | 2 fat |
| Serving: 16 fl. oz. | | | | | | | | | | |
| Vanilla Shake | 430 | 73 | 13 | 9 | 5 | 30 | 330 | 2 | 5 | 5 other carb. |
| | | | | | | | | | | 2 fat |
| **Dipping Sauces/Condiment Sauces** | | | | | | | | | | |
| Barbecue | 35 | 9 | 0 | 0 | 0 | 0 | 400 | 0 | ½ | ½ other carb. |
| Serving: 1 oz. pkt. | | | | | | | | | | |
| Honey Flavored | 90 | 23 | 0 | 0 | 0 | 0 | 10 | 0 | 1½ | 1½ other carb. |
| Serving: 1 oz. pkt. | | | | | | | | | | |
| Honey Mustard | 90 | 10 | 0 | 6 | 1 | 10 | 150 | 0 | ½ | ½ other carb. |
| Serving: 1 oz. pkt. | | | | | | | | | | 1 fat |
| Ranch | 170 | 2 | 0 | 17 | 3 | 0 | 200 | 0 | 0 | 3 fat |
| Serving: 1 oz. pkt. | | | | | | | | | | |
| Sweet & Sour | 45 | 11 | 0 | 0 | 0 | 0 | 50 | 0 | 1 | 1 other carb. |
| Serving: 1 oz. pkt. | | | | | | | | | | |
| Bull's Eye® BBQ | 20 | 5 | 0 | 0 | 0 | 0 | 140 | 0 | 0 | Free |
| Serving: ½ oz. pkt. | | | | | | | | | | |
| King Sauce | 70 | 2 | 0 | 7 | 1 | 4 | 70 | 0 | 0 | 1 fat |
| Serving: ½ oz. pkt. | | | | | | | | | | |
| Tartar Sauce | 260 | 0 | 0 | 29 | 4 | 20 | 330 | 0 | 0 | 6 fat |
| Serving: 1½ oz. pkt. | | | | | | | | | | |

## Pizza Hut®

| | Calories | Carbohydrate (gm) | Protein (gm) | Total Fat (gm) | Saturated Fat (gm) | Cholesterol (mg) | Sodium (mg) | Dietary Fiber (gm) | Total Carb Exchange | Suggested Exchange Value |
|---|---|---|---|---|---|---|---|---|---|---|
| **Stuffed Crust Pizza (Medium)** (serving size = 1 of 8 slices) | | | | | | | | | | |
| Cheese | 445 | 46 | 22 | 19 | 10 | 24 | 1090 | 3 | 3 | 3 starch<br>2 med. fat meat<br>2 fat |
| Beef Topping | 466 | 46 | 23 | 22 | 10 | 30 | 1137 | 3 | 3 | 3 starch<br>2 med. fat meat<br>2 fat |
| Ham | 404 | 27 | 24 | 22 | 12 | 39 | 1190 | 2 | 2 | 2 starch<br>3 med. fat meat<br>1 fat |
| Pepperoni | 438 | 45 | 21 | 19 | 9 | 27 | 1116 | 3 | 3 | 3 starch<br>2 med. fat meat<br>2 fat |
| Italian Sausage | 478 | 46 | 22 | 23 | 10 | 35 | 1164 | 3 | 3 | 3 starch<br>2 med. fat meat<br>3 fat |
| Pork Topping | 461 | 46 | 22 | 21 | 10 | 29 | 1176 | 3 | 3 | 3 starch<br>2 med. fat meat<br>2 fat |
| Meat Lover's® | 543 | 46 | 26 | 29 | 13 | 48 | 1427 | 3 | 3 | 3 starch<br>2 med. fat meat<br>4 fat |
| Veggie Lover's® | 421 | 48 | 20 | 17 | 8 | 19 | 1039 | 3 | 3 | 3 starch<br>1 med. fat meat<br>2 fat |
| Pepperoni Lover's® | 525 | 46 | 26 | 26 | 13 | 40 | 1413 | 3 | 3 | 3 starch<br>2 med. fat meat<br>3 fat |
| Supreme | 487 | 47 | 24 | 23 | 11 | 33 | 1227 | 3 | 3 | 3 starch<br>2 med. fat meat<br>3 fat |
| Super Supreme | 505 | 46 | 25 | 25 | 11 | 44 | 1371 | 3 | 3 | 3 starch<br>2 med. fat meat<br>3 fat |
| Chicken Supreme | 432 | 47 | 24 | 17 | 8 | 32 | 1111 | 3 | 3 | 3 starch<br>2 med. fat meat<br>1 fat |

## Pizza Hut®—*Continued*

| | Calories | Carbohydrate (gm) | Protein (gm) | Total Fat (gm) | Saturated Fat (gm) | Cholesterol (mg) | Sodium (mg) | Dietary Fiber (gm) | Total Carb Exchange | Suggested Exchange Value |
|---|---|---|---|---|---|---|---|---|---|---|
| **Thin 'N Crispy® Pizza (Medium)** (serving size = 1 of 8 slices) | | | | | | | | | | |
| Cheese | 243 | 27 | 11 | 10 | 5 | 11 | 653 | 2 | 2 | 2 starch<br>1 med. fat meat<br>1 fat |
| Beef Topping | 305 | 28 | 14 | 15 | 7 | 24 | 814 | 3 | 2 | 2 starch<br>1 med. fat meat<br>2 fat |
| Ham | 212 | 27 | 10 | 7 | 3 | 15 | 662 | 2 | 2 | 2 starch<br>1 med. fat meat |
| Pepperoni | 235 | 27 | 10 | 10 | 4 | 14 | 672 | 2 | 2 | 2 starch<br>1 med. fat meat<br>1 fat |
| Italian Sausage | 325 | 28 | 14 | 18 | 7 | 32 | 865 | 3 | 2 | 2 starch<br>1 med. fat meat<br>2 fat |
| Pork Topping | 298 | 28 | 14 | 15 | 6 | 23 | 875 | 3 | 2 | 2 starch<br>1 med. fat meat<br>2 fat |
| Meat Lover's® | 339 | 28 | 15 | 19 | 8 | 35 | 970 | 3 | 2 | 2 starch<br>1 med. fat meat<br>3 fat |
| Veggie Lover's® | 222 | 30 | 9 | 8 | 3 | 7 | 621 | 3 | 2 | 2 starch<br>1 med. fat meat<br>1 fat |
| Pepperoni Lover's® | 289 | 28 | 13 | 14 | 6 | 22 | 859 | 2 | 2 | 2 starch<br>1 med. fat meat<br>2 fat |
| Supreme | 284 | 29 | 13 | 13 | 6 | 20 | 784 | 3 | 2 | 2 starch<br>1 med. fat meat<br>2 fat |
| Super Supreme | 304 | 29 | 14 | 15 | 6 | 26 | 902 | 3 | 2 | 2 starch<br>1 med. fat meat<br>2 fat |
| Chicken Supreme | 232 | 29 | 13 | 7 | 3 | 19 | 681 | 3 | 2 | 2 starch<br>1 med. fat meat |

## Pizza Hut®—*Continued*

| | Calories | Carbohydrate (gm) | Protein (gm) | Total Fat (gm) | Saturated Fat (gm) | Cholesterol (mg) | Sodium (mg) | Dietary Fiber (gm) | Total Carb Exchange | Suggested Exchange Value |
|---|---|---|---|---|---|---|---|---|---|---|

### Thin 'N Crispy® Pizza (Medium)—*Continued*
(serving size = 1 of 8 slices)

| | Calories | Carbohydrate (gm) | Protein (gm) | Total Fat (gm) | Saturated Fat (gm) | Cholesterol (mg) | Sodium (mg) | Dietary Fiber (gm) | Total Carb Exchange | Suggested Exchange Value |
|---|---|---|---|---|---|---|---|---|---|---|
| Taco Pizza | 260 | 27 | 12 | 11 | 5 | 20 | 860 | 2 | 2 | 2 starch<br>1 med. fat meat<br>1 fat |
| Meatless Taco Pizza | 230 | 27 | 9 | 9 | 4 | 10 | 700 | 2 | 2 | 2 starch<br>1 med. fat meat<br>1 fat |
| Beef Taco Pizza | 260 | 29 | 13 | 10 | 5 | 20 | 850 | 2 | 2 | 2 starch<br>1 med. fat meat<br>1 fat |
| Chicken Taco Pizza | 260 | 26 | 11 | 12 | 5 | 20 | 850 | 2 | 2 | 2 starch<br>1 med. fat meat<br>1 fat |

### Pan Pizza (Medium) (serving size = 1 of 8 slices)

| | Calories | Carbohydrate (gm) | Protein (gm) | Total Fat (gm) | Saturated Fat (gm) | Cholesterol (mg) | Sodium (mg) | Dietary Fiber (gm) | Total Carb Exchange | Suggested Exchange Value |
|---|---|---|---|---|---|---|---|---|---|---|
| Cheese | 361 | 44 | 13 | 15 | 6 | 11 | 678 | 3 | 3 | 3 starch<br>1 med. fat meat<br>2 fat |
| Beef Topping | 399 | 45 | 15 | 18 | 7 | 20 | 773 | 4 | 3 | 3 starch<br>1 med. fat meat<br>3 fat |
| Ham | 331 | 44 | 12 | 12 | 4 | 15 | 687 | 3 | 3 | 3 starch<br>1 med. fat meat<br>1 fat |
| Pepperoni | 353 | 44 | 12 | 14 | 5 | 14 | 697 | 3 | 3 | 3 starch<br>1 med. fat meat<br>2 fat |
| Italian Sausage | 415 | 45 | 15 | 20 | 7 | 26 | 805 | 3 | 3 | 3 starch<br>1 med. fat meat<br>3 fat |
| Pork Topping | 394 | 45 | 15 | 18 | 6 | 20 | 820 | 4 | 3 | 3 starch<br>1 med. fat meat<br>3 fat |
| Meat Lover's® | 428 | 45 | 16 | 21 | 7 | 29 | 607 | 3 | 3 | 3 starch<br>1 med. fat meat<br>3 fat |

## Pizza Hut®—*Continued*

| | Calories | Carbohydrate (gm) | Protein (gm) | Total Fat (gm) | Saturated Fat (gm) | Cholesterol (mg) | Sodium (mg) | Dietary Fiber (gm) | Total Carb Exchange | Suggested Exchange Value |
|---|---|---|---|---|---|---|---|---|---|---|
| **Pan Pizza (Medium)—*Continued* (serving size = 1 of 8 slices)** | | | | | | | | | | |
| Veggie Lover's® | 333 | 46 | 11 | 12 | 4 | 7 | 601 | 4 | 3 | 3 starch<br>1 med. fat meat<br>1 fat |
| Pepperoni Lover's® | 370 | 44 | 13 | 16 | 5 | 18 | 767 | 3 | 3 | 3 starch<br>1 med. fat meat<br>2 fat |
| Supreme | 385 | 45 | 14 | 17 | 6 | 18 | 757 | 4 | 3 | 3 starch<br>1 med. fat meat<br>2 fat |
| Super Supreme | 401 | 46 | 15 | 18 | 6 | 22 | 854 | 4 | 3 | 3 starch<br>1 med. fat meat<br>3 fat |
| Chicken Supreme | 343 | 45 | 15 | 12 | 4 | 16 | 671 | 3 | 3 | 3 starch<br>1 med. fat meat<br>1 fat |
| Taco Pizza | 310 | 36 | 12 | 13 | 5 | 15 | 800 | 3 | 2 | 2 starch<br>1 med. fat meat<br>2 fat |
| Meatless Taco Pizza | 290 | 36 | 10 | 12 | 4 | 10 | 680 | 3 | 2 | 2 starch<br>1 med. fat meat<br>1 fat |
| Beef Taco Pizza | 300 | 36 | 12 | 12 | 5 | 15 | 770 | 3 | 2 | 2 starch<br>1 med. fat meat<br>1 fat |
| Chicken Taco Pizza | 320 | 36 | 12 | 15 | 5 | 15 | 830 | 3 | 2 | 2 starch<br>1 med. fat meat<br>2 fat |
| **Personal Pan Pizza® (serving size = 1 pizza)** | | | | | | | | | | |
| Cheese | 813 | 110 | 31 | 27 | 12 | 24 | 1581 | 8 | 7 | 7 starch<br>2 med. fat meat<br>3 fat |
| Pepperoni | 810 | 111 | 30 | 28 | 11 | 32 | 1661 | 8 | 7 | 7 starch<br>2 med. fat meat<br>3 fat |

## Pizza Hut® —*Continued*

| | Calories | Carbohydrate (gm) | Protein (gm) | Total Fat (gm) | Saturated Fat (gm) | Cholesterol (mg) | Sodium (mg) | Dietary Fiber (gm) | Total Carb Exchange | Suggested Exchange Value |
|---|---|---|---|---|---|---|---|---|---|---|
| **Personal Pan Pizza®—*Continued* (serving size = 1 pizza)** | | | | | | | | | | |
| Supreme | 808 | 111 | 30 | 27 | 10 | 28 | 1579 | 8 | 7 | 7 starch<br>2 med. fat meat<br>3 fat |
| Taco Pizza | 780 | 90 | 27 | 35 | 10 | 30 | 1900 | 7 | 6 | 6 starch<br>2 med. fat meat<br>5 fat |

## Subway®

| | Calories | Carbohydrate (gm) | Protein (gm) | Total Fat (gm) | Saturated Fat (gm) | Cholesterol (mg) | Sodium (mg) | Dietary Fiber (gm) | Total Carb Exchange | Suggested Exchange Value |
|---|---|---|---|---|---|---|---|---|---|---|
| **Subs (serving size = 6-inch sub)** | | | | | | | | | | |
| Classic Italian B.M.T.® on Italian Roll | 445 | 39 | 21 | 21 | 8 | 56 | 1652 | 3 | 3 | 3 starch<br>1 vegetable<br>2 med. fat meat<br>2 fat |
| Cold Cut Trio on Italian Roll | 362 | 39 | 19 | 13 | 4 | 64 | 1401 | 3 | 3 | 3 starch<br>1 vegetable<br>2 med. fat meat<br>1 fat |
| Ham on Italian Roll | 287 | 39 | 18 | 5 | 1 | 28 | 1308 | 3 | 3 | 3 starch<br>1 vegetable<br>1 lean meat<br>1 fat |
| Pizza Sub on Italian Roll | 448 | 41 | 19 | 22 | 9 | 50 | 1609 | 3 | 3 | 3 starch<br>1 vegetable<br>2 med. fat meat<br>2 fat |
| Meatball on Italian Roll | 404 | 44 | 18 | 16 | 6 | 33 | 1035 | 3 | 3 | 3 starch<br>1 vegetable<br>1 med. fat meat<br>2 fat |
| Roast Beef on Italian Roll | 288 | 39 | 19 | 5 | 1 | 20 | 928 | 3 | 3 | 3 starch<br>1 vegetable<br>2 lean meat |

## Subway®—Continued

### Subs—Continued (serving size = 6-inch sub)

| | Calories | Carbohydrate (gm) | Protein (gm) | Total Fat (gm) | Saturated Fat (gm) | Cholesterol (mg) | Sodium (mg) | Dietary Fiber (gm) | Total Carb Exchange | Suggested Exchange Value |
|---|---|---|---|---|---|---|---|---|---|---|
| Roasted Chicken Breast on Italian Roll | 332 | 41 | 26 | 6 | 1 | 48 | 967 | 3 | 3 | 3 starch<br>1 vegetable<br>3 very lean meat<br>1 fat |
| Subway Seafood & Crab® on Italian Roll w/light mayonnaise (processed seafood & crab blend) | 332 | 39 | 19 | 10 | 2 | 32 | 873 | 3 | 3 | 3 starch<br>1 vegerable<br>2 very lean meat<br>2 fat |
| Steak & Cheese on Italian Roll | 383 | 41 | 29 | 10 | 6 | 70 | 1106 | 3 | 3 | 3 starch<br>1 vegetable<br>3 med. fat meat |
| Subway Club® on Italian Roll | 297 | 40 | 21 | 5 | 1 | 26 | 1341 | 3 | 3 | 3 starch<br>1 vegetable<br>2 lean meat |
| Subway Melt™ on Italian Roll | 366 | 40 | 22 | 12 | 5 | 42 | 1735 | 3 | 3 | 3 starch<br>1 vegetable<br>2 med. fat meat |
| Tuna on Italian Roll w/light mayonnaise | 376 | 39 | 18 | 15 | 2 | 32 | 928 | 3 | 3 | 3 starch<br>1 vegetable<br>1 very lean meat<br>3 fat |
| Turkey Breast on Italian Roll | 273 | 40 | 17 | 4 | 1 | 19 | 1391 | 3 | 3 | 3 starch<br>1 vegetable<br>1 very lean meat<br>1 fat |
| Turkey Breast & Ham on Italian Roll | 280 | 39 | 18 | 5 | 1 | 24 | 1350 | 3 | 2½ | 2½ starch<br>1 vegetable<br>1 lean meat<br>1 fat |
| Veggie Delight on Italian Roll | 222 | 38 | 9 | 3 | 0 | 0 | 582 | 3 | 2½ | 2½ starch<br>1 vegetable |

## Subway®—*Continued*

| | Calories | Carbohydrate (gm) | Protein (gm) | Total Fat (gm) | Saturated Fat (gm) | Cholesterol (mg) | Sodium (mg) | Dietary Fiber (gm) | Total Carb Exchange | Suggested Exchange Value |
|---|---|---|---|---|---|---|---|---|---|---|
| **Salads** (serving size = 1) | | | | | | | | | | |
| Classic Italian B.M.T.® Salad+ | 274 | 11 | 14 | 20 | 7 | 56 | 1379 | 1 | 0 | 2 vegetable 2 med. fat meat 2 fat |
| Cold Cut Trio Salad+ | 191 | 11 | 13 | 11 | 3 | 64 | 1127 | 1 | 0 | 2 vegetable 2 med. fat meat |
| Ham Salad+ | 116 | 11 | 12 | 3 | 1 | 28 | 1034 | 1 | 0 | 2 vegetable 1 lean meat |
| Meatball Salad+ | 223 | 16 | 12 | 14 | 5 | 33 | 761 | 2 | 1 | 1 starch 2 vegetable 1 med. fat meat 2 fat |
| Pizza Salad+ | 277 | 13 | 12 | 20 | 8 | 50 | 1336 | 2 | 0 | 2 vegetable 1 med. fat meat 3 fat |
| Roast Beef Salad+ | 117 | 11 | 12 | 3 | 1 | 20 | 654 | 1 | 0 | 2 vegetable 1 lean meat |
| Roasted Chicken Breast Salad+ | 162 | 13 | 20 | 4 | 1 | 48 | 693 | 1 | 0 | 2 vegetable 3 very lean meat |
| Steak & Cheese Salad+ | 212 | 13 | 22 | 8 | 5 | 70 | 832 | 1 | 0 | 2 vegetable 3 lean meat |
| Subway Melt™ Salad | 195 | 12 | 16 | 10 | 4 | 42 | 1461 | 1 | 0 | 2 vegetable 2 med. fat meat |
| Subway Seafood & Crab® w/ light mayonnaise (processed seafood & crab blend) | 161 | 11 | 13 | 8 | 1 | 32 | 599 | 2 | 0 | 2 vegetable 2 very lean meat 1 fat |
| Subway Club® Salad+ | 126 | 12 | 14 | 3 | 1 | 26 | 1067 | 1 | 0 | 2 vegetable 2 lean meat |
| Tuna Salad w/light mayonnaise | 205 | 11 | 12 | 13 | 2 | 32 | 654 | 1 | 0 | 2 vegetable 1 very lean meat 2 fat |
| Turkey Breast Salad+ | 102 | 12 | 11 | 2 | 1 | 19 | 1117 | 1 | 0 | 2 vegetable 1 very lean meat |
| Turkey Breast & Ham Salad+ | 109 | 11 | 11 | 3 | 1 | 24 | 1076 | 1 | 0 | 2 vegetable 1 lean meat |
| Veggie Delight™ Salad+ | 51 | 10 | 2 | 1 | 0 | 0 | 308 | 1 | 0 | 2 vegetable |

## Subways® — *Continued*

| | Calories | Carbohydrate (gm) | Protein (gm) | Total Fat (gm) | Saturated Fat (gm) | Cholesterol (mg) | Sodium (mg) | Dietary Fiber (gm) | Total Carb Exchange | Suggested Exchange Value |
|---|---|---|---|---|---|---|---|---|---|---|
| **Salad Dressings** (serving size = 1 tbsp.) | | | | | | | | | | |
| French | 70 | 5 | 0 | 6 | 1 | 0 | 100 | 0 | 0 | 1 fat |
| Fat Free French | 18 | 4 | 0 | 0 | 0 | 0 | 98 | 0 | 0 | Free |
| Creamy Italian | 65 | 3 | 0 | 7 | 1 | 4 | 133 | 0 | 0 | 1 fat |
| Fat Free Italian | 5 | 1 | 0 | 0 | 0 | 0 | 153 | 0 | 0 | Free |
| Ranch | 88 | 2 | 0 | 10 | 2 | 6 | 118 | 0 | 0 | 2 fat |
| Fat Free Ranch | 15 | 4 | 0 | 0 | 0 | 0 | 178 | 0 | 0 | Free |
| 1000 Island | 65 | 3 | 0 | 7 | 1 | 8 | 155 | 0 | 0 | 1 fat |

## Long John Silver's®

## Specialties

| | Calories | Carbohydrate (gm) | Protein (gm) | Total Fat (gm) | Saturated Fat (gm) | Cholesterol (mg) | Sodium (mg) | Dietary Fiber (gm) | Total Carb Exchange | Suggested Exchange Value |
|---|---|---|---|---|---|---|---|---|---|---|
| Regular Battered Fish<br>Serving: 1 piece | 230 | 15 | 12 | 14 | 5 | 30 | 560 | N/A | 1 | 1 starch<br>1 med. fat meat<br>2 fat |
| Junior Battered Fish<br>Serving: 1 piece | 140 | 10 | 6 | 9 | 3 | 15 | 360 | N/A | 1 | 1 starch<br>1 med. fat meat<br>1 fat |
| Battered Chicken Plank<br>Serving: 1 piece | 130 | 10 | 7 | 7 | 3 | 15 | 380 | N/A | 1 | 1 starch<br>1 med. fat meat |
| Battered Shrimp<br>Serving: 1 piece | 35 | 2 | 1 | 2 | <1 | 10 | 75 | N/A | 0 | 1 fat |
| Breaded Clams<br>Serving: 1 piece | 250 | 26 | 9 | 14 | 4 | 35 | 560 | N/A | 2 | 2 starch<br>1 med. fat meat<br>2 fat |
| Lemon Crumb Fish<br>Serving: 2 piece | 240 | 10 | 23 | 12 | 4 | 55 | 790 | N/A | 1 | 1 starch<br>3 med. fat meat |
| Lemon Crumb Fish a-la-carte<br>Serving: 2 piece w/ rice | 480 | 52 | 27 | 17 | 5 | 55 | 1490 | N/A | 4 | 4 starch<br>2 med. fat meat<br>1 fat |
| Lemon Crumb Fish Add-A-Piece<br>Serving: 1 piece w/rice | 150 | 9 | 12 | 7 | 2 | 30 | 460 | N/A | ½ | ½ starch<br>1 med. fat meat |

## Long John Silver's®—*Continued*

| | Calories | Carbohydrate (gm) | Protein (gm) | Total Fat (gm) | Saturated Fat (gm) | Cholesterol (mg) | Sodium (mg) | Dietary Fiber (gm) | Total Carb Exchange | Suggested Exchange Value |
|---|---|---|---|---|---|---|---|---|---|---|
| **Meals** (serving size = 1 meal) | | | | | | | | | | |
| 2 Junior Fish w/Fries | 620 | 57 | 15 | 37 | 9 | 30 | 1380 | N/A | 4 | 4 starch<br>1 med. fat meat<br>6 fat |
| 2 Chicken Planks w/Fries | 600 | 57 | 18 | 33 | 9 | 35 | 1420 | N/A | 4 | 4 starch<br>1 med. fat meat<br>6 fat |
| 5 Shrimp w/Fries | 500 | 47 | 10 | 30 | 7 | 50 | 1030 | N/A | 3 | 3 starch<br>6 fat |
| 1 Chicken Plank/ 3 Shrimp w/Fries | 550 | 51 | 14 | 32 | 8 | 45 | 1230 | N/A | 3 | 3 starch<br>1 med. fat meat<br>5 fat |
| 1 Junior Fish/1 Chicken Plank w/Fries | 610 | 57 | 17 | 35 | 9 | 30 | 1400 | N/A | 4 | 4 starch<br>1 med. fat meat<br>6 fat |
| 1 Junior Fish/1 Chicken Plank w/Fries | 610 | 57 | 17 | 35 | 9 | 30 | 1400 | N/A | 4 | 4 starch<br>1 med. fat meat<br>6 fat |
| 1 Junior Fish/3 Shirmp w/Fries | 560 | 52 | 13 | 34 | 8 | 45 | 1210 | N/A | 3½ | 3½ starch<br>7 fat |
| Lemon Crumb Fish Meal | 730 | 89 | 31 | 29 | 6 | 60 | 1720 | N/A | 6 | 6 starch<br>2 med. fat meat<br>4 fat |
| **Sandwiches** (serving size = 1) | | | | | | | | | | |
| Ultimate Fish™ | 430 | 44 | 18 | 21 | 7 | 35 | 1340 | N/A | 3 | 3 starch<br>1 med. fat meat<br>3 fat |
| Fish Grab 'n Go | 340 | 40 | 11 | 15 | 4 | 20 | 800 | N/A | 2½ | 2½ starch<br>1 med. fat meat<br>2 fat |
| Fish Grab 'n Go w/Cheese | 390 | 40 | 14 | 20 | 9 | 35 | 1050 | N/A | 2½ | 2½ starch<br>1 med. fat meat<br>3 fat |
| Chicken Grab 'n Go | 330 | 40 | 13 | 13 | 4 | 20 | 820 | N/A | 2½ | 2½ starch<br>1 med. fat meat<br>2 fat |

## Long John Silver's®—*Continued*

| | Calories | Carbohydrate (gm) | Protein (gm) | Total Fat (gm) | Saturated Fat (gm) | Cholesterol (mg) | Sodium (mg) | Dietary Fiber (gm) | Total Carb Exchange | Suggested Exchange Value |
|---|---|---|---|---|---|---|---|---|---|---|
| **Sandwiches—*Continued*** (serving size = 1) | | | | | | | | | | |
| Chicken Grab 'n Go w/Cheese | 380 | 40 | 16 | 18 | 9 | 35 | 1070 | N/A | 2½ | 2½ starch<br>1 med. fat meat<br>3 fat |
| Wraps | 840 | 99 | 20 | 41 | 10 | 50 | 2180 | N/A | 6½ | 6½ starch<br>8 fat |
| **Side Items** | | | | | | | | | | |
| Cheese Sticks<br>Serving: 5-piece | 160 | 12 | 6 | 9 | 4 | 10 | 360 | N/A | 1 | 1 starch<br>2 fat |
| Cole Slaw<br>Serving: 4 oz. | 170 | 23 | 2 | 7 | 0 | 0 | 310 | N/A | 1 | 1 other carb.<br>1 vegetable<br>1 fat |
| Corn Cobbette<br>Serving: 1 | 80 | 19 | 3 | <1 | 0 | 0 | 0 | 0 | 1 | 1 starch |
| Corn Cobbette (w/butter)<br>Serving: 1 | 140 | 19 | 3 | 8 | 2 | 0 | 0 | 0 | 1 | 1 starch<br>2 fat |
| Fries<br>Serving: regular | 250 | 28 | 3 | 15 | 3 | 0 | 500 | 3 | 2 | 2 starch<br>3 fat |
| Fries<br>Serving: large | 420 | 46 | 5 | 24 | 4 | 0 | 830 | 4 | 3 | 3 starch<br>5 fat |
| Hushpuppy<br>Serving: 1 | 60 | 0 | 1 | 3 | 0 | 0 | 25 | 0 | ½ | 1 fat |
| Rice<br>Serving: 4 oz. | 180 | 34 | 3 | 4 | <1 | 0 | 560 | N/A | 2 | 2 starch<br>1 fat |
| **Salads** (serving size = 1) | | | | | | | | | | |
| Ocean Chef Salad+ | 130 | 15 | 14 | 2 | 0 | 60 | 540 | N/A | 1 | 3 vegetable |
| Grilled Chicken Salad+ | 140 | 10 | 20 | 3 | <1 | 45 | 260 | N/A | 0 | 2 vegetable<br>2 very lean meat |
| Garden Salad+ | 45 | 9 | 3 | 0 | 0 | 0 | 25 | N/A | 0 | 2 vegetable |
| Side Salad+ | 20 | 3 | 1 | 0 | 0 | 0 | 10 | N/A | 0 | 1 vegetable |

## Long John Silver's®—*Continued*

| | Calories | Carbohydrate (gm) | Protein (gm) | Total Fat (gm) | Saturated Fat (gm) | Cholesterol (mg) | Sodium (mg) | Dietary Fiber (gm) | Total Carb Exchange | Suggested Exchange Value |
|---|---|---|---|---|---|---|---|---|---|---|
| **Salad Dressings** (serving size = 1 oz.) | | | | | | | | | | |
| Fat-Free French | 40 | 10 | 0 | 0 | 0 | 0 | 240 | N/A | ½ | ½ other carb. |
| Italian | 90 | 2 | 0 | 9 | 2 | 0 | 290 | N/A | 0 | 2 fat |
| Ranch | 170 | 1 | 0 | 18 | 3 | 10 | 260 | N/A | 0 | 4 fat |
| Fat-Free Ranch | 40 | 9 | 0 | 0 | 0 | 0 | 290 | N/A | ½ | ½ other carb. |
| 1000 Island | 120 | 5 | 0 | 10 | 2 | 15 | 290 | N/A | 0 | 2 fat |
| **Desserts** (serving size = 1 slice) | | | | | | | | | | |
| Pineapple Creme Cheesecake Pie | 310 | 36 | 4 | 17 | 9 | 5 | 105 | N/A | 2 | 2 other carb. 3 fat |
| Chocolate Creme Pie | 260 | 29 | 4 | 17 | 8 | 15 | 125 | N/A | 2 | 2 other carb. 3 fat |
| Double Lemon Pie | 350 | 41 | 6 | 18 | 10 | 40 | 180 | N/A | 3 | 3 other carb. 4 fat |
| Strawberries 'n Creme Pie | 260 | 32 | 4 | 15 | 8 | 15 | 130 | N/A | 2 | 2 other carb. 3 fat |
| Key Lime Creme Cheese Pie | 310 | 33 | 4 | 19 | 11 | 20 | 140 | N/A | 2 | 2 other carb. 4 fat |
| Pecan Pie | 390 | 53 | 3 | 19 | 4 | 40 | 250 | N/A | 3½ | 3½ other carb. 4 fat |

# The Good Diet

In addition to weight control, can sensible eating increase health status? Very definitely! One way in which this can happen is due to the effect of food and its nutrients on the immune system. To bolster the immune system with nutrients may mean fewer colds, viruses, and even cancers and quicker recovery if you should become ill. Is nutrition a panacea for dis-

From *Nutrition in the Fast Lane*. Reprinted by permission of the publisher, Frankling Publishing, Inc., Indianapolis, Indiana (1-800-634-1993).

## A Look at the Calories in Our Cocktails...

You might want to think of your beer, wine or cocktail glass as leaving the following "rings"...

**Beer**
Calories per ounce: 12.5

**Wine**
Calories per ounce: 24.3

**Hard liquor (80 proof)**
Calories per ounce: 69.3

The above percentages represent not volume or weight, but rather the percentage of each beverage's total calories that come in the form of the nutrients listed.

| | CALORIES | CARBO-HYDRATES (grams) | ALCOHOL (grams) |
|---|---|---|---|
| **DISTILLED LIQUORS** | | | |
| Liqueurs (cordials) — 1 cordial glass | | | |
| Anisette | 75 | 7.0 | 7.0 |
| Apricot brandy | 65 | 6.0 | 6.0 |
| Benedictine | 70 | 6.6 | 6.6 |
| Creme de menthe | 67 | 6.0 | 7.0 |
| Curacao | 55 | 6.0 | 6.0 |
| Brandy, California — 1 brandy glass | 73 | — | 10.5 |
| Brandy, cognac — 1 brandy glass | 73 | — | 10.5 |
| Cider, fermented — 6 oz. | 71 | 1.8 | 9.4 |
| Gin, rum, vodka, whiskey (rye/scotch) — 1 jigger | | | |
| 80-proof | 104 | 0.0 | 15.0 |
| 86-proof | 112 | 0.0 | 16.2 |
| 90-proof | 118 | 0.0 | 17.1 |
| 94-proof | 124 | 0.0 | 17.9 |
| 100-proof | 133 | 0.0 | 19.1 |
| **WINES** — 1 wine glass | | | |
| Champagne, domestic | 85 | 3.0 | 11.0 |
| Dessert (18.8% alcohol by volume) | 137 | 7.7 | 15.3 |
| Madeira | 105 | 1.0 | 15.0 |
| Muscatel/port | 158 | 14.0 | 15.0 |
| Red, California | 85 | — | 10.0 |
| Sauterne, California | 85 | 4.0 | 10.5 |
| Sherry, dry, domestic | 85 | 4.8 | 9.0 |
| Table (12.2% alcohol by volume) | 85 | 4.2 | 9.9 |
| Vermouth, dry (French) | 105 | 1.0 | 15.0 |
| Vermouth, sweet (Italian) | 167 | 12.0 | 18.0 |
| **MALT LIQUORS (American)** — 12 oz. | | | |
| Ale, mild | 148 | 12.0 | 13.1 |
| Beer, Budweiser | 150 | 12.8 | 13.2 |
| Beer, lite | 96 | 2.8 | 12.1 |
| Beer, Michelob | 160 | 14.9 | 14.2 |
| Beer, Natural Light | 100 | 5.5 | 11.6 |
| **COCKTAILS** | | | |
| Daiquiri — 1 cocktail | 125 | 5.2 | 15.1 |
| Eggnog (Christmas) — 4 oz. | 335 | 18.0 | 15.0 |
| Gin rickey — 8 oz. | 150 | 1.3 | 21.0 |
| Manhattan — 1 cocktail | 165 | 7.9 | 19.2 |
| Martini — 1 cocktail | 140 | 0.3 | 18.5 |
| Mint julep — 10 oz. | 212 | 2.7 | 29.2 |
| Old-fashioned — 4 oz. | 180 | 3.5 | 24.0 |
| Planters punch — 4 oz. | 175 | 7.9 | 21.5 |
| Rum sour — 4 oz. | 165 | — | 21.5 |
| Tom collins — 10 oz. | 180 | 9.0 | 21.5 |
| Whiskey sour — 1 cocktail | 138 | 7.7 | — |
| **MIXERS** — 4 oz. | | | |
| Club soda | 0 | 0.0 | 0 |
| Tonic water | 44 | 11.0 | 0 |
| Bitter lemon | 64 | 14.1 | 0 |
| Collins mixer | 42 | 10.8 | 0 |
| Ginger ale | 45 | 11.3 | 0 |
| Cola | 43 | 12.0 | 0 |
| Orange juice | 28 | 6.0 | 0 |
| Tomato juice | 24 | 5.2 | 0 |

*Glass Sizes:* Cordial ⅔ oz.; brandy 1 oz.; jigger 1½ oz.; sherry 2 oz.; cocktail 3 oz.; wine 4 oz.; champagne 5 oz.

Source: From *Food Values of Portions Commonly Used, 15th Edition* by Helen Nichols Church, B.S. and Jean A.T. Pennington, Ph.D., R.D. Copyright © 1980, 1985, 1989 by Helen Nichols Church, B.S. and Jean. A.T. Pennington, Ph.D., R.D. Reprinted by permission of HarperCollins Publishers, Inc.

ease? No! But it can help. Some suggestions include: Cruciferous vegetables like broccoli, cabbage, and cauliflower may aid in reducing cancer risk because they contain indoles; foods high in vitamin C content, such as citrus fruits (green peppers included), act as antioxidants (retard aging) and enhance cellular immunity; fish (specifically those found in cold waters) rich in omega-3 fatty acids may aid in reducing cancer and heart disease risk; zinc, a mineral vital for the immune system, can be found in oysters, most other seafoods, and meats as well as a variety of legumes; and vitamins A and E serve as antioxidants and, therefore, make cells more resistant to cancer.

# Dietary Guidelines for Americans/Nutrition and Your Health

1. *Eat a variety of foods daily.* Include these foods every day: fruits and vegetables, whole-grain and enriched breads and cereals and other products made from grains; milk and milk products; meats, fish, poultry, and eggs; and dried peas and beans.
2. *Maintain healthy weight.* To increase calorie expenditure, increase physical activity. To decrease calorie intake, control overeating by eating slowly, taking smaller portions, and avoiding "seconds"; eat fewer fatty foods and sweets and less sugar, drink fewer alcoholic beverages, and eat more foods that are low in calories and high in nutrients.
3. Choose a diet low in fat, saturated fat, and *cholesterol.* Choose low-fat protein sources such as lean meats, fish, poultry, and dry peas and beans; use eggs and organ meats in moderation; limit intake of fats on and in foods; trim fats from meats; broil, bake, or boil—don't fry; limit breaded and deep-fried foods; read food labels for fat contents.
4. *Choose a diet with plenty of vegetables, fruits, and grain products.* Substitute starchy foods for foods high in fats and sugars; select whole-grain breads and cereal, fruits and vegetables, and dried beans and peas, to increase fiber and starch intake.
5. *Use sugars only in moderation.* Use less sugar, syrup, and honey; reduce concentrated sweets like candy, soft drinks, cookies, and the like; select fresh fruit or fruits canned in light syrup or their own juices; read food labels—sucrose, glucose, dextrose, maltose, lactose, fructose, syrups, honey are all sugars; eat sugar less often to reduce dental caries.
6. *Use salt and sodium only in moderation.* Learn to enjoy the flavors of unsalted foods; flavor foods with herbs, spices, and lemon juice; reduce

salt in cooking; add little or no salt at the table; limit salty foods like potato chips, pretzels, salted nuts, popcorn, condiments (soy sauce, steak sauce, and garlic salt), some cheese, pickled foods and cured meats, and some canned vegetables and soups; read food labels for sodium or salt contents, especially in processed and snack foods; use lower-sodium products when available.

7. *If you drink alcoholic beverages, do so in moderation.* For individuals who drink, limit all alcoholic beverages (including wine, beer, liquors, and so on) to one (for women) or two (for men) drinks per day. "One drink" means 12 oz of beer, 3 oz of wine, or 1- 1/2 oz of distilled spirits. People who should *not* drink alcohol include pregnant women, those who must drive, those taking medication, those who have trouble limiting alcohol intakes, and children and adolescents.

---

Source: U.S. Department of Agriculture, U.S. Department of Health and Human Services, *Nutrition and your Health: Dietary Guidelines for Americans*, 3rd edition (Washington, D.C.: Government Printing Office, 1990).

# Eating Problems

Our society seems to be preoccupied with "thinness." Unrealistic expectations become commonplace and can drive one toward disordered eating patterns. Our cultural and societal messages about appearance create tremendous pressure on one to try and conform, to an "ideal" weight, and/or physique. This expectation can lead to unhealthy eating patterns such as **bulimia** and **anorexia nervosa**. The pursuit of "the perfect fitness appearance" can contribute to these problems.

Anorexia nervosa is a "body image" problem. Some people believe they are or look "too fat" and severely restrict food intake to the point where hospitalization may be necessary.

Bulimia involves an attempt at controlling caloric intake by engaging in frequent episodes of binging (eating large volumes of food) and purging (self-induced vomiting, fasting, or laxative abuse).

Disorders of eating behaviors can also include chronic dieting and regain of weight (yo-yo syndrome), following VLCDs and pursuing body weight and food as an obsession.

The key to fitness and body weight control is to pursue healthful behaviors, which include regulation of exercise and diet, allowing for optimal function.

# Summary

The old expression "you are what you eat" may be more true than ever expected. It has become obvious that diet is extremely important in preventing and combating disease processes. Much research supports the concept that a very low fat diet, in conjunction with exercise, may actually reduce existing plaque buildup in arteries. Remember, it is a two-sided coin where diet is concerned—not only what you eat but also how much.

Care must be taken with vitamin and/or mineral supplementation. Toxicity (physiological problems) can be created by overdosing with vitamins and minerals. Consult a reliable source of information for vitamin/mineral overdosing.

Three questions are important relative to dietary selections and, therefore, impact on health status:

1. Are the majority of foods I have chosen good sources of complex carbohydrates?
2. Have I included good sources of vitamins A, C, and E in my daily meals?
3. Have I included a good source of protein that is low in fat?

# Check Out These Websites

http://www.MyPyramid.gov - an outstanding website for food source information; calorie content; energy expenditure; dietary guidelines

http://vm.cfsan.fda.gov/~dms/supplmnt.html - all about supplements from the Food and Drug Administration

http://www.shapeup.org/kitchen/frameset1.htm - the cyberkitchen allows for meal planning based on information provided by you. Very interactive.

http://www.cspinet.org/quiz-quizzes - about food, vitamins, rate your diet quiz sponsored by Center for Science in the Public Interest

# "Healthy" Weight

Our culture provides the perfect recipe for the development of problems associated with nutritional practices: an abundant food supply and a sedentary life-style. When we combine these with an unrealistic standard of thinness by which people are judged, it is easy to understand why dieting is probably the number one nutrition pursuit.

Over the last 10 years, the advice offered in the Dietary Guidelines for Americans published by the U.S. Department of Agriculture has ranged from maintaining an "ideal weight," then a "desirable weight," and most recently a "healthy weight." This "healthy weight" is recognized as the point at which there is little if any risk for weight/fat-related diseases. Three questions will aid in determining "healthy weight" and any need for change: (1) Are you within an acceptable weight range for your age, height, and somatotype? (2) Is your waist-to-hip ratio below the recommended values of .90 for women and .85 for men? and (3) Do you have an existing condition that would benefit from weight reduction, such as diabetes or hypertension?

# Review Questions

1. What does VLCD mean and what are potential problems associated with it?

2. What are the six classes of nutrients? Which ones contain calories?

3. What is a complete and incomplete protein?

4. Can you explain calorie density and nutrient density?

5. What do vitamins and minerals do?

6. What are two eating disorders associated with thinness?

CHAPTER ACTIVITY

# Determining Energy Requirements

## Purpose

To assess the daily caloric requirements for basal metabolic requirements and daily activity requirements.

Energy (caloric) requirements vary among individuals, depending on body size, gender, and daily activities. Energy needs are for two main purposes: interval function for life called basal metabolism, and for daily activities. To estimate how much energy (total calories) you need each day, the following **calorie calculator*** is used.

Simply follow the directions to determine the number of calories needed for (1) basal metabolism and (2) daily caloric requirement. It must be remembered that this daily requirement is that needed to maintain present body weight.

## Procedure

1. Using a pin as a marker, locate your actual weight on line 1.
2. Setting the edge of a ruler against the pin, swing the other end to your height on line 6.
3. Remove the pin and place it at the point where the ruler crosses line 2.
4. Keeping the edge of the ruler firmly against the pin on line 2, swing the right-hand edge to your sex and age on line 7, using the age of your nearest birthday for the purpose.

---

*Hewitt, Donald W., M.D., *Reduce and Be Happy*, The Pacific Press Publishing Assoc., Calif., 1955. Reprinted with permission.

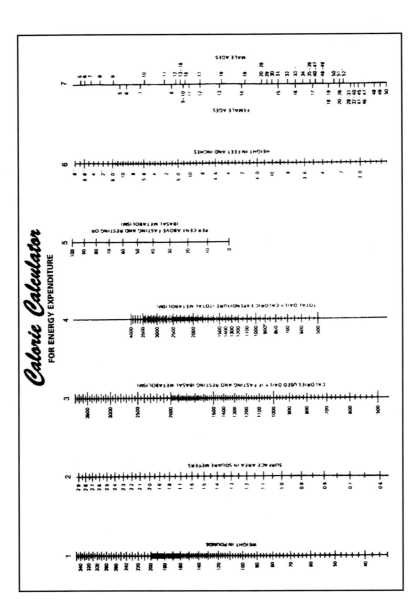

5. Remove the pin and place it where the ruler crosses line 3. This gives you the calories used daily (in 24 hrs.) if you are resting and fasting (basal metabolism).

6. To the basal calories thus determined, add the percentage above fasting and resting for your type of activity using the Activity Level Guide. Leaving the pin in line 3, swing the edge of the ruler to the right to the proper percentage on line 5. Where the ruler crosses line 4, you will find the number of calories necessary to maintain your present weight.

## Activity Level Guide for Use with Calorie Calculator

The following percentages should be added depending on daily activities.

**20 percent** should be added to the basal caloric needs of individuals who are bed patients, or those whose activities are confined to sitting in a wheel chair.

**30 percent** should be added for ambulatory patients who are in need of more rest than are normal individuals, but who are able to engage in limited physical exercise such as is obtained by short walks.

**40 percent** should be added for individuals of somewhat greater activity, but whose energy output is still considerably below par. In this class may be cited such persons as housewives who engage in various social activities, but who hire others to do housework and students who are not participating in regular physical activity but are primarily engaged in study. Usually they are nonworking students whose physical activity is primarily limited to walking to and from classes.

**50 percent** should be added for individuals engaged in clerical duties, various machine operators, cooks, domestics of various sorts, chauffeurs, and others doing similar semisedentary work. Students who work at clerical jobs such as the library or as laboratory assistants are included in this area. Their physical activity includes about two hours of walking or standing daily.

**60 percent** should be added for manual laborers, truck drivers, farmers of various types, roofers, and the like. Teenager children who are overweight are included in this classification. College students who, in addition to their academic studies, participate in limited physical exercises such as are offered in the physical education activity courses, or intramural sports of a moderate nature are included, as are those students who attend dances and other social activities regularly and walk or stand about two hours each day.

**70 percent** should be added for individuals who engage in heavy work, such as construction work, mining, and stevedoring. In this group also are college students participating in physical education classes and individual sport and exercise activity programs on a regular, daily basis, and those on intercollegiate teams of a moderate nature with daily practices and weekly contests.

**80-100 percent** should be added for those engaged in the heaviest type of work described in the 70 percent category, and for those students participating in intercollegiate sport activities that have the highest rate of calories expenditure as shown on the activity chart (basketball, track, etc.).

# Laboratory 6 Results Sheet

1. According to the Calorie Calculator, how many calories are being consumed per day, enabling you to maintain present body weight?

    _____ Total Calories

2. Approximately how many of the total calories are used for basal metabolism?

    _____ Calories for BMR

3. Approximately how many calories are being used for daily activities above basal metabolism?

    $$\underline{\hspace{3cm}} - \underline{\hspace{3cm}} = \underline{\hspace{3cm}}$$
    (total calories)         (BMR calories)         (Activity calories)

4. For what purposes are calories (energy) used at rest?

5. What is the most significant determiner of calories used for RMR? (see Chapter 3)

6. As age increases what should you consider so that healthy weight and body composition can be maintained?

CHAPTER ACTIVITY

# Calorie Expenditure— Calorie Ingestion

## Part A

The amount of energy you burn off during a day depends on your activity. Sedentary activity burns off relatively few calories while activities that use your whole body in strenuous exercise burn off high levels of energy.

Listed below are several activities and the calorie burn-off that occurs during an hour of each activity for people of various weights.

1. Record your physical activity for a 24-hour period and place the breakdown of hours in the appropriate space under "No. of Hours."
2. Refer to the chart for calorie value of activities for 1 hour. Multiply the calories expended in an hour for your weight times the hours in activity and record under "No. of Calories."
3. Add up total calories for 24-hour period and record under "Total Calories."

| Activity | No. of Hours | No. of Calories |
| --- | --- | --- |
| Sleeping | _____ | _____ |
| Sitting | _____ | _____ |
| Walking | _____ | _____ |
| Light—clerical or sales work or equivalent | _____ | _____ |
| Low intensity—housekeeping, bowling | _____ | _____ |
| Moderate intensity—singles tennis, racquetball, walking 4–5 mph | _____ | _____ |

| Activity | No. of Hours | No. of Calories |
|---|---|---|
| High intensity—running 6 mph or more | _____ | _____ |
| Other recreational activities— tennis, basketball | _____ | _____ |

You will note that the energy expenditure for the 200-lb person is twice the expenditure for the 100-lb person doing the same activity. You will also note that vigorous activities do, indeed, bum many calories. Not all activities are listed, but you should be able to make a reasonable determination of energy used in other activities by these examples.

| Activity | Calories/Hr, Based on Body Weight | | | | |
|---|---|---|---|---|---|
| | 100 | 110 | 120 | 130 | 140 |
| Sleeping | 43 | 47 | 52 | 56 | 60 |
| Lying awake | 50 | 55 | 60 | 65 | 70 |
| Sitting, not working | 65 | 72 | 78 | 85 | 91 |
| Sitting, reading | 69 | 76 | 83 | 90 | 97 |
| Standing, relaxing | 69 | 76 | 83 | 90 | 97 |
| Dressing | 77 | 85 | 92 | 100 | 108 |
| Typing rapidly | 91 | 100 | 109 | 118 | 129 |
| Light exercise, i.e. filing in office | 110 | 121 | 132 | 143 | 154 |
| Walking slowly | 130 | 143 | 156 | 169 | 182 |
| Carpentry | 156 | 172 | 187 | 203 | 218 |
| Active exercise, i.e. volleyball | 188 | 207 | 226 | 244 | 263 |
| Walking average rate | 195 | 215 | 234 | 254 | 273 |
| Severe exercise, i.e. sit ups, push ups | 292 | 321 | 350 | 380 | 408 |
| Swimming, non-competitive | 325 | 358 | 390 | 423 | 455 |
| Jogging | 370 | 407 | 444 | 481 | 518 |
| Very severe exercise, i.e. wrestling, hard running; hard rowing | 390 | 429 | 468 | 507 | 548 |

| Calories/Hr, Based on Body Weight | | | | | |
|---|---|---|---|---|---|
| 150 | 160 | 170 | 180 | 190 | 200 |
| 65 | 69 | 73 | 77 | 82 | 86 |
| 75 | 80 | 85 | 90 | 95 | 100 |
| 98 | 104 | 111 | 117 | 124 | 130 |
| 104 | 110 | 117 | 124 | 132 | 138 |
| 104 | 110 | 117 | 124 | 132 | 138 |
| 116 | 123 | 131 | 139 | 146 | 154 |
| 137 | 146 | 155 | 164 | 173 | 182 |
| 165 | 176 | 187 | 193 | 209 | 220 |
| 195 | 208 | 221 | 234 | 247 | 260 |
| 234 | 250 | 265 | 281 | 296 | 312 |
| 282 | 301 | 320 | 338 | 357 | 376 |
| 293 | 312 | 332 | 351 | 371 | 390 |
| 438 | 467 | 496 | 526 | 555 | 584 |
| 488 | 520 | 553 | 585 | 618 | 650 |
| 555 | 592 | 629 | 666 | 703 | 740 |
| 585 | 624 | 663 | 712 | 741 | 780 |

# Part B

Maintenance of body weight requires an equal expenditure of energy and intake of calories through food. There is a general list of calorie value in chapter 3. Other calories values are available in most cookbooks.

List the calorie values for the food that you have eaten during the same 24-hour period recorded in Part A.

Calorie intake and expenditure vary with each day, so Part A and Part B may not represent a balance. However, the lab will demonstrate that foods have very different calorie values and careful selection of foods may be required to control the amount of calories ingested. Physical activity also varies with each day, so your recordings will reflect your activity for one day only. A log kept over a longer period of time would be indicative of the balance effect that occurs on a long-term basis.

| Breakfast | | Lunch | | Dinner | | Other | |
|---|---|---|---|---|---|---|---|
| Food | Cal. | Food | Cal. | Food | Cal. | Food | Cal. |
| ——————— | | ——————— | | ——————— | | ——————— | |
| ——————— | | ——————— | | ——————— | | ——————— | |
| ——————— | | ——————— | | ——————— | | ——————— | |
| ——————— | | ——————— | | ——————— | | ——————— | |
| ——————— | | ——————— | | ——————— | | ——————— | |
| ——————— | | ——————— | | ——————— | | ——————— | |
| ——————— | | ——————— | | ——————— | | ——————— | |
| ——————— | | ——————— | | ——————— | | ——————— | |
| ——————— | | ——————— | | ——————— | | ——————— | |
| **Total** | | Total | | Total | | Total | |

Total calories for 24-hour period _____

# CHAPTER 5

# Cardiovascular Fitness and Health

Cardiovascular problems are the leading cause of death in the United States. Approximately 50% of all deaths are attributable to heart and blood vessel disease. Over 1 million people experience a heart attack each year wtih about one-third dying. For every American dying of cancer, 3 will die resulting from heart related disease.

The economic cost of this health disaster resulting from medical costs, loss of earnings and productivity were in excess of $250 billion in 1998. Although there has been a slight decline in coronary heart disease (**CHD**), approximately 80 percent of the deaths occur in people less than 65 years of age.

Coronary heart disease can include artherosclerosis, hypertension (high blood pressure), stroke (brain attack), peripheral vascular disease and congestive heart failure. The first three are unfortunately far too common.

There are many factors that contribute to the development of coronary heart disease. Some are uncontrollable such as age, gender and inherited characteristics. Others are largely life-style issues such as physical activity and fitness level, diet, obesity, smoking and stress.

The American Heart Association recognizes **physical inactivity** as a primary risk for CHD similar to smoking, high cholesterol and hypertension. Epidemiological studies show that an increase in physical activity and fitness are associated with a decreased death rate from all causes as well as from CHD.

**Cardiovascular disease** occurs when a part of the cardio (heart) vascular (blood vessels) system can no longer function adequately enough to deliver blood throughout the body. The failure of the cardiovascular system can be due to many reasons. It is characteristically caused by a reduction in the open space (lumen) through which blood flows to the heart muscle (myocardium) and supplies it with blood and oxygen.

The heart is a four-chambered double pump that beats roughly 100,000 times a day to pump blood through 60,000 miles of blood vessels. The right side of the heart receives blood after it has been returned with carbon dioxide from the body and sends the blood to the lungs. The lungs cleanse the blood of the carbon dioxide and provide oxygen from respiration. The oxygenated blood is returned to the left side of the heart where it is pumped out to the body. The number of times the heart pumps per minute will vary between 60 and 95 in normal hearts. A heart rate below 60 is called **bradycardia** while a heart rate above 95 is called **tachycardia**.

**Atherosclerosis** is a progressively slow buildup of fat inside arteries which results in a decrease in blood flow through that artery. The **lumen** (the space inside the artery) becomes smaller due to this fat build up called **plaque**. The plaque formation results from a substance called **cholesterol** (this is discussed later in the chapter).

**Heart attack** is not usually a surprise. The predisposing causes of the disease such as atherosclerosis have been building up for years, but the victim has been unaware of the process. A blood clot or thrombus forms in a narrowed artery causing a **coronary thrombosis**, which may completely eliminate the flow of blood to the heart. The stoppage of blood to the heart results in a **myocardial infarction**, which is the death of heart tissue and subsequent scar formation. The question of a victim surviving a heart attack may depend on the extent of the myocardial infarction and whether coronary **collateral circulation** is present. Coronary collateral circulation

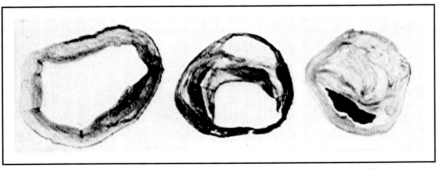

**Figure 5.1**    *The deterioration of a normal artery (left) is seen as atherosclerosis develops and begins depositing fatty substances and roughening the channel lining (center) until a clot forms (right) and plugs the artery to deprive the heart muscle of vital blood which results in heart attack.*

provides a series of small blood vessels to carry blood when the larger coronary arteries are blocked. These vessels may be working prior to an attack as more coronary vessels become clogged. It is thought that exercise plays a key role in creating these collateral arteries and that trained people have a better chance of surviving a heart attack because of the additional blood flow.

The victim of a heart attack may have had some early warning from **angina pectoris**. Chest pains develop during a heart attack, but they often occur at times prior to the actual attack. A lack of oxygen caused by diminished blood flow can be mild or oppressive as in a heart attack. The symptoms should not be ignored. Pain usually occurs during physical exertion and may be absent at rest.

**Stroke** or "brain attack," occurs when the brain does not receive enough oxygen. A common cause of stroke is a clot or thrombus in cerebral arteries. An embolus can also cause a stroke. A stroke may be induced by the

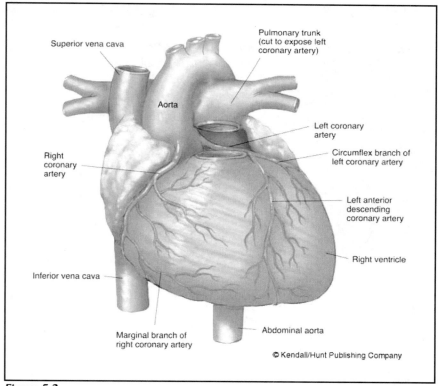

*Figure 5.2*

breaking of a blood vessel supplying the brain, which distends and dam-
ages brain tissue. Stroke can cause difficulty in walking, paralysis, and loss
of memory. The extent of the impairment will depend on how much damage is caused to the brain tissue. Cerebral hemorrhage (stroke) is often
associated with high blood pressure.

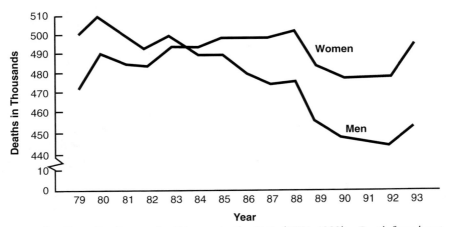

**Mortality from Cardiovascular Disease in the U.S. (1979–1993)**   *Death from heart
disease has been declining among men for about 20 years but has increased slightly
among women.*

Source: American Heart Association

# A Primer on Vascular Disease

It kills more Americans than any other illness, including cancer. The root causes are still something of a mystery, but we know how the disease progresses. And we're learning more about how to prevent it.

**How the body's response to injury can slowly destroy a coronary artery.**

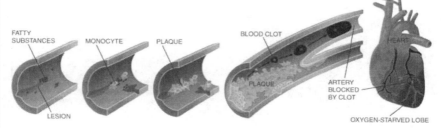

1. A blood-borne irritant such as homocysteine injures the arterial wall, and fatty substances accumulate
2. Circulating immune cells known as monocytes rush to the site of injury, causing inflammation
3. Arterial cells proliferate in an effort to heal the lesion, causing plaque to form on the vessel lining
4. As the plaque grows, it narrows the arterial opening and impedes blood flow. When pieces of the tough, brittle plaque break loose, they can seed clots that lodge in other parts of the vessel.
5. When a clot blocks a coronary artery, it can destroy the heart muscle by depriving it of oxygen

## Heart facts

- About 250,000 people die each year of a heart attack within one hour of symptoms and before reaching a hospital.

  Heart attacks accounted for 1 of every 4.7 deaths in the United States in 1994. Forty-five percent of all heart attacks occur in people under the age of 65.

  About 1.5 million Americans this year will have a first or repeat heart attack. Roughly one third of them will die.

## Leading killer

Cardiovascular disease was the leading cause of death in the U.S. for men and women of all racial and ethnic groups in 1994.

HIV (AIDS)
■ 41,930

ACCIDENTS
■ 90,140

CORONARY HEART DISEASE
■ 487,490

CANCER
■ 536,860

ALL CARDIOVASCULAR DISEASE
■ 954,720

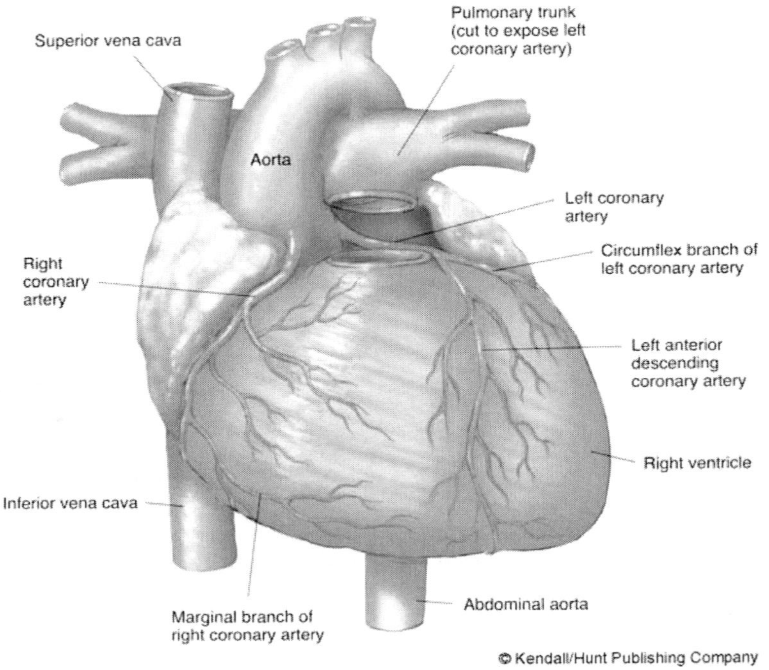

Labels in figure:
Superior vena cava
Pulmonary trunk (cut to expose left coronary artery)
Aorta
Left coronary artery
Circumflex branch of left coronary artery
Right coronary artery
Left anterior descending coronary artery
Right ventricle
Inferior vena cava
Abdominal aorta
Marginal branch of right coronary artery
© Kendall/Hunt Publishing Company

*Figure 5.5*    *The human heart, like the heart in all mammals, has four chambers. Two of these chambers (one atrium and one ventricle) perform systemic circulation. The two remaining chambers carry out pulmonary circulation. There is a wall between the chambers (the septum) which prevents oxygenated blood from mixing with deoxygenated blood. Valves between the atria and ventricles prevent backward flow when the heart contracts. From Gray and Matson,* Health Now.

# Uncontrollable Factors Related to Heart Disease

**Age**—Generally, the older a person gets, the more susceptible he or she becomes to cardiovascular disease. The risk increases significantly above fifty years of age, although we continue to see an increase in debilitating heart attacks striking people as young as 30 or 40. One in four victims of heart attack deaths is under the age of 65. Stroke, which is considered to be a disease of the older person, strikes people at an increasingly younger age. One in six of all stroke deaths occurs under the age of 65. The specific cause can probably be attributed to a number of contributing factors, including the deterioration of the cardiovascular system with age.

**Sex**—Cardiovascular disease is the leading cause of death for both men and women. Women tend to develop artery disease about 10 years later than men. Men, ages 25-64, have twice the incidence of heart disease of women in that age group. After age 65, heart disease rates for men and women are similar. The theory is that the hormone estrogen may protect females against heart attack while the hormone testosterone in males may actually increase the chances of heart problems.

**Heredity**—We inherit many characteristics from our parents and grandparents. Evidently, we may inherit a tendency toward susceptibility to disease in the circulatory system. Although there is no direct evidence that heart attack and stroke or the process of atherosclerosis is hereditary, the incidence is higher in some families than others. The susceptibility to a number of the factors that increase risk are probably inherited. Certain families inherit specific tendencies to cardiovascular disease and have limited life expectancy as a result.

# Heart Disease Risk Factors That You Can Control

**Cholesterol**—an elevation of this blood fat (lipid) is highly correlated to coronary heart disease. Fatty streaks appear on the lining of arteries as a result of lipid deposition. The lipid materials continue to build up and form solid deposits called plaque. This process begins early in life and continues to a point in adulthood where blood flow and oxygen supply are affected. This is most crucial in the coronary and cerebral arteries which supply the heart and brain respectively. *Atherosclerosis* (the build up of plaque) can hit throughout the body creating blockages. A 1993 study based on autopsies of 1532 teenagers and young adults found that all had fatty patches in their aortas. Fifty percent had heart disease. Cholesterol is produced by the liver as well as being ingested in the typical American diet. Cholesterol levels may reflect genetic influences which cause the liver to produce very high levels of lipids. It is recommended that cholesterol levels be maintained below 170 mg. Many times this can be accomplished by regulating diet and exercise. With genetic causes, medication is necessary. The blood lipids (cholesterol and triglycerides) must combine with a protein as they are produced in the liver, hence the name lipoprotein. There are two major classifications—HDL (High Density Lipids) and LDL (Low Density Lipids). LDL consists of about 60-75% cholesterol (with very little protein)

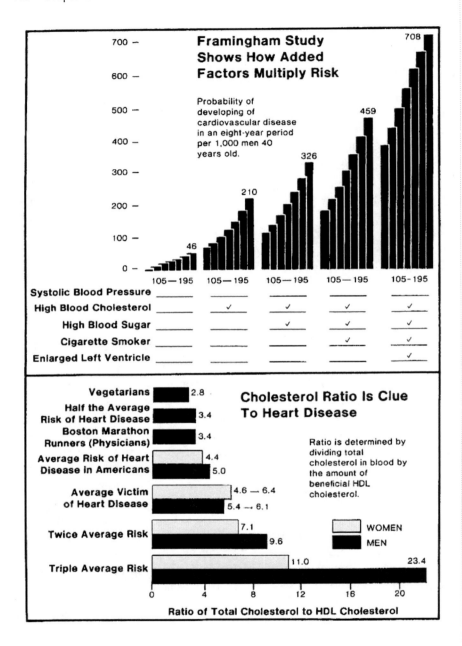

Source: The New York Times Company.

and is the major carrier of cholesterol to the cells. Therefore it is of greatest concern in developing the fatty plaques in the arteries. The HDL's appear to aid in decreasing the effect of LDL's by removing it from cells via enzymatic effect and by preventing the deposition of LDL in arterial cells. As a result of a large protein coating, the HDL's appear to be able to take on the cholesterol from the LDL's. This is a process called **reverse cholesterol transport**. Many studies suggest that high levels of HDL protect against CHD. HDL level is the best simple predictor of future coronary artery disease and can be increased after a few months of regular aerobic exercise. To determine the degree of risk it is necessary to know total cholesterol level and HDL level. Then create a **HDL ratio** by dividing the total cholesterol by the HDL level. Lower ratios would indicate lower risk. **A ratio of 5 for men and 4 for women suggest average risk**.

Lipid/HDL ratio example:      $\frac{200}{45} = 4.44$
Total cholesterol = 200 mg
HDL level = 45 mg

    **High Blood Pressure (Hypertension)**—Blood pressure is the force of the blood against the arterial walls. The force is generated by the heart as it pumps to keep blood moving through the arteries. The artery walls are muscular and elastic. The blood pressure increases as the heart pumps and decreases as the heart relaxes.

    Blood pressure is elevated in many people. The cause is not specifically known but the high level could be caused by change in body chemistry (due to a defect in an organ such as a kidney), emotional stress, and possible hereditary implication. High blood pressure causes the heart to overwork. The elevation of blood pressure against the arterial walls causes the heart to pump more often and it will eventually weaken. The arterial walls will eventually lose their elasticity, thus contributing to **arteriosclerosis (hardening of the arteries)**. Risk of premature cardiovascular disease and death rise sharply with increase in blood pressure. The vessels may not be able to deliver enough oxygen to the body. A blood pressure reading of 120/80 is thought to be normal. However, upper level readings **(systolic)** between 100 and 140 are also thought to be normal as well as lower level readings **(diastolic)** of 60 to 90. Some symptoms of high blood pressure include dizziness, light-headedness, fatigue, shortness of breath, and headaches.

|  | Amount | Rating |
|---|---|---|
| **Total Cholesterol** | < 200 mg/dl | Desirable |
|  | 200–239 mg/dl | Borderline high |
|  | ≥ 240 mg/dl | High risk |
| **LDL-Cholesterol** | < 130 mg/dl | Desirable |
|  | 130–159 mg/dl | Borderline high |
|  | ≥ 160 mg/dl | High risk |

|  | **Men** | **Women** | **Rating** |
|---|---|---|---|
| **HDL-Cholesterol** | ≥ 45 mg/dl | ≥ 55 mg/dl | Desirable |
|  | 36–44 mg/dl | 46–54 mg/dl | Moderate risk |
|  | ≤ 35 mg/dl | ≤ 45 mg/dl | High Risk |

From National Cholesterol Education Program

Medicines are very effective in lowering blood pressure to acceptable limits and maintaining those limits. Change in diet to lower fat levels, and cessation of smoking are also important considerations.

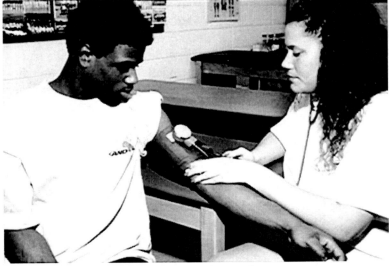

*Blood pressure measurement is easy to do and very informative*

**Obesity**—additional weight as body fat becomes problematic due not only to the added work of the heart but also because of a **comorbidity with hypertension, diabetic tendencies and elevated blood lipid levels**. All of these risk factors usually improve with increases in physical activity accompanied by prudent selection of food types and amounts.

**Homocysteine**—this amino acid appears to increase the tendency of plaque formation in arteries thus contributing to blockage. Like all amino acids homocysteine contributes to metabolism of the body. It results from the breakdown of other amino acids. This breakdown requires vitamin B6. This has led to the recommendation that includes a daily consumption of this vitamin since some people have high levels of homocysteine. Daily consumption of fruits and vegetables can usually help in providing adequate amounts of vitamin B6. As is true in many cases this elevated level of homocysteine may be genetically determined.

**Smoking**—this is the most preventable cause of illness and death in our society. It is a contributor to cardiovascular disease, cancer, bronchitis, emphysema and accelerates the process of artherosclerosis. It contributes to sudden death in the event of a myocardial infarction. Smoking increases heart rate, blood pressure and can create heart arrhythmias. Research indicates that HDL cholesterol and the ability of blood to carry oxygen are decreased by smoking. Interestingly, the risks for cardiovascular disease and cancer begin to decrease almost immediately with the cessation of smoking.

**Exercise**—The level of exercise is of special importance in its relationship to heart disease. Vigorous, rational exercise can decrease the blood lipid levels in the bloodstream and increase the amount of blood available to the body by increasing the stroke volume of the heart. The **stroke volume** is the amount of blood that the heart pumps with each contraction. A heart muscle that is trained can pump more blood as it beats less times per minute. The amount of blood supplied to the cells per minute is the cardiac output. As the stroke volume increases due to training, less heart beats are needed to maintain the cardiac output, and the resting heart rate will drop as the stroke volume increases. The exercised heart will also have a better chance at surviving a heart attack through the development of coronary collateral blood vessels that enable blood to supply the heart despite a blockage in a main coronary artery.

Research studies of various occupations have found a lack of exercise to be correlated with development of the disease. Studies of bus drivers and conductors, postal clerks and telegraphers, and railroad clerks and railroad maintenance workers, among others, indicate higher incidence of CHD deaths among sedentary people than among active people. Current avail-

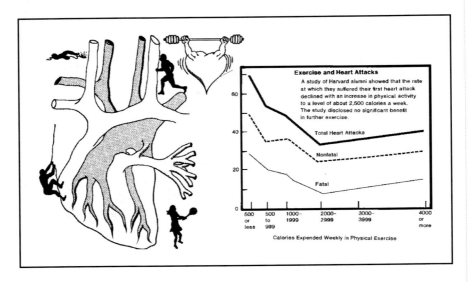

able evidence indicates that a physically inactive person has a higher risk of heart disease than a person who is physically active. In addition, evidence indicates that the chances of recovery from a heart attack are better for a person who has been physically active.

The American Heart Association has concluded, from existing evidence, that a lack of exercise is a risk factor in heart disease. Interestingly, "according to new findings presented to the American Heart Association, those who engage in vigorous exercise on a regular basis are likely to reduce in many ways the risk of developing heart disease. Studies of thousands of active individuals show that achieving physical fitness is associated with significant drops in weight, blood pressure, cholesterol levels and other factors associated with an increased risk of heart disease."[5]

Exercise also appears to elevate the level of **high-density lipoproteins** in the blood. These high-density lipoproteins seem to purge the blood of cholesterol. Certain types of these lipoproteins are higher in women and may be a factor in women being less prone to heart disease.

Studies of a large group of Harvard alumni (see following illustration) showed that highly active people have significantly fewer heart attacks.

> "Physicians who have studied the effects of exercise on heart function maintain that to derive significant benefits, exercisers should 'work up a sweat' for 20 minutes at least three times a week. Such a 'moderate' amount of activity would use up about 1,200 calories a week.

The continuing study of nearly 17,000 Harvard alumni has demonstrated that moderate physical exercise in adult life can significantly increase life expectancy."[6]

The study conducted by Dr. Ralph S. Paffenberger Jr. of Stanford University indicates that those men who use more than 2,000 calories a week in exercise had death rates one-quarter to one-third lower than the least active people even if the exercisers were not active prior to graduation.

The study further showed that exercise could diminish potential health threats posed by cigarette smoking and high blood pressure. Expenditures of 2,000 calories a week is the equivalent of walking briskly 20 miles a week. Advantages of exercising beyond 3,500 calories a week are minimal and suggest that moderate exercising may provide as much benefit as very strenuous exercise. As Dr. Paffenberger states "There are lots of skeptics who say people are active because they are healthy. I believe you're healthy because you're active."[7]

# Symptoms of Heart Disease

Many people fail to recognize the symptoms (signs) of cardiovascular defects. Often these symptoms are generalized and may indicate a number of problems. The symptoms may be mild or severe but they should be checked promptly in any event.

The **symptoms of heart attack are:**

- shortness of breath
- pain in the chest running down the left arm
- dizziness, light-headedness
- swelling in the extremities
- headache
- fatigue
- vague indigestion

# Summary

Heart disease is the leading killer in the United States. Heart disease is striking more people in their 20s and 30s than ever before. The risk of heart disease depends on several factors. Some factors cannot be controlled by you; these include age, sex, and heredity. Older people, men, and people with family histories of heart disease seem to be more susceptible to heart disease. The controllable factors that contribute to heart disease are elevated blood lipids or fats (cholesterol and triglycerides), elevated blood pressure, obesity, smoking (length of time and amount of cigarettes per day), and lack of exercise. You should recognize the symptoms of heart disease. They include shortness of breath, pain in the chest running down the left arm, dizziness, light-headedness, swelling in ankles, headache, fatigue, and vague indigestion.

No matter what a person's age, moderate exercise not only improves all-round health but also appears to ward off early death.

- Regular exercisers have lower mortality rate and morbidity from cardiovascular disease than do sedentary people.
- Research has supported the fact that light-to-moderate exercise is better than remaining inactive. Inactivity carries with it a risk almost as high as the relative risk of smoking a pack of cigarettes a day.
- Exercise effectively reduces or prevents the effects of most risk factors such as high blood pressure, obesity, blood lipid profiles, and cigarette smoking.
- Exercise after a myocardial infarction may decrease mortality.

# Exercise: The CHD Prescription

In 1989 a report prepared by a United States Preventive Services Task Force recommended that physicians advise all patients to engage in regular physical activity. In the last 25 years more than 40 major scientific studies have linked exercise to cardiovascular health-morbidity and mortality. Though a number of controversies remain, there is general agreement that exercise exerts a positive impact on many health variables.

Exercise scientists regard aerobic capacity as the best indicator of fitness level, since it represents the functional capacity of the cardiovascular system. In addition, it is accepted as a measure of the health status of the heart, blood vessels, and lungs.

Exercise is a valuable tool in modifying those factors that put people at risk of CHD. People who exercise are less likely to smoke than those who are sedentary. Also, with regard to every level of smoking (from not at all to heavy), exercisers have a lower risk of developing CHD. Other predictors of CHD such as obesity, blood pressure, blood lipids, family history, and blood glucose levels are all affected favorably by exercise.

Apparently, study results indicate that not a very large increase in activity and fitness is required to reduce the risk of CHD. Exercise should be undertaken with consideration given to the following components:

Aerobic activities that involve large muscle movements will promote cardiorespiratory improvement.

Muscular strength and endurance exercise can supplement aerobic exercise and aid in enhancing health and fitness as well.

Exercise should occur three to five times per week and last for 20 to 60 minutes each time.

When fitness improves, a decision must be made regarding continued change or maintaining the achieved level, that is, creating a change or preventing a change from occurring.

# Review Questions

1. What is the leading cause of death in the U.S. and what is the "trend" for men ages 25–44?

2. Briefly describe the process called atherosclerosis.

3. What does coronary collateral circulation have to do with heart attack?

4. How are angina pectoris and heart attack related?

5. What are the "big four" risk factors in developing heart disease?

6. What are the three "uncontrollable" risk factors? What factors are controllable?

7. What are the signs and symptoms of heart attack?

CHAPTER ACTIVITY

# RISKO: Your Chance of Having a Heart Attack

## Purpose

To assess your chances of suffering a heart attack based on the interplay of risk factors recognized by the American Heart Association.

## Procedure

Follow the directions indicated, then compare your score with the scale that accompanies the game. (Note: The purpose of this game is to yield only an estimate.)

## RISKO

The game is played by making squares that—from left to right—represent an increase in your RISK FACTORS. These are medical conditions and habits associated with an increased danger of heart attack. Not all risk factors are measurable enough to be included in this game; see back of sheet for other RISK FACTORS.

## Rules

Study each RISK FACTOR and its row. Find the box applicable to you and circle the large number in it. For example, if you are 37, circle the number in the box labeled 31—40.

After checking out all the rows, add the circled numbers. This total—your score—is an estimate of your risk.

_____

RISKO. © Michigan Heart Association

| | | | | | | |
|---|---|---|---|---|---|---|
| **AGE** | 10 to 20 | 21 to 30 | 31 to 40 | 41 to 50 | 51 to 60 | 61 to 70 and over |
| **HEREDITY** | No known history of heart disease | 1 relative with cardiovascular disease Over 60 | 2 relatives with cardiovascular disease Over 60 | 1 relative with cardiovascular disease Under 60 | 2 relatives with cardiovascular disease Under 60 | 3 relatives with cardiovascular disease Under 60 |
| **WEIGHT** | More than 5 lbs. below standard weight | −5 to +5 lbs. standard weight | 6-20 lbs. over weight | 21-35 lbs. over weight | 36-50 lbs. over weight | 51-65 lbs. over weight |
| **TOBACCO SMOKING** | Non-user | Cigar and/or pipe | 10 cigarettes or less a day | 20 cigarettes a day | 30 cigarettes a day | 40 cigarettes a day or more |
| **EXERCISE** | Intensive occupational and recreational exertion | Moderate occupational and recreational exertion | Sedentary work and intense recreational exertion | Sedentary occupational and moderate recreational exertion | Sedentary work and light recreational exertion | Complete lack of all exercise |
| **CHOLES-TEROL OR FAT % IN DIET** | Cholesterol below 180 mg.% Diet contains no animal or solid fats | Cholesterol 181-205 mg.% Diet contains 10% animal or solid fats | Cholesterol 206-230 mg.% Diet contains 20% animal or solid fats | Cholesterol 231-255 mg.% Diet contains 30% animal or solid fats | Cholesterol 256-280 mg.% Diet contains 40% animal or solid fats | Cholesterol 281-300 mg.% Diet contains 50% animal or solid fats |
| **BLOOD PRESSURE** | 100 upper reading | 120 upper reading | 140 upper reading | 160 upper reading | 180 upper reading | 200 or over upper reading |
| **SEX** | Female under 40 | Female 40-50 | Female over 50 | Male | Stocky male | Bald stocky male |

## Heredity

Count parents, grandparents, brothers, and sisters who have had heart attack and/or stroke.

## Tobacco Smoking

If you inhale deeply and smoke a cigarette way down, add one to your classification. Do not subtract because you think you do not inhale or smoke only a half inch on a cigarette.

## Exercise

Lower your score one point if you exercise regularly and frequently.

## Cholesterol or Saturated Fat Intake Level

A cholesterol blood level is best. If you can't get one from your doctor, then estimate honestly the percentage of solid fats you eat. These are usually of animal origin—lard, cream, butter, and beef and lamb fat. If you eat much of this, your cholesterol level probably will be high. The U.S. average, 40%, is too high for good health.

## Blood Pressure

If you have no recent reading but have passed an insurance or industrial examination chances are you are 140 or less.

## Sex

This line takes into account the fact that men have from 6 to 10 times more heart attacks than women of child-bearing age.

# Chapter Activity Results Sheet

Risk score for AGE is _____

Risk score for HEREDITY is _____

Risk score for WEIGHT is _____

Risk score for SMOKING is _____

Risk score for EXERCISE is _____

Risk score for CHOLESTEROL is _____

Risk score for BLOOD PRESSURE is _____

Risk score for SEX is _____

Total Risk score is _____

## If You Score

6-11—Risk well below average      25-31 —Risk moderate
12-17 —Risk below average         32-40 —Risk at a dangerous level
18-24 —Risk generally average     41-62 —Danger urgent
                                          See your doctor now.

## Based On Total Score My Risk Is: (circle one)

Well below average      Below average      Generally average
Moderate risk           Dangerous risk     Danger urgent

## Questions:

1. Based on your score what should you consider doing creating a change or preventing a change from occurring?

2. What specific controllable risk factors need to be changed and what will you do to accomplish this?

3. If you need to maintain a favorable risk level, how will you do that?

CHAPTER ACTIVITY

# Measurement and Evaluation of Blood Pressure

Blood pressure is the amount of force that the blood exerts against the arterial walls. It is expressed in millimeters of mercury. There are two phases of blood pressure—one produced during the contraction phase of the heart, called the systolic pressure; and the second produced during the relaxation phase of the heart cycle, called the diastolic pressure. Blood pressure may be measured with instruments called a sphygmomanometer (blood pressure cuff) and a stethoscope. Normal limits range from 110–140 systolic and 60–90 diastolic.

## Purpose

To determine individual blood pressure at rest.

## Part A—Measurement of Resting Blood Pressure

1. Place the cuff around the subject's upper arm so that the lower edge of the cuff is about 1 to 1 inches above the bend at the elbow. The arm should be at a right angle and in a relaxed, supported position.
2. Place the diaphragm of the stethoscope firmly over the midpoint at the bend of the elbow (antecubital space), directly over the site of the brachial pulse.
3. Be sure the valve control on the pump is completely shut. Inflate the pressure to approximately 160 mm, or approximately 30 mm beyond a brachial pulse cutoff.

4. Slowly release the pressure by opening the control valve so that pressure decreases at about 2 to 3 mm per second.
5. While decreasing pressure listen for the following sounds:
   a. a "sharp thud" (the first Korotkoff sound), this is accepted as the level of systolic pressure.
   b. the last sound followed by silence marks the diastolic pressure.

Resting Blood Pressure:

systolic = _____

diastolic = _____

| Rating | Systolic | Diastolic |
|---|---|---|
| Ideal | ≤ 120 | ≤ 80 mm Hg |
| Borderline high | 121–139 | 81–89 mm Hg |
| Hypertension | ≥ 140 | ≥ 90 mm Hg |

## Questions

1. What are the ranges for normal blood pressure?

   systolic: from _____ to _____

   diastolic: from _____ to _____

2. What long-term benefits does exercise have on blood pressure, and Why?

3. What are at least three dangers of hypertension?

# CHAPTER 6

# Principles of Exercise

The human body is a remarkably adaptable organism. Exercise causes the body to adapt to the exercise in a number of ways. The adaptations that are made are collectively referred to as **the training effect**. The training effect are those beneficial changes in structure and function that provide for improved health status, improved appearance, and improved function.

When few or no physical demands are made on the body there is a decline in function, or a negative adaptation. This is a classic example of the **"use it or lose it principle."**

Most people will admit that exercise is beneficial. Logical questions to consider would be:

- What kind of exercise?
- How much exercise?
- How often should the exercise be done?
- How hard should the exercise be done?

What is necessary to remember is that in order for the optimal benefit to be achieved exercise should be used following a prescription form. The **exercise prescription** will define the answers to the previous questions.

The variables that form an **exercise prescription** are: **exercise type** (aerobic or anaerobic); **exercise frequency** (how often); **exercise duration** (how long) and **exercise intensity** (how hard).

The exercise prescription can be designed to produce very specific adaptations. For example, an exercise prescription designed to create muscular strength would be quite different from one that would be designed to improve cardiorespiratory fitness.

**Frequency**—the recommended number of exercise sessions per week is **3**. This number is sufficient to create adaptation although more times per week is often desirable.

**Intensity**—there are a number of ways of measuring exercise intensity. The most common is to use heart rate. By calculating a **target heart rate**, which is based on various percentages of maximum heart, appropriate levels of exercise can be prescribed. As dicussed in an earlier chapter these various percentages of maximum can be described as **exercise lite** or **exercise heavy**. Intensity is the most critical variable to consider when creating a change in the body. Ideally, **60% to 90% of maximum is ideal**.

Another way to determine intensity is to use the **Rating of Perceived Exertion scale** developed by Borg. This rating scale allows a number to be chosen that would describe how someone feels (**"listening to your body"**) during exercise. This rating tends to correspond closely to heart rate. Opportunities to calculate your target heart rate and view the RPE scale appear at the end of the chapter.

**Duration**—there is no magic number that appears to be best. There is good evidence that **15 minutes at target heart rate** appears to be minimum. Of course exercise time can be extended to hours in some cases. Highly recommended duration is **30 minutes**.

Physical Activity recommendations for exercise include the following from the Center for Disease Control, the American College of Sports Medicine and the National Center for Disease Prevention and Health Promotion:

- **Adults should engage in moderate-intensity physical activities for at least 30 minutes on 5 or more days of the week** (CDC/ACSM)
- **Adults should engage in vigorous-intensity physical activity 3 or more days per week for 20 or more minutes per occasion** (Healthy People 2010)

The chart that follows shows average maximal attainable heart rates for specific age levels and the respective "target zones." The target heart rate zone represents the heart rate range which will best create the training effect.

It describes 5 different Target Heart Rate Zones (THRZ) based on the age-predicted maximum HR. To get an estimate of your HRmax, simply subtract your age from 220. The result is your age-predicted HRmax in beats per minute (bpm). This is a fairly accurate method for determining your HRmax (+ or – 15 bpm). There are other methods of determining your HRmax more accurately, but most require the supervision of a qualified individual such as a doctor.

## Target Heart Rate Zones

| Age, years | Moderate Activity Zone 50%–60% HRmax | Weight Management Zone 60%–70% HRmax | Aerobic Zone 70%–80% HRmax | Anaerobic Threshold Zone 80%–90% HRmax | Red Line Zone 90%–100% HRmax |
|---|---|---|---|---|---|
| 20–24 | 98–120 | 117–140 | 137–160 | 156–180 | 176–200 |
| 25–29 | 95–117 | 114–137 | 133–156 | 152–176 | 171–195 |
| 30–34 | 93–114 | 111–133 | 130–152 | 148–171 | 167–190 |
| 35–39 | 90–111 | 108–130 | 126–148 | 144–167 | 162–185 |
| 40–44 | 88–108 | 105–126 | 123–144 | 140–162 | 158–180 |
| 45–49 | 85–105 | 102–123 | 119–140 | 136–158 | 153–175 |
| 50–54 | 83–102 | 99–119 | 116–136 | 132–153 | 149–170 |
| 55–59 | 80–99 | 96–116 | 112–132 | 128–149 | 144–165 |
| 60–64 | 78–95 | 93–112 | 109–128 | 124–144 | 140–160 |

# American College of Sports Medicine Recommendations

The American College of Sportsmedicine (ACSM) has developed recommendations on exercise for healthy (asymptomatic) adults. The recommendations include both aerobic and resistance training guidelines, which are summarized as follows:

Frequency—3 to 5 times per week

Intensity—60% to 90% of maximum heart rate; or 50% to 85% of heart rate reserve method using Karvonen determination.

Duration—20 to 30 minutes; or 2 to 3 miles per workout (if walking, jogging) or the expenditure of approximately 250-300 calories.

Resistance Training—8 to 10 exercises; performed for 8 to 12 repetitions, twice per week as a minimum.

# Mode (Type) of Exercise

There are two general types of exercise: **aerobic** and **anaerobic**. Each has specific characteristics related to the biochemistry of energy production in the body. These characteristics are based on the amount of oxygen that can be supplied, delivered, and used during exercise.

## Aerobic Exercise Characteristics

Aerobic literally means "with air or oxygen." When applied to exercise it would involve activities which require large amounts of oxygen to be supplied, delivered and used over extended periods of time. As such, there are three characteristics which categorize an exercise as aerobic. They are:

1. Sustained exercise for 15 minutes or longer at *steady state of heart rate or RPE.*
2. Gross (total) body movement (big muscles are active)
3. Repetitive movement (same pattern repeated)

## Anaerobic Exercise Characteristics

Anaerobic literally means "without air or oxygen." When applied to the exercise setting it would involve activities which much be slowed down or stopped because not enough oxygen is being supplied, delivered and used. As such, an appropriate characteristic which categorizes an exercise as anaerobic is:

1. Muscular activity that forces a slowdown or cessation (stop) in less than three minutes. The best example is resistance training (lifting weights) where the muscles become fatigued and slow down or stop in very short periods of time, certainly less than three minutes.

The same exercise (running, for example) can be an aerobic effort for some people and anaerobic for others. This is due to individual differences in fitness level that reflect the ability to supply, deliver, and use oxygen. The primary factor in determining whether an exercise is aerobic or anaerobic is the intensity of effort. Generally, high-effort levels are anaerobic and lower-effort levels are aerobic.

# How to Exercise

The following chart illustrates a training or *exercising pattern*. It shows the progression from **warm-up**, to training **stimulus level**, to cool-down. Please note that exercise at the proper intensity is approximately 20 minutes. The period of time at the 60% to 90% level should be preceded by a warm-up so that the body's systems necessary to support activity are not suddenly taxed. The exercise period should be followed by a gradual return to normal called a cool-down. This allows the body to regain **homeostasis** more easily.

Some of the benefits of a warm-up include:

* Gradual increase in heart rate
* Gradual increase in blood pressure
* Increased blood flow to muscles
* Increased muscle temperature
* Increased circulatory and respiratory function

## The Aerobic Workout

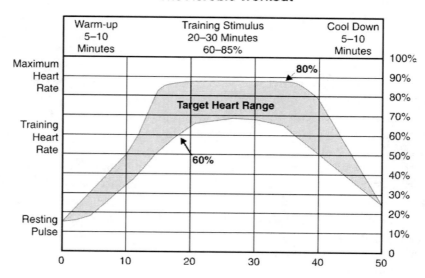

From *The Aerobic Workout* by Newlife Technologies. Copyright © 1999 by Newlife Technologies. Reprinted by permission.

The cool-down is an important part of the exercise training pattern. Dilated blood vessels in exercising muscles may cause a fall in blood pressure, pooling of blood in the veins, and diminished return of blood to the heart if exercise is terminated abruptly. When a person walks or engages in another activity involving rhythmic contraction of the leg muscles during the cool-down phase, blood is milked out of these vessels and circulation is aided. The cool-down produces the same benefit as the warm-up, except allowing for gradual decreases in function back toward resting levels.

A proper sequence of an exercise session would be to warm up, stretch, work out, and cool down. Stretching can also be used as part of the cool-down phase.

# The Use of S.O.A.P.

In addition to some of the basic considerations of exercise reflecting intensity, duration, and frequency, the idea of S.O.A.P. becomes important. S.O.A.P. not only represents what you should use after exercising, but also the four basic principles related to any exercise program. They are:

- Specificity
- Overload
- Adaptation
- Progression

**Specificity** as applied to exercise means that you get what you train for if your program is strength oriented, the gain will be primarily strength; endurance-oriented activities produce greater endurance. The body adapts specifically to the demands placed on it regulated by the intensity, duration, and types of activities.

To prompt positive change in the body, **overload** must be employed. This principle involves the increase in the demands made upon the body during exercise. Overload can be in the form of greater intensity (strenuousness), duration (longer exercise sessions), or frequency (number of exercise sessions). If resistance training is the type of exercise program, sets, repetitions, and resistance can be forms of overload.

**Adaptation** is a principle of exercise that merely involves the changes that occur in the body because of the specific exercise program. All aspects of the training effect are examples of this principle.

The last principle of exercise programs is that of **progression**. To induce the training effect in the body you must *progress gradually but con-*

*tinuously.* This principle involves the application of exercise variables that are not too demanding for you but at the same time will be enough to ensure positive gains. On occasion, you may experience **retrogression** in response to any form of overload. During this time your physiology is beginning adaptation, which is manifested in reduced performance level and lingering discomforts. However, this is not a permanent condition, and exercise should be continued at a reduced level after a recovery day.

**Maintenance** is a principle that should be employed once you are in good condition. It is never necessary to always employ overload. At some point "enough is enough." The guideline is once you look better, feel better, and function better, maintain that exercise prescription; don't overload— anything more is a psychological desire, not a physical need.

## Precautions and Considerations

No one exercise program can be used for all people. Fitness goals should be realistic and reflect your needs, interests, and desires—in the present and future. Sometimes, frustration, disappointment, and even a decrease in ability (regression) will occur. It will be helpful in avoiding these possibilities if the following exercise precautions and considerations are kept in mind:

1. Be realistic about what you need and desire from exercise as well as what exercise will and will not do.
2. Choose a form of exercise that will help fulfill your needs, one that will be enjoyable yet demanding.
3. Realize that there are no "shortcut, easy methods" of exercising. It takes time and effort.
4. Choose appropriate clothing for your exercise and the prevailing environmental conditions (temperature, terrain, etc.).
5. Understand that some degree of discomfort seems to be an inescapable adjunct of vigorous muscular activity.
6. If you exercise with someone, try to exercise with a person in the same level of fitness and relative ability and interests.
7. Keep your enthusiasm in perspective; too much exercise— over-stressing—can be dangerous, especially at the start of a program. Some signs and symptoms of *overconditioning* include:
   Insomnia
   Prolonged washed out feeling and muscular soreness

Extreme weight loss
Chronic fatigue
Irritability
Lowered general resistance (evidenced by sniffles, headaches, fever blisters, etc.)

8. If you are 35 years of age or older, consider it absolutely necessary to have a thorough physical examination before beginning an exercise program. This is especially necessary if you possess any of the heart disease risk factors or have been sedentary for months or years. Even if you are under 35 years of age, a physical exam before starting a program would be an intelligent course of action.

9. Remember, fitness is a lifelong value—to maintain the physical, mental, and emotional benefits, exercise must be a lifetime endeavor. It requires considerable self-discipline, but the rewards are worth the effort.

**How much exercise?** There does seem to be a point of diminishing return, depending on the person. The following diagram illustrates the fact that beyond a certain point there is little if any benefit. Too much exercise, too often, too hard, and too long is not good.

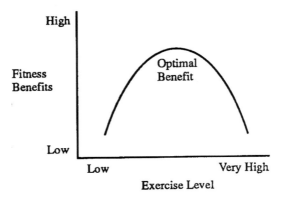

# Some Considerations for Exercise, Fitness and Health

- The mode of aerobic exercise is not important. Many activities give the same benefit, so choose an activity that you enjoy. Injuries tend to increase with the amount of exercise, so don't overdo.
- Low-to-moderate training intensities are best for most adults. Higher intensities increase risk of injury and the probability of becoming an exercise dropout.
- Monitor your heart rate on a regular basis when you exercise, on a regular basis but not necessarily every workout.
- If your first goal is to lose weight, exercise more often and longer but at low-to-moderate intensity.
- Exercising less than twice a week usually does not improve fitness and benefits level off after more than three days per week.
- You must keep exercising to preserve your benefit. Cardiorespiratory fitness drops after 10 days of detraining. After 10 weeks you've lost all benefit.
- Age does not hinder endurance training. Improvements in fitness in middle-aged and older people can rival those seen in young people.
- You need a well-rounded program to exercise all the major muscle groups of the body. Strength training, aerobic exercise, and flexibility exercise are all necessary.

# Calories Burned During Exercise and Activities

Calories burned during exercise is affected by body weight, intensity of workout, conditioning level and your metabolism. Data is based on research from Medicine and Science in Sports and Exercise, the "Official Journal of the American College of Sports Medicine."

The *Activity Profile* of **NutriStrategy Nutrition and Fitness Software** has hundreds of examples of calories burned during exercises and activities, based on your individual body weight. Calories burned per hour is shown below for the body weights of 140 and 195 pounds. Exercises and activities from Aerobics to Weight Lifting are alphabetized below.

| Activity (1 hour) | 140 lbs | 195 lbs |
|---|---|---|
| Aerobics, general | 381 | 531 |
| Aerobics, high impact | 445 | 620 |
| Aerobics, low impact | 318 | 443 |
| Archery (non-hunting) | 222 | 310 |
| Backpacking | 445 | 620 |
| Badminton, social | 286 | 398 |
| Basketball, game | 508 | 708 |
| Basketball, officiating | 445 | 620 |
| Basketball, shooting baskets | 286 | 398 |
| Basketball, wheelchair | 413 | 575 |
| Bicycling, <10 mph, leisure | 254 | 354 |
| Bicycling, 10–11.9 mph, light effort | 381 | 531 |
| Bicycling, 12–13.9 mph, moderate effort | 508 | 708 |
| Bicycling, 14–15.9 mph, vigorous effort | 636 | 885 |
| Bicycling, 16–19 mph, very fast, racing | 763 | 1062 |
| Bicycling, >20 mph, racing | 1017 | 1416 |
| Bicycling, Mountain or BMX | 540 | 753 |
| Bicycling, stationary, general | 318 | 443 |
| Bicycling, stationary, very light effort | 350 | 487 |
| Bicycling, stationary, light effort | 350 | 487 |
| Bicycling, stationary, moderate effort | 445 | 620 |
| Bicycling, stationary, vigorous effort | 667 | 930 |
| Bicycling, stationary, very vigorous effort | 795 | 1107 |
| Billiards | 159 | 221 |
| Bowling | 191 | 266 |
| Boxing, in ring, general | 763 | 1062 |
| Boxing, punching bag | 381 | 531 |
| Boxing, sparring | 572 | 797 |
| Broomball | 445 | 620 |
| Calisthenics (pushups, sit-ups), light/moderate effort | 286 | 398 |
| Calisthenics, vigorous effort | 508 | 708 |
| Canoeing, on camping trip | 254 | 354 |
| Canoeing, rowing, light effort | 191 | 266 |
| Canoeing, rowing, moderate effort | 445 | 620 |
| Canoeing, rowing, crewing, >6 mph, vigorous effort | 763 | 1062 |
| Circuit training | 508 | 708 |
| Cleaning house, general | 222 | 310 |
| Cleaning, light, moderate effort | 159 | 221 |

| Activity (I hour) | 140 lbs | 195 lbs |
|---|---|---|
| Cleaning, heavy, vigorous effort | 286 | 398 |
| Coaching, football, soccer, basketball, etc. | 254 | 354 |
| Cricket (batting, bowling) | 318 | 443 |
| Croquet | 159 | 221 |
| Curling | 254 | 354 |
| Dancing, aerobic, swing, ballet or modern, twist | 381 | 531 |
| Dancing, ballroom, slow | 191 | 266 |
| Dancing, ballroom, fast | 350 | 487 |
| Fencing | 381 | 531 |
| Fishing, general | 254 | 354 |
| Football or baseball, playing catch | 159 | 221 |
| Football, competitive | 572 | 797 |
| Football, touch, flag | 508 | 708 |
| Frisbee playing | 191 | 266 |
| Frisbee, ultimate | 222 | 310 |
| Gardening, general | 318 | 443 |
| Golf, carrying clubs | 350 | 487 |
| Golf, pulling clubs | 318 | 443 |
| Golf, using power cart | 222 | 310 |
| Golf, miniature or driving range | 191 | 266 |
| Hacky sack | 254 | 354 |
| Handball | 763 | 1062 |
| Health club exercise | 350 | 487 |
| Hiking, cross country | 381 | 531 |
| Hockey, field | 508 | 708 |
| Hockey, ice | 508 | 708 |
| Horse grooming | 381 | 531 |
| Horseback riding, walking | 159 | 221 |
| Horseback riding, trotting | 413 | 575 |
| Horseback riding, galloping | 508 | 708 |
| Hunting | 318 | 443 |
| Jai alai | 763 | 1063 |
| Jogging | 445 | 620 |
| Judo, karate, kick boxing, tae kwon do | 636 | 885 |
| Kayaking | 318 | 443 |
| Lacrosse | 508 | 708 |
| Marching band, playing instrument, walking | 254 | 354 |
| Mowing lawn | 350 | 487 |
| Paddleboat | 254 | 354 |
| Polo | 508 | 708 |

| Activity (1 hour) | 140 lbs | 195 lbs |
|---|---|---|
| Race walking | 413 | 575 |
| Racquetball, casual | 445 | 620 |
| Racquetball, competitive | 636 | 885 |
| Raking lawn | 254 | 354 |
| Rock climbing, ascending rock | 699 | 974 |
| Rope jumping, moderate | 636 | 885 |
| Rowing, stationary, moderate effort | 604 | 841 |
| Rugby | 636 | 885 |
| Running, 5 mph (12 minute mile) | 508 | 708 |
| Running, 5.2 mph (11.5 minute mile) | 572 | 797 |
| Running, 6 mph (10 minute mile) | 636 | 885 |
| Running, 6.7 mph (9 minute mile) | 699 | 974 |
| Running, 7 mph (8.5 minute mile) | 731 | 1018 |
| Running, 7.5 mph (8 minute mile) | 795 | 1107 |
| Running, 8 mph (7.5 minute mile) | 858 | 1195 |
| Running, 8.6 mph (7 minute mile) | 890 | 1239 |
| Running, 9 mph (6.5 minute mile) | 953 | 1328 |
| Running, 10 mph (6 minute mile) | 1017 | 1416 |
| Running, 10.9 mph (5.5 minute mile) | 1144 | 1594 |
| Running, stairs, up | 953 | 1328 |
| Sailing, in competition | 318 | 443 |
| Shoveling snow | 381 | 531 |
| Skateboarding | 318 | 443 |
| Skating, ice | 445 | 620 |
| Skating, ice, speed, competitive | 953 | 1328 |
| Skating, roller | 445 | 620 |
| Ski machine | 604 | 681 |
| Skiing, cross-country, slow or light effort | 445 | 620 |
| Skiing, cross-country, moderate effort | 508 | 708 |
| Skiing, cross-country, vigorous effort | 572 | 797 |
| Skiing, cross-country, uphill, maximum effort | 1049 | 1461 |
| Skiing, snow, downhill light effort | 318 | 443 |
| Skiing, snow, downhill, moderate effort | 381 | 531 |
| Skiing, snow, downhill, vigorous effort | 508 | 708 |
| Skiing, water | 381 | 531 |
| Skin-diving, scuba diving | 445 | 620 |
| Sledding, tobogganing, bobsledding, luge | 445 | 620 |
| Snowmobiling | 222 | 310 |
| Soccer, casual | 445 | 620 |
| Soccer, competitive | 636 | 885 |

| Activity (1 hour) | 140 lbs | 195 lbs |
|---|---|---|
| Softball or baseball | 318 | 443 |
| Squash | 763 | 1062 |
| Stair machine | 381 | 531 |
| Stretching, hatha yoga | 254 | 354 |
| Surfing, body or board | 191 | 266 |
| Swimming laps, freestyle, light/moderate effort | 508 | 708 |
| Swimming laps, freestyle, fast, vigorous effort | 636 | 885 |
| Swimming, backstroke | 508 | 708 |
| Swimming, breaststroke | 636 | 885 |
| Swimming, butterfly | 699 | 974 |
| Swimming, leisurely | 381 | 531 |
| Table tennis, ping pong | 254 | 354 |
| T'ai chi | 254 | 354 |
| Tennis, singles | 508 | 708 |
| Tennis, doubles | 381 | 531 |
| Volleyball, competitive | 254 | 354 |
| Walk/run—playing with children, moderate | 254 | 354 |
| Walking, 2.0 mph, slow pace | 159 | 221 |
| Walking, 3.0 mph, moderate pace | 222 | 310 |
| Walking, 4.0 mph, very brisk pace | 254 | 354 |
| Walking, upstairs | 508 | 708 |
| Wallyball | 445 | 620 |
| Water aerobics | 254 | 354 |
| Water polo | 636 | 885 |
| Weight lifting, light or moderate effort | 191 | 266 |
| Weight lifting or bodybuilding, vigorous effort | 381 | 531 |

Source: NutriStrategy.com

# Summary

The training effect is the change in the body resulting from the physical demands of exercise. Three variables affect the degree of the training effect. They are frequency (how often), intensity (how hard or vigorous), and duration (how long). Among other factors that influence the training effect is specificity. Specificity means that you get what you train for. Another factor is the degree of overload. Overload requires that you place increased demands on your musculature to improve performance. Adaptation is the way in which your body changes as a result of exercise. Progression is needed to continue the improvement of your body's performance until good fitness levels are attained. Then, maintenance of the exercise regimen will help to retain the acquired benefit or training effect.

# Check Out These Websites

www.phys.com - Allows you to ask your business questions, learn ways to begin or get back into exercising no matter what your excuse, and find tips, forums, chat rooms, and much more.

www.enduranceplus.com/workouts.html - provides a complete list of training moves for every muscle group that exists! Provides descriptions along with helpful photos to help maintain proper form. Also gives a three day a week workout, and special workouts for women.

# Listening to Your Body—Perceptions of Work

Exercise intensity (heart rate) is the most difficult variable to deal with in the exercise setting. The ability to exercise at a prescribed heart rate (effort) will vary from person to person even though they may be the same age. Actually, our bodies are usually quite good at letting us know what a "hard workout" is or isn't. The "whole body" perceptions become just as important as a particular heart rate—"my legs are beat," "my lungs are burning," or "this feels easy" are good measures of exertion. This *perceived exertion* is the way in which we can listen to our body and determine sufficient exertion or intensity.

Dr. Gunnar Borg developed a simple method of applying a number value to perceived exertion. It was developed using stress tests (treadmill tests), during which time a patient would indicate how they felt by choosing a number on a scale like the one below.

**Perceived exertion scale\***

| | |
|---|---|
| 6 | |
| 7 | Very very light |
| 8 | |
| 9 | Very light |
| 10 | |
| 11 | Fairly light |
| 12 | |
| 13 | Somewhat hard |
| 14 | |
| 15 | Hard |
| 16 | |
| 17 | Very hard |
| 18 | |
| 19 | Very very hard |
| 20 | |

\*This scale was developed in the early 1960s by Swedish physiologist Gunnar Borg. Borg observed that people were quite good at perceiving the physical costs of various work loads. Through several years of research, he constructed a self-report scale to assess these perceptions.

Very frequently, the perceived exertion will approximate a heart rate. The Rate of Perceived Exertion (RPE) scale is numbered vertically from 6 to 20. A 6 reflects a restful condition with virtually no exertion and a 20 reflects near maximum exertion. The purpose is to combine all feelings—legs, breathing, arms, heart, and so on when choosing one of the numbers. Therefore, it becomes possible to exercise at a particular RPE, based on listening to your body, that coincides nicely with objective measures of exercise intensity like heart rate.

# Review Questions

1. What is the "training effect" and give 5 specific examples of this phenomenon? (see chapter 2 for additional information).

2. What are the variables included in an exercise prescription and what are the guidelines which apply to each?

3. Name two ways in which intensity can be measured. What does training heart rate range mean? What does RPE mean?

4. To what do the letters S.O.A.P. refer? What does each mean?

5. What are three signs/symptoms of overconditioning?

CHAPTER ACTIVITY

# Heart Rate as a Measure of Exercise Intensity

To obtain the greatest aerobic benefits from exercise, the effort must not be too high or too low. Generally, it is always better and safer to exercise too easily rather than too hard. The accepted measure of effort is heart rate in beats per minute. For exercise to be productive it must be performed at a predetermined level. The Karvonen method of determining ideal training heart rate has been endorsed by the American College of Sports Medicine. The proper intensity is actually a range, rather than a single heart rate. This intensity is based on age and resting heart rate. Follow these procedures to determine resting heart rate and proper training intensity.

## *Purpose*

To determine resting heart rate (RHR) and training rate range.

## Part A—Resting Heart Rate

Take heart beat while seated by counting either the carotid pulse (either side of larynx) or the radial pulse (thumb side of wrist) for ten (10) seconds and multiply by six to convert to a minute base (BPM).

RHR     TRIAL 1 _____ BPM
            TRIAL 2 _____ BPM
            TRIAL 3 _____ BPM

SUM OF 3 TRIALS  =  _____

AVERAGE RHR    =  _____ (sum divided by 3)

# Part B

1.    220
   − ☐ (age)
   ───────
   ☐ Estimated
      Maximum
      Heart rate
      (EMHR)

2. ☐ (EMHR)
   − ☐ (RHR)
   ───────
   ☐ Adjusted
      rate

3. ☐ Adjusted
      rate
   × .40 (40%)
   ───────
   ☐ (Work rate)

4. ☐ (Work rate)
   + ☐ (RHR)
   ───────
   ☐ Training
      rate @
      40% level

1.    220
   − ☐ (age)
   ───────
   ☐ (EMHR)

2. ☐ (EMHR)
   − ☐ (RHR)
   ───────
   ☐ Adjusted
      rate

3. ☐ Adjusted
      rate
   × .60 (60%)
   ───────
   ☐ (Work rate)

4. ☐ (Work rate)
   + ☐ (RHR)
   ───────
   ☐ Training
      rate @
      60% level

1.    220
   − ☐ (age)
   ───────
   ☐ (EMHR)

2. ☐ (EMHR)
   − ☐ (RHR)
   ───────
   ☐ Adjusted
      rate

3. ☐ Adjusted
      rate
   × .90 (90%)
   ───────
   ☐ (Work rate)

4. ☐ (Work rate)
   + ☐ (RHR)
   ───────
   ☐ Training
      rate @
      90% level

1. What do these training heart rates mean?

2. How do these training heart rates affect frequency and duration?

3. What should you do if you are unable to sustain your 60-90% heart rate level for a prescribed length of time?

CHAPTER ACTIVITY

# Aerobic Fitness Walk Test

## Rockport Fitness Walking Test— a do it yourself test

The amount of oxygen that you can process (supply, deliver and use) is the best indicator of health-related fitness status. This measure is referred to as aerobic fitness and can be evaluated in various ways. This is a major fitness test based on walking developed by Dr. James M. Rippe at the University of Massachusetts Medical Center in Worcester, Massachusetts. The test will tell you only about cardiovascular endurance—*not heart disease.*

## *Purpose*

To evaluate aerobic fitness level, not heart disease.

## *Procedure*

Please remember: the two necessary pieces of information are the time it takes to walk the mile and your heart rate when finished.

1. Warm-up for 3 minutes and stretch.
2. Walk 1 mile as briskly as possible (no running).
3. Note time (in minutes) and heart rate (neck or wrist, count 15 sec. x 4 for BPM)
4. Using the appropriate age adjusted chart for males and females respectively draw a line horizontally from your heart rate and vertically from your time.
5. Where these lines intersect is an indicator of your relative aerobic fitness.

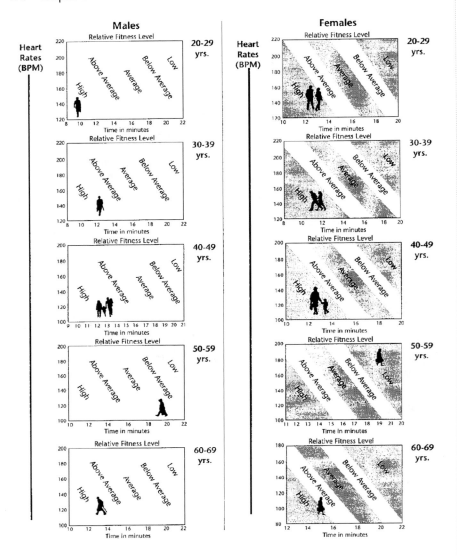

CHAPTER ACTIVITY

# The Back Fitness Test

One of the common musculoskeletal problems afflicting adult Americans is low back pain. Most backaches are due to weaknesses in the muscles that support the vertebrae. This can lead to spinal nerve and disc problems, which create the chronic low back syndrome.

## Purpose

To perform a single assessment of back fitness relative to the potential of future back problems.

## Procedure

Perform the specific tests as described and determine the grades in the four categories.

## Part A—The Sit-Up

1. Do not allow anyone to hold your feet down.
2. Be sure to perform the sit-up with adequate padding under your back.

| TEST | GRADE I<br>Excellent | GRADE II<br>Average | GRADE III<br>Fair | GRADE IV<br>Poor |
|------|----------------------|---------------------|-------------------|------------------|
| A.<br>THE<br>SIT-UP | Able to sit up with knees bent and hands on shoulders. | Able to sit up with knees bent and arms folded across chest. | Able to sit up with knees bent and arms held out straight. | Unable to sit up with knees bent. |

Result: Grade _____

## Part B—The Double Leg Raise

| | GRADE I Excellent | GRADE II Average | GRADE III Fair | GRADE IV Poor |
|---|---|---|---|---|
| B. THE DOUBLE LEG RAISE | Able to keep back flat against the floor while raising the legs 6 inches for 10 counts. | Able to raise the legs for several counts but back curves partway through the test. | Able to lift the legs but back curves immediately when the legs are raised. | Unable to lift both legs for 10 counts and/or lifting legs causes pain. |

Result: Grade _____

## Part C—The Lateral Trunk Lift

| | GRADE I Excellent | GRADE II Average | GRADE III Fair | GRADE IV Poor |
|---|---|---|---|---|
| C. THE LATERAL TRUNK LIFT | Able to raise the shoulders 12 inches off the floor without difficulty, holding for 10 counts. | Able to raise the shoulders 12 inches off the floor but with difficulty. Cannot hold for 10 counts. | Able to raise shoulders slightly off the floor and with difficulty. | Unable to raise shoulders off the floor. |

Result: Grade _____

From *Goodbye Backache*, by Dr. David Imrie with Colleen Dimson. (Arco, 1983)

## Part D—The Hip Flexors

1. Be sure to measure both sides, right and left.

| | GRADE I<br>Excellent | GRADE II<br>Average | GRADE III<br>Fair | GRADE IV<br>Poor |
|---|---|---|---|---|
| **D.**<br>**THE**<br>**HIP**<br>**FLEXORS** | Able to hold one leg firmly against the chest with the other leg flat against the floor. | With effort able to hold one knee against the chest while straightening the other leg flat to the floor. | With one knee fixed firmly against the chest the other leg raises off the floor. | Unable to get one leg firmly against the chest without causing pain or discomfort. |

Result: Grade _____

## Questions

Based on your results, what considerations should be made in the type of exercise needed to create change or to prevent change (i.e., to promote improvement or to prevent further deterioration)?

# CHAPTER 7

# Systems of Exercise— What Do I Do?

If you have asked the question, "What kind of exercise do I do?" a major obstacle has already been overcome. By asking that question you have hopefully admitted (at least to yourself) that exercise is a necessary part of life-style in our society. The answer to the question is . . . "it depends." The type of exercise program "depends" on many factors, such as:

- What aspect of fitness do I need most?
- What do I want from exercise?
- What exercise do I enjoy?
- Where will I be exercising (school, home, health club)?
- Will I be exercising with someone or alone?
- What skills do I need?
- Will I need special equipment?

Exercise programs have different outcomes—some will produce gains primarily in endurance; others are conducive to increases in strength, muscular endurance, or flexibility. Some are better for weight gain, others are better for weight loss and a change in body composition. Regardless of what a specific system of exercise will or will not do, all involve a manipulation of the variables mentioned in chapter 7 (frequency, intensity, duration).

Basically, **systems of exercise** can be easily classified into four general categories:

- Aerobic
- Circuit Training
- Resistance Training
- Interval Training

*Exercise choices are varied and can be fun.*

Some consideration of each will aid in answering, "What do I do?"

# Aerobics

Aerobic exercise (also called "Cardio") will inherently lead to improvements in circulatory, respiratory and vascular (blood) function. Cardiovascular or cardiorespiratory exercise are other names attached to aerobics. The factor which is unique to aerobics of any description is steady state heart rate or a steady RPE rating.

**Aerobic exercise** gained considerable attention primarily due to the professional efforts of Dr. Kenneth H. Cooper, M.D., who is the author of several books dealing with the idea behind aerobics. The term *aerobic* literally means "with air or oxygen." When placed in the context of exercise it includes those exercises which force your body to process large amounts of oxygen without producing or creating an oxygen debt. An inherently aerobic exercise exhibits these three characteristics simultaneously:

1. It can be performed continuously for at least 15 minutes;
2. It involves gross body movement (total body movement); and
3. It involves a repetitive type movement pattern.

The aerobic system of exercise as developed by Dr. Cooper has many distinct advantages: It has adjusted the exercise variables for age, gender, and level of fitness at the start; it has preestablished programs of exercise for various levels of fitness and activity; it tells you how to determine your individual level of fitness; it has established the necessary amounts of exercise to attain and maintain a good fitness level; and the programs have been scientifically formulated based on stringent clinical, laboratory, and field research.

The aerobics system works by using a point system designed to develop cardiovascular efficiency. Exercise performed at a certain activity level will be worth a prescribed number of points based on the amount of energy expended; exercise at a high energy level will earn more points than exercise at a low energy level for the same time period. Points are also earned toward fitness benefit through the duration and frequency of exercise.

According to Dr. Cooper, the exercises that are best for inducing the training effect are running, swimming, and cycling. Points are awarded for many other activities, providing they can be classified as being aerobic.

The aerobics program of Dr. Cooper supports a gradual increase in exercise level until an average of 30 points are being earned on a weekly basis (actual point levels are 27 points for women and 32 points for men). It should be remembered that the primary goal of the aerobics program is to improve fitness levels and thus to impact health status. Consequently, if other goals or needs are desired, this program should be supplemented with other programs. The addition of stretching and strengthening exercises would aid in greater total benefit. The most important factor is to earn the required number of points per week, and not to exercise in a particular manner or at any particular effort level. The following is an example of many exercise programs in Dr. Cooper's book.

## Walking Exercise Program
(Under 30 Years of Age)

| Week | Distance (miles) | Time Goal (minutes) | Freq/Wk | Points/Wk |
|------|------------------|---------------------|---------|-----------|
| 1 | 2.0 | 34:00 | 3 | 12.2 |
| 2 | 2.0 | 32:00 | 4 | 18.0 |
| 3 | 2.0 | 30:00 | 5 | 25.0 |
| 4 | 2.5 | 38:00 | 5 | 31.8 |
| 5 | 2.5 | 37:00 | 5 | 33.2 |
| 6 | 2.5 | 36:00 | 5 | 34.6 |
| 7 | 3.0 | 45:00 | 5 | 40.0 |
| 8 | 3.0 | 44:00 | 5 | 41.3 |
| 9 | 3.0 | 43:00 | 5 | 42.9 |
| 10 | 3.0 | 42:00 | 4 | 35.4 |

By the tenth week, an adequate level of aerobic condition has been reached and can be maintained with a four-time-per-week schedule. This level of exercise equals 35 aerobic points per week, consistent with the good category of aerobic fitness.

Note: Points determined from the equations for walking, jogging, and running. If the point charts in the Appendix are used, the total point values may vary slightly.

## Running/Jogging Exercise Program
(Under 30 Years of Age)

| Week | Activity | Distance (miles) | Time Goal (minutes) | Freq/Wk | Points/Wk |
|------|----------|------------------|---------------------|---------|-----------|
| 1 | walk | 2.0 | 32:00 | 3 | 13.5 |
| 2 | walk | 3.0 | 48:00 | 3 | 21.7 |
| 3 | walk/jog | 2.0 | 26:00 | 4 | 24.9 |
| 4 | walk/jog | 2.0 | 24:00 | 4 | 28.0 |
| 5 | jog | 2.0 | 22:00 | 4 | 31.6 |
| *6 | jog | 2.0 | 20:00 | 4 | 36.0 |
| 7 | jog | 2.5 | 25:00 | 4 | 46.0 |
| 8 | jog | 2.5 | 23:00 | 4 | 49.5 |
| 9 | jog | 3.0 | 30:00 | 4 | 56.0 |
| 10 | jog | 3.0 | 27:00 | 4 | 61.3 |

*By the sixth week, a minimum aerobic fitness level has been reached (36 aerobic points per week), but it is suggested that a higher level of fitness be achieved. By the tenth week of the above program, a total of 61 points per week is being earned, consistent with the excellent category of aerobic fitness. Excerpt from THE AEROBICS WAY by Kenneth H. Cooper. Copyright © 1977 by Kenneth H. Cooper. Used by permission of Bantam Books, a division of Bantam Doubleday Dell Publishing Group, Inc.

Many types of exercise programs are aerobic in design. There are many variations of **rhythmically choreographed exercise programs** that include exercise movements done to musical background. Some examples are jazzercise and step aerobics or step training.

# Circuit Training

One of the most widely used exercise programs is **circuit training**. This method of exercise was developed during the 1950s and is used primarily to improve general body condition. It is truly the "smorgasbord" approach to exercise. Circuit training involves a series of exercises performed one after the other in as continuous fashion as possible. Therefore, since different exercise movements are put together, the end result is some improvement in virtually all aspects of fitness—a smorgasbord effect.

The exercises selected can be of calisthenic type, as is popular in most exercise classes, or involve the use of resistance exercises, which create greater degrees of muscular strength and muscular endurance.

The most common program of circuit training involves 10 to 15 exercise stations or exercises arranged so that they can be performed one after the other. After choosing the amount of work (repetitions of exercise and/or resistance) to be performed at each station, the time to complete three complete circuits is taken. This time is reduced by one-third and becomes a "target time." When someone completes the three complete circuits in the target time, the amount of work at each station is increased (overload principle). A new target time is then established.

This form of exercise system can be as simple or as complicated as you care to make it. Exercise movements that involve all major muscle groups should be included.

The following chart is an example of a "20 Minute" circuit training program. Each exercise is performed for one minute in succession with choices listed for the "cardio" segments (numbers 1, 3, 5, 7, 11, 13, 15, 17, 19).

| Exercise/Machine | Time (minutes) | Exercise/Machine | Time (minutes) |
|---|---|---|---|
| 1. Bicycle or Run in Place | 1 | 11. Bicycle/Run in Place/ Jump Rope | 1 |
| 2. Leg Press | 1 | 12. Rower | 1 |
| 3. Jump Rope or Run in Place | 1 | 13. Bicycle/Run in Place/ Jump Rope | 1 |
| 4. Knee Extension | 1 | 14. Lat. Pull | 1 |
| 5. Bicycle/Jump Rope/ Run in Place | 1 | 15. Bicycle/Treadmill/ Jump Rope | 1 |
| 6. Knee Flexion (leg curl) | 1 | 16. Abdominal Machine | 1 |
| 7. Bicycle/Treadmill/ Run in Place | 1 | 17. Bicycle/Run in Place/ Jump Rope | 1 |
| 8. Chest Press | 1 | 18. Triceps Press | 1 |
| 9. Bicycle/Treadmill/ Run in Place | 1 | 19. Bicycle/Run in Place/ Jump Rope | 1 |
| 10. Shoulder Press | 1 | 20. Arm Curls | 1 |

In the exercise industry the franchise known as **Curves** uses circuit training as the basis for the exercise program offered for women.

# Resistance Training (Strength Training)

Progressive Resistance Exercise (PRE) is a general exercise system that incorporates three different forms of exercise. This system has been shown to be effective in rehabilitation, increasing athletic performance, and changing physical appearance. The three forms are weight training, **weight lifting**, and **bodybuilding**. All are similar in that they involve the use of resistance (weights) in gradually progressive amounts. However, each is different from the other in terms of outcome of the exercise system. The primary gains for any of the PRE forms are **muscular strength** and **muscular endurance**. The specific gain depends on how the variables associated with this type of exercise system are manipulated. These variables include:

**Intensity**—(effort) determined by the amount of resistance (weight) that is being moved. (Heart Rate is not important)

**Sets**—the number of times an exercise of specific reps will be performed, that is, a group of reps.

**Repetitions**—number of times an exercise movement is repeated.

**Resistance**—the amount of weight that is being moved.

The sets, repetitions, and resistance are combined in an infinite number of ways. Classically, one example of a combination that would guarantee strength gain is as follows:

**Sets**—3
**Repetitions**—less than 10
**Resistance**—10 RM (this would be the amount of weight that could be moved only 10 times, not more—a 10 "repetition maximum")

This combination would change to include the following if muscular endurance and tone were the objective:

**Sets**—3
**Repetitions**—15 or more
**Resistance**—15 RM

Strength training has been studied extensively by many investigators. Differences of opinion based on practical experience as well as the result of scientific research are endless. There is no "one way" to change muscle and its ability to produce force. Recently, one investigator has found that a three set, 6 RM regimen provided the best results when compared to other combinations such as: 5 sets, 8 to 12 RM; 3 sets, 10 to 12 RM; 1 set, 8 to 12 RM. The general rule that can be applied is that increases in resistance (<10RM will create strength, whereas increases in repetitions (15RM +) will create increases in muscular endurance.

Equipment is necessary in resistance training and may take many forms: free weights involving barbells, dumbbells, a variety of machines; large elastic bands or tubing of various degrees of thickness; and weighted rods or bars. Some exercises using free weights while seated on a **stability ball**

**or standing on an unstable surface** are used to increase **core strength** and **balance control**.

Weight training is that part of resistance training which involves the use of resistance exercises in the development of strength and/or muscular endurance as an aid in general body conditioning, improvement of sport skills, and changes in body contour (physical appearance) and lean body mass.

Weight lifting involves a competitive approach to resistance training where the primary goal is maximum lift capacity in selected exercises or lifts. Weight lifting is an Olympic sport as well as being an international competitive event. Power lifting is an adjunct form of training and competition.

Bodybuilding practiced by men and women is also a form of resistance training, which has as its goal the creation of maximum muscular hypertrophy and body symmetry. The individuals who enjoy this approach have competition that leads to such IFBB titles as Mr./Ms. America, Mr./Ms. Universe, and Mr./Ms. World. It is not unusual for individuals pursuing this goal to have incredible degrees of muscle hypertrophy. This degree of hypertrophy is not always the normal result of resistance training. Often times anabolic steroids are used to accelerate the growth of muscle and strength. The use of these substances outside of normal medical prescription has significant deleterious effects. Since they alter the normal function of the body, their use should be restricted to medical purposes only.

Until rather recently, resistance training had been considered the domain of "men only." Fortunately, this taboo has been broken and women have become familiar with the offerings that weight training holds. Contrary to popular opinion the idea of "muscle-boundness" does not occur with this system of training. Women do not have to fear the tremendous degrees of hypertrophy that make them look "too masculine." The reason is that the hormone testosterone will control the degree of hypertrophy and this hormone is present in much higher levels in men than in women. However, there are cases where some women athletes have maximized their inherited tendencies with weight training to produce considerable muscularity.

---

## Relative Adverse Effects of Anabolic Steroids on Males and Females

Liver lesions and cancer
Decreased HDL levels
Increased serum cholesterol
Increased blood pressure
Decreased glucose tolerance
Testicular atrophy
Increased hirsutism (hair
    development)

Irreversible clitoral enlargement
Menstrual abnormalities
Aggressive behavior
Psychological disorders
Premature epiphyseal closure
    in youths leading to growth
    abnormalities
Decreased sperm count

---

## Interval Training

One attractive feature of interval training is that you *get to rest*. This rest phase sets this system of exercise apart from others. The idea behind interval training is that greater quantity and quality of exercise can be achieved if the work phase is broken into segments separated by rest phases, that is, more work, less fatigue.

The time of the work segment is alternated with the rest phase, which is also timed. The work phase is usually of short duration because of the high intensity. The rest phase can be either "complete or active rest." Complete rest would involve cessation of activity, whereas active rest might include a walk rather than a jog during the rest phase. When a program of interval training is developed for training, it would involve specific "work to rest" time ratios. For example, a ratio of 1 to 3 might mean work 1 minute, rest 3, or rest 3 times as long as the work. By manipulating the work and rest times, "overload" can be controlled. Due to the nature of this combination, cardiorespiratory benefit is the principal gain.

Heart rate responses to the work-rest idea will be variable as indicated by the following chart of an interval workout (solid line) compared to an "aerobic" workout (dotted line).

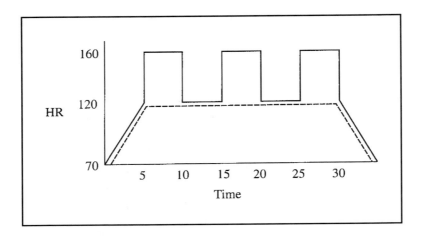

# Cross-Training

Cross-training is a method of combining different exercise types in an attempt to create the elusive "total fitness." This training was originally made popular by the triathlon—swimming, running, and cycling. Traditionally, fitness has been regarded as a measure of aerobic endurance. Cross-training involves developing the five major components of fitness: cardiovascular, muscular strength, muscular endurance, body composition, and flexibility. In a cross-training approach one, two, three, or four "tracks" of exercise can be used. Each track represents a particular form of exercise; for example, combining a swimming workout with two weight-training workouts, with a three-day jogging program.

The advantages to pursuing cross-training may include: overall total fitness; reduction of monotony; enhanced energy expenditure, therefore, fat loss; and reduction of the risk of overtraining and injury.

# Summary

There are four general classifications of systems of exercise. Aerobics is a system of exercise in which a person will exercise a long period of time before exhaustion. The primary training effects of aerobics is cardiorespiratory fitness. Circuit training uses progressive resistance exercises that have to be completed within a time framework. The desired training effect is muscle strength, muscle endurance, and cardiovascular fitness. Resistance exercises place an overload or group of muscles. The overload usually used is a weight or group of weights. The purpose of resistance training is muscular strength and muscular endurance. The principle of progressive resistance exercises can be achieved through isotonic exercises (e.g., push-ups) or isometric exercises (e.g., pushing against a doorway). Each will contribute to muscular strength. Interval training involves maximum effort interspersed with a resting or submaximum phase. The resting time is often shortened as performance improves. The primary result of interval training is cardiorespiratory improvement. For those dedicated to fitness, cross-training is one method of programming that achieves balanced fitness—the elusive total fitness.

## Check Out These Websites

k2.kirtland.cc.mi.us/~balbachl/fitness.html - This is one of the few websites written and maintained by a certified personal trainer and aerobics instructor, which gives many fitness tips and answers to common questions. Also provides an enormous links page!

www.sportfit.com - This amazing sports-minded website covers almost every aspect of training. A major focus of this site is sports-specific training for the beginner to the advanced athlete. Find virtual personal training, training logs and tips, a fitness glossary to help clear up confusing fitness lingo, and more!

www.enteract.com/bradapp/docs/rec/stretching_5.html#SEC40 - This comprehensive stretching site covers literally every possible aspect of stretching, including warm-up, cool-down, the many different types of stretches and when to use them, and more. The one-stop site for stretching!

# Creating a Plan of Action

Creating a Plan of Action Exercise can be regarded as a systematic approach to creating or maintaining fitness. Following are some considerations that should help in putting yourself in motion.

Establish realistic goals: Remember, exercise can do great things but there are limitations.

Develop a specific plan: What are you going to do?, how hard?, how long?, how often? Use monthly, weekly, and daily plans.

Involve others for motivation: Seek advice from competent experts (books, videos, personal) and ask others for their support, even exercising with them.

Vary your exercise: Use your plan to establish occasional changes in routine, that is, place pace, distance, time, sets, reps, resistance, equipment, and so on.

Progress slowly: Life is an endurance effort, not a sprint.

Avoid injury: Be sensible, use good techniques, good equipment, proper warm-up, cool-down, and underdo, don't overdo.

Keep a record: Seeing your achievements as a result of your plan provides motivation and information for continued progress.

Reward yourself: Patting yourself on the back to recognize effort and achievement is good to do; tangible results aid motivation.

# Review Questions

1. What are some factors which determine exercise choice?

2. What are the four major systems of exercise?

3. How many "points" of aerobic exercise per week is good and how are these "points" earned?

4. What exercise system creates the "smorgasbord" effect and how does it do this?

5. What is unique about Interval Training when compared to other exercise systems?

6. What are the two primary gains from Resistance Training?

# CHAPTER 8

# Examples of Exercise Programs—Recipes for Fitness

To help you select the exercises you need to improve your physical condition or to maintain your present level of fitness it becomes necessary to evaluate the many existent programs of exercise.

It is important to keep in mind several factors that may determine the appeal and consequent benefit attained from any exercise program. Some things to consider in choosing or developing an exercise program are the following:

- Present physical fitness levels—reflecting body composition, cardiovascular efficiency, strength, flexibility, and neuromuscular skills.
- The need for special equipment or facilities.
- Adaptability to a variety of ages.
- The specific time requirement for each exercise session.
- The relative contribution to the components of fitness.
- Adaptability to a variety of locations—school, home, indoors, outdoors, city, suburbs, etc.

In addition to these considerations it must be remembered that if any exercise program is to be of optimal benefit the variables *frequency, intensity,* and *duration* must be employed and adjusted to appropriate age, sex, and fitness levels. By manipulating the variables of exercise it is then possible to create a "cycle" in the exercise program that will aid in avoiding both physical and psychological monotony. This cycle training or "periodization" creates different emphasis on frequency, intensity, and duration as well as type of training during a specified calendar time. For example, approximately every two to four months (eight to sixteen weeks) the em-

209

phasis would change to reflect greater frequency, intensity, or duration in the exercise program. Cycling may also include the addition of a different type of exercise into the existing program. For example, resistance training may be added to supplement a jogging program.

You will recall that different exercise programs have different benefits and you must select accordingly. The following examples of programs may help to acquaint you with a variety of possibilities and aid in making an intelligent choice.

# Aerobics Program

Dr. Kenneth Cooper developed the exercise system of aerobics based on the relationship between energy expenditure and points. The number of points earned determines the relative fitness level. The best aerobic-type exercises from a fitness standpoint are running, swimming, and cycling. For complete examples of each of these programs as well as others consult *Aerobics, The New Aerobics,* and *Aerobics for Women.*

Following are four examples of aerobic fitness maintenance programs adapted from *The Aerobics Program for Total Well-being* by Dr. Kenneth Cooper. The entire program and their sex and age adjustments can be found in his book.

## Sample Maintenance Programs

The following charts illustrate how to maintain 30 or more aerobic points per week.

Included are four programs for walking, running, and swimming; five programs for cycling; and a weekly program incorporating a variety of activities.

An initial walk-jog-run program may be modeled after the following example:

1st week—3-4 days/week.

1. Warm-up-stretching and calisthenics 5—10 minutes.
2. Alternate jogging and walking for 15 minutes.

## Maintenance Programs for the Person Already Conditioned (all ages)

### Walking

| Distance (miles) | Time Requirement (min) | Freq/Wk | Points/ Wk |
|---|---|---|---|
| 2.0 | 24:01–30:00 | 6 | 30 |
| or | | | |
| 3.0 | 36:01–45:00 | 4 | 32 |
| or | | | |
| 4.0 | 48:01–60:00 | 3 | 33 |
| or | | | |
| 4.0 | 60:01–80:00 | 5 | 35 |

### Running

| Distance (miles) | Time Requirement (min) | Freq/Wk | Points/ Wk |
|---|---|---|---|
| 1.0 | 6:41–8:00 | 6 | 30 |
| or | | | |
| 1.5 | 10:01–12:00 | 4 | 32 |
| or | | | |
| 1.5 | 12:01–15:00 | 5 | 32.5 |
| or | | | |
| 2.0 | 16:01–20:00 | 4 | 36 |
| or | | | |
| 2.0 | 13:21–16:00 | 3 | 33 |

### Cycling

| Distance (miles) | Time Requirement (min) | Freq/Wk | Points/ Wk |
|---|---|---|---|
| 5.0 | 15:01–20:00 | 5 | 30 |
| or | | | |
| 6.0 | 18:01–24:00 | 4 | 30 |
| or | | | |
| 7.0 | 21:01–28:00 | 4 | 36 |
| or | | | |
| 8.0 | 24:01–32:00 | 3 | 31.5 |

## Maintenance Programs (*continued*)

### Swimming

| Distance (yards) | Time Requirement (min) | Freq/Wk | Points/ Wk |
|---|---|---|---|
| 600 | 10:01–15:00 | 6 | 30 |
| or | | | |
| 800 | 13:21–20:00 | 4 | 30.5 |
| or | | | |
| 900 | 15:01–22:30 | 4 | 36 |
| or | | | |
| 1000 | 16:41–25:00 | 3 | 31 |

### Progressive Treadmill Exercise

| Treadmill Speed (mph) | Incline (%) | Time (min) | Freq/Wk | Points/ Wk |
|---|---|---|---|---|
| 6.0 | flat | 30:00 | 3 | 42 |
| 5.0 | flat | 30:00 | 4 | 36 |
| 4.5 | 5% | 30:00 | 4 | 30 |
| 4.0 | flat | 45:00 | 5 | 40 |
| 4.0 | 5% | 45:00 | 4 | 35 |

### Aerobic Dancing and Other Exercise Programs Conducted to Music

| Time (min) | Heart Rate Max* (beats/min) | Freq/Wk | Points/ Wk |
|---|---|---|---|
| 45:00 | above 140 | 3 | 27 |
| 40:00 | above 140 | 4 | 32 |
| 30:00 | above 140 | 5 | 30 |

*Heart rate determined at 3 or more equal intervals during the exercise based on a 10 second x 6 count.

2nd and 3rd Week—2-4 days/week.

1. Warm-up-stretching and calisthenics 5—10 minutes.
2. Jogging and walking for 15—18 minutes.
3. Run comfortably for 5 minutes.
4. Walk for 5 minutes.

4th and 5th Week—3-4 days/week.

1. Warm-up same as above 5 minutes.
2. Alternate jogging and running for 15 minutes.
3. Run comfortably for 5—10 minutes.
4. Walk for 5 minutes.

6th Week—3-4 days/week.

1. Warm-up same as above.
2. Jog for 5 minutes.
3. Run for 15 minutes.
4. Jog 5 minutes.
5. Walk 5 minutes.

# Circuit Training or Circuit Weight Training (CWT)

The term circuit refers to a given number of exercises arranged in a continuous order. It is usually set up in an exercise room or gymnasium and each place where a specific exercise is performed is called a station. The type of circuit is dependent on time, equipment, space, and desired objectives.

The Adult Physical Fitness Program based on a circuit training format was a progressive program of calisthenics and endurance activities was developed under the direction of the President's Council on Physical Fitness.

There are exercises for men and women at five levels of difficulty. Progression from level to level is determined by increases in fitness.

The first three levels of the programs for men and women follow and can be found in detail in the book *Adult Physical Fitness* from the President's Council on Physical Fitness in Washington, D.C.

A circuit-training program (CWT) can be designed in which free weights and/or machines are used. Typically, exercises that involve all major muscle groups are selected and one exercise is performed per muscle group per exercise session. These exercises usually involve multijoint movement and usually 15 to 20 repetitions are performed in only one set. The rest period between exercises is typically very short, usually no more than 15 seconds. The amount of weight or resistance is kept relatively low to allow for the performance of 15 or more repetitions. This type of training can accomplish a great deal in a relatively short workout session.

## First Three Levels of Adult Physical Fitness Program for Women

| Exercise | Level I | Level II | Level III |
|---|---|---|---|
| 1. Toe touch | 5 | 10 | 20 |
| 2. Sprinter | 8 | 12 | 16 |
| 3. Sitting stretch | 10 | 15 | 15 |
| 4. Knee push-up | 8 | 12 | 20 |
| 5. Sit-up | 5 each leg | 10 each leg | 15 each leg |
| 6. Leg raise | 5 | 10 | 16 |
| 7. Flutter Kick | 20 | 30 | 40 |
| 8. Circulatory activity (choose one for each workout) | | | |
| Walking/jogging | ½ mile (120 steps/min.) | ½ mile (jog 50 yd.; walk 50 yd.) | ¾ mile (jog 50 yd.; walk 50 yd.) |
| Rope skipping | 2 series (skip 30 sec.; rest 60 sec.) | 3 series (skip 30 sec.; rest 60 sec.) | 3 series (skip 45 sec.; rest 30 sec.) |
| Running-in-place | 2 min. | 3 min. | 4 min. |

## First Three Levels of Adult Physical Fitness Program for Men

| Exercise | Level I | Level II | Level III |
|---|---|---|---|
| 1. Toe touch | 10 | 20 | 30 |
| 2. Sprinter | 12 | 16 | 20 |
| 3. Sitting stretch | 12 | 18 | 24 |
| 4. Knee push-up | 4 | 10 | 20 |
| 5. Sit-up | 5 | 20 | 30 |
| 6. Leg raise | 12 each leg | 16 each leg | 20 each leg |
| 7. Flutter Kick | 30 | 40 | 50 |
| 8. Circulatory activity (choose one for each workout) | | | |
| Walking/jogging | 1 mile (120 steps/min.) | 1 mile (jog 100 yd.; walk 100 yd.) | 1½ miles (jog 200 yd.; walk 100 yd.) |
| Rope skipping | 3 series (skip 30 sec.; rest 30 sec.) | 3 series (skip 1 min.; rest 1 min.) | 3 series (skip 1 min.; rest 1 min.) |
| Running-in-place | 2 min. | 3 min. | 4 min. |

An example of a circuit training workout would be the following where each exercise (station) is performed for one minute (for a total time of 20 minutes). Since there is some aerobic type exercise and some resistance exercise done in continuous fashion the benefits derived exhibit the "smorgasbord" effect.

The following chart is an example of a "20 Minute" circuit training program. Each exercise is performed for one minute in succession with choices listed for the "cardio" segments (numbers 1, 3, 5, 7, 9, 11, 13, 15, 17, 19).

From the booklet *Adult Physical Fitness*, President's Council on Physical Fitness and Sports, Washington, D.C.

| | Exercise/Machine | Time (minutes) | | Exercise/Machine | Time (minutes) |
|---|---|---|---|---|---|
| 1. | Bicycle or Run in Place | I | 11. | Bicycle/Run in Place/ Jump Rope | I |
| 2. | Leg Press | I | 12. | Rower | I |
| 3. | Jump Rope or Run in Place | I | 13. | Bicycle/Run in Place/ Jump Rope | I |
| 4. | Knee Extension | I | 14. | Lat. Pull | I |
| 5. | Bicycle/Jump Rope/ Run in Place | I | 15. | Bicycle/Treadmill/ Jump Rope | I |
| 6. | Knee Flexion (leg curl) | I | 16. | Abdominal Machine | I |
| 7. | Bicycle/Treadmill/ Run in Place | I | 17. | Bicycle/Run in Place/ Jump Rope | I |
| 8. | Chest Press | I | 18. | Triceps Press | I |
| 9. | Bicycle/Treadmill/ Run in Place | I | 19. | Bicycle/Run in Place/ Jump Rope | I |
| 10. | Shoulder Press | I | 20. | Arm Curls | I |

# Weight Training—Resistance Exercise

This is the best way to make more muscle—and muscle means metabolism.

Care should be taken to select exercises that involve all major muscle groups in the body. This involves a concept called "**muscle balance**." Muscles function best when all become stronger, and since muscles work in groups, it is prudent to include exercises for all those groups—muscles on the front side (anterior) of the body; the back side (posterior) of the body; the right side and the left side.

Remember, resistance training will not turn fat into muscle. These two tissues are entirely different—one stores energy, the other does all the work.

# What Good Is Resistance Training?

- Bone density increases
- Strength increases
- Lean Body Mass increases
- Body fat decreases
- Blood pressure at rest tends to decrease
- Resting metabolism increases
- Glucose metabolism (insulin regulation) increases
- Activities of daily living are improved

Selection of exercises to accomplish this is easy because there are literally hundreds of specific exercises for different muscle groups. The following exercises would fulfill the muscle balance principle with each one having several variations. These exercises can be performed with free weights or with machines such as Universal or Nautilus, among many others.

Squat or Leg Press: for hips, legs, and back
Bench Press: for chest, shoulders, and arms
Military (Shoulder) Press: for upper back, shoulders, and arms
Upright Row: for shoulders and upper back
Bent over Row: for arms, shoulders, and upper back
Curls: for upper arm
Sit-ups or Crunches: for abdominal and trunk muscles

The following photographs illustrate these particular exercises.

*The Squat Exercise: Support weight across shoulders in a standing position; feet are about shoulder-width apart; perform a squat movement until thighs are about parallel to the floor and return to the standing position.*

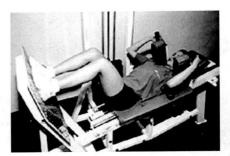

*The squat exercise movement can be performed using a machine.*

*The Bench Press: While lying on a bench, hold the weight with arms straight; then slowly lower until it makes contact with the chest; then push up to the starting position with the arms straight.*

*A similar exercise can be performed using a machine.*

*The Military (Shoulder) Press: Begin with the weight supported across the front of the chest with hands about shoulder width apart; then push the weight up until the elbows are straight and then return to the starting position.*

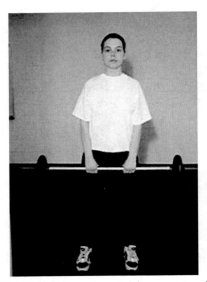 

*The Upright Row: In a standing position, hold the weight across the thighs with the arms straight; then pull the weight up until the hands are at neck level and return to the starting position.*

*Bent over Row: Begin with the weight held at about knee height, hands about shoulder-width apart, chest held parallel to the floor, head up; lift the weight up toward the chest and return to the starting position, thus creating a rowing motion.*

*A rowing movement can also be performed on a machine.*

*The Curl: Hold the weight with palms up across the front of the thighs with hands about shoulder-width apart. Lift the weight so that the elbows bend and finish with the weight across the body at shoulder level; return to the starting position.*

*The curl exercise can be performed using a machine.*

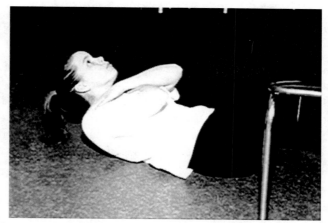

The Crunch: Start with the lower leg on a bench or chair so that the hips and knees are flexed; hands across the chest; curl the upper body up and return to the starting position. This may also be performed with a twisting movement.

Abdominal/trunk exercise can be performed using a machine.

# Flexibility Exercises—Stretching

Flexibility is the ability of body joints to move through a full range of movement. Bones, muscle, tendons, and ligaments all contribute to this movement. Individuals with good flexibility of joints have greater ease of movement, less stiffness in muscles, and a lesser chance of injury during movement. Exactly how much flexibility you should have is difficult to define. Everyone should try to prevent losses of flexibility that accompany inactivity and aging.

**Static stretching** (stretch and hold) and ballistic stretching (bouncing movements) are used to create flexibility. The use of fast, bouncing movements can induce the stretch reflex, which can create discomfort and injury. Static stretching is recommended because it does not induce a stretch reflex and is more productive. Any stretching should not progress to the point of pain. Typically, stretching movements should be held for 20 seconds for good benefit.

In some instances more than one stretch held for 20 seconds is advocated and can be performed in sets similar to that of resistance training, that is, three sets of the same stretch can be performed, each held for 20 seconds.

The following figures show some stretching movements that can benefit different muscles and joints of the body.

*For low back and back of the legs.*

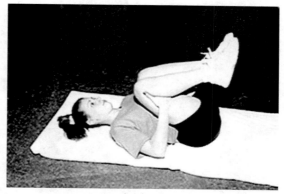

*Low back release.*

*For low back, back of legs, and groin.*

*For back, low back, and buttocks.*

*For front of thigh and hip.*

*For back of lower leg.*

*For front of upper arm and chest.*

*For shoulder and back of upper arm.*

# Interval Training

In recent years interval training systems have evolved for use in competitive athletics as well as general conditioning programs. Interval training stresses the "quality" of work effort as well as the "quantity" found in continuous type programs.

This kind of training involves a higher intensity and consequently should be undertaken after a good base of conditioning has been found.

It's as easy as 1-2-3-4-5 and takes only 30 minutes. This can be used with walking, jogging, running, swimming, cycling, rollerblading.

1 minute easy, 1 minute "harder"; 2 minutes easy, 2 minutes "harder"; 3 minutes easy, 3 minutes "hard"; 4 minutes easy, 4 minutes "hard"; 5 minutes easy, 5 minutes "hard";—total 30 minutes.

It can be easily seen that as fitness level increases, the amount of rest decreases while the work output remains constant. The variables that may be changed are distance, time, rest, and repetitions.

A similar approach may be used with programs involving walking, cycling, swimming, and weight training, each with its specific benefits.

# An Exercise Program for the Low Back

Dr. David Imrie, author of *Goodbye Backache,* has developed a group of simple exercises that build in difficulty to match the ability level of each person's muscles that support the back. Depending on the results, that is, Grade I, II, III, or IV from the measures of this laboratory experience, the appropriate exercise is selected. If results were not good in each of the four measures, then the entire program should be performed at appropriate levels ranging from easy to hard. These exercises can be used to recondition a poorly functioning back as well as to maintain strength and flexibility in a low back that scores well and is pain-free.

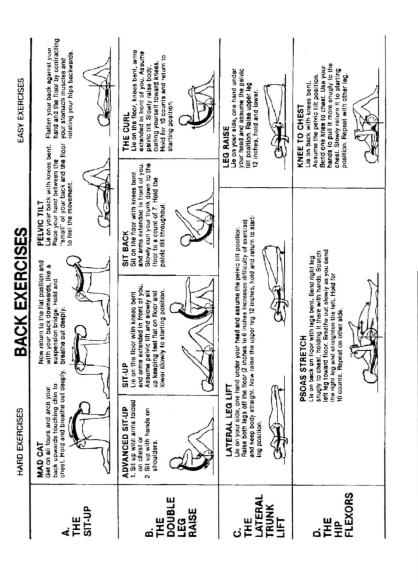

From *Goodbye Backache*, by Dr. David Imrie with Colleen Dimson. (Arco, 1983)

# Summary

The number of exercise programs are virtually endless. The bases and considerations of selected programs have been presented to aid in developing one of your own. It must be remembered that any program should be based on sound principles of physiology to ensure both safety and benefit.

Remember—with any exercise program

1. Warm-up and cool-down
2. Use heart rate or RPE as a guide to effort
3. Include some stretching for flexibility
4. Under-do rather than over-do

# Check Out These Websites

home.ait.ac.nz/staff/pmellow - This New Zealand site gives very hard to find information (such as: Should you exercise with a cold?), along with many links to other fitness sport and health related websites.

www.fitness.ukf.com - This "Be healthy gym" is packed full of info on topics such as blood pressure and exercise, vitamins and their uses, weight training and athletes, stretching, and so much more!

www.fit-net.com/exercise/index.cfm - This very helpful site offers very useful information, such as: When is the best time to exercise, 20 ways to turn your hotel room into a gym, stretching out back pain, and more!

# Strolling through Life

In a competitive sense, walking is a bona fide track event. As a more casual undertaking it can be an incredibly effective strategy for fitness and health.

To begin a walking program, keep in mind that you are in no big hurry—life is an endurance race, not a sprint. For now, forget the watches, heart rates, and distances. Just go for a walk at a comfortable pace somewhere between a stroll and a "hurry-up." You don't have to walk in a particular way but some considerations will help reap benefits.

Posture—Lean slightly forward from the ankles, not the waist. Keep your head level and chin up.

Arm Swing—This makes walking a total body activity. Elbows should be held at a 90-degree angle and arms swing from the shoulder. Hands come up shoulder-high in front and elbows rise on the backswing so that the upper arm is parallel to the ground.

Stride—Make your stride comfortably long and smooth. Remember to step out onto your heel and push off the big toe of the rear foot.

The proper technique is not as important as getting out there and doing something. Schedule regular walks with a friend if you need an extra push; walk first thing in the morning before other commitments creep in; or vary your routine to provide a change in scenery. Maybe you shouldn't think of it as exercise but as time you've set aside for yourself.

# Review Questions

1. What is "periodization" and why might this be done?

2. Which of the exercise program examples would be best for you, and why?

3. Since exercise types can be combined which two would be best, and why?

CHAPTER ACTIVITY

# Resistance Training

Resistance Training involves three unique variables: sets, repetitions and resistance (weight). Resistance is the measure of intensity or how hard you work. A good question is "how much weight should I lift?" If you are presently doing resistance training then you already know the answer. However, if you are **just beginning,** try the following calculations based on your body weight.

## *Purpose*

To determine resistances (weights) for upper and lower body exercises.

## *Procedure*

Perform the following calculations to determine training weights based on body weight. The weight ranges (+ or –) allow for **differences in age, experience, fitness level, somatotype, single or multi joint movements and any musculoskeletal problem (injury).**

**Females:**

Upper Body exercise: $\dfrac{TBW}{4}$ = _____ + or – 10 lbs.

Lower Body exercise: $\dfrac{TBW}{3}$ = _____ + or – 20 lbs.

**Males:**

Upper Body exercise: $\dfrac{\text{TBW}}{4}$ = _____ + or – 10 lbs.

Lower Body exercise: $\dfrac{\text{TBW}}{3}$ = _____ + or – 20 lbs.

# CHAPTER 9

# Exercise-Related Injuries
## (How to Be Your Own Doctor...Sometimes)

Exercise that is of sufficient frequency, duration and intensity to produce a beneficial training effect does not go without risk. An inescapable adjunct of exercise is some degree of discomfort resulting from the stress on the body. There are times when risk results in a **traumatic injury** or as the result of repeated stress, an **overuse injury**.

An area of expertise within the medical profession referred to as **Sportsmedicine** deals with exercise related injury relative to prevention, diagnosis, and treatment. There are many occasions when medical help is necessary and should not be delayed. However, there are other occasions when the recognition and treatment of certain injuries can be performed by oneself. Some common injuries and annoyances warrant consideration so that you might be your own doctor...sometimes.

## R.I.C.E. as Therapy

The body responds to tissue injury with inflammation (swelling) as it attempts to "cast" the injured part and repair the damage. This inflammatory response causes pain, swelling, redness, and heat. Pain can be reduced, inflammation kept at a minimum, and normal movement resumed if early treatment is begun.

The use of R.I.C.E. in the immediate treatment of injury is a widely advocated procedure in dealing with new injuries. Each letter represents a portion of the treatment to be used.

**R= rest.** Do not continue exercise. Rest may mean 3 days, 3 weeks, or 3 months depending on the injury. In many cases it may involve resting (not using) the injured area, not the entire body. For example, a person with a sprained ankle could swim or perform upper body resistance exercise but walking, jogging, or cycling would be out of the question.

**I = ice application.** The injured area should feel cold to the touch, but be careful not to frostbite. Generally, ice may be applied for 15 minutes and removed for 30 minutes as often as possible for the first two to three days. For chronic injury, ice should be applied after exercise sessions to reduce any inflammation.

**C = compression.** An ace bandage can be used to hold ice in place as well as to provide compression (gentle squeezing). Compression of the injured area limits the swelling and resulting pain. Numbness, pain, and cramping are signs of too much compression. Always begin compression (wrapping) from a point farthest from the heart, working toward the heart.

**E = elevation.** Every attempt should be made to keep the injured area at the level of the heart or higher. If the injured part is below the waist, the person should lie down or elevate the part on a stool, chair, or bed while sitting. If the injury is to the arm, wrist or hand the part should be kept at shoulder level with appropriate support.

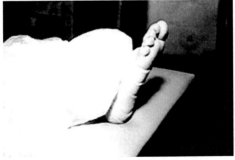

*For best results—wet the ace bandage first, wrap the injury, then apply the ice.*

The R.I.C.E. approach should be continued for at least 48 hours after the injury has occurred.

## Types of Injuries

**Muscle soreness.** DOMS—delayed onset muscle soreness. This common problem usually appears within the first 12 to 24 hours following exertion. Many theories relate the discomfort to chemical changes in the muscle, fluid accumulation, and microscopic tears in the muscle fiber and connective tissue. The soreness may be very significant and persist for one to two days. It will gradually diminish. This discomfort/pain may be relieved by taking aspirin, unless you are sensitive to this substance, in which case an aspirin-free medication containing acetaminophen may be used. In addition, light massage, gentle static stretching, and mild exercise will prove helpful, if tolerable.

**Blisters.** A localized problem caused by friction, which creates heat and results in tissue damage and fluid accumulation. Oftentimes "hot spots" can be felt before the actual blistering of the skin occurs. At the site of this friction, fluid begins to accumulate between the layers of skin in an attempt to prevent further tissue damage. This fluid may be clear in color or bloody, creating a "blood blister."

Once a blister has formed it can be extremely debilitating and painful. If the blister has broken, it must be treated as if it were an open wound; that is, it must be cleansed, sterile dressing applied, and it must be kept clean. If the blister is unbroken, two approaches may be considered. First, it may be protected from pressure by applying appropriate gauze padding over the blister or cutting a foam "doughnut" a circular-shaped piece of foam with a hole, which is slightly larger than the blister size, cut in the center. Second, the blister may be punctured at its side with a sterilized needle to release accumulated fluid. Then it must be treated with an antiseptic and covered tightly. The dressing must be kept clean to reduce the chances of infection. Never remove the layer of skin that covers a blister. The skin covering will aid in protecting the sensitive underlying layer of skin.

**Strain.** A tear in a muscle sometimes referred to as a muscle pull. Most times it is caused by an abnormal or excessive muscular contraction. A severe weakness and a loss of function are indications of this condition. Ice applications and compression are recommended for pain reduction and minimization of hemorrhage. Rest and a gradual return to activity are to be expected.

**Sprain.** A traumatic injury occurring at a joint resulting in damage to the supportive structures, that is, ligaments. The damage can range from microscopic tears to a complete avulsion (break) of the ligament(s). Immediate application of ice and an elastic compression bandage is advocated accompanied by no weight bearing for as long as 24 to 48 hours, depending on the severity.

**Tendinitis.** An inflammation of the specialized fibrous tissue that connects muscle to bone. This condition is created over a period of time and is usually chronic. It should be treated as soon as possible with as many forms of moist heat as are available. Ice application may be used to ease the acute discomfort of an existing condition. Extended rest with activity held to a minimum is advisable.

**Contusion.** Results from a hard blow to some part of the body (usually soft tissue). This contact results in a hemorrhage (bleeding) within the tissue involved. There is no break in the skin. The result is pain and tightness in the region of the injury. Immediate application of ice and elastic wrap is necessary to minimize the hemorrhagic tendencies.

**Heat Injuries.** Most heat-related problems involve a combination of high environmental temperature, high humidity, and dehydration (less than adequate fluid levels in body tissue). Signs of heat problems include muscle cramps, excessive fatigue, diminished coordination, nausea, and dizziness. All symptoms may appear simultaneously and are classified as **hyperthermia** injuries.

Remember, **thirst is a poor indicator of your need for water**. Dehydration can begin with as little as 2% loss of total body weight as fluid and start to create problems. A good rule to follow to avoid dehydration is to consume **6 to 8 ounces of water every 15 to 20 minutes of exercise**.

1. **Heat Stroke** is a true medical emergency. This condition may occur suddenly without the classic symptoms. It is characterized by hot, dry skin and a rising body temperature, which may reach 106°. Every attempt must be made to cool the body—ice massage, cool water immersion, and any other means for immediate cooling. Seek medical aid immediately.

2. **Heat Exhaustion** is characterized by profuse sweating accompanied by dizziness and extreme weakness. On occasion unconsciousness may ensue. Fluids should be taken immediately and continuously until symptoms/signs have passed. Physical activity should be halted and attempts should be made to cool the body—cold water, wet towels, ice massage, and shade.

**Hypothermia** (low body temperature). Occurs when the heat production of the body is exceeded by heat loss. Symptoms (felt by the involved person) include intense shivering; muscle tensing, fatigue, numbness, drowsiness, and disorientation and stumbling. Hypothermia usually occurs in extended exposure to cold weather and may be accompanied by frostbite. The best approach is to prevent low body temperature from occurring. The most critical concern is the wind chill factor. Layers of clothing that are loose fitting are more effective in conserving heat and thereby preventing hypothermia. See the following chart for the wind chill index and danger zone.

### Wind Chill Index

| Actual temperature | With wind blowing at speed, in m.p.h., listed below, it feels as if the temperature is: | | | | | | | | |
|---|---|---|---|---|---|---|---|---|---|
| | Calm | 5 | 10 | 15 | 20 | 25 | 30 | 35 | 40 |
| +30 | 30 | 27 | 16 | 9 | 4 | 0 | −2 | −4 | −6 |
| +20 | 20 | 16 | 4 | −5 | −10 | −15 | −18 | −20 | −21 |
| +10 | 10 | 6 | −9 | −18 | −25 | −29 | −33 | −35 | −37 |
| 0 | 0 | −5 | −21 | −36 | −39 | −44 | −48 | −49 | −53 |
| −10 | −10 | −15 | −33 | −45 | −53 | −59 | −63 | −67 | −69 |
| −20 | −20 | −26 | −46 | −58 | −67 | −74 | −79 | −82 | −85 |

DANGER AREA

Courtesy of THE RECORD.

## Summary

There are truly a multitude of exercise-related problems. The medical profession has realized the birth of specializations, which include sports podiatry, sports psychology, and sports medicine. The chances are great that you may never have any injury-related problem while being involved in an exercise program. In the case of severe injury or prolonged discomfort, it is advisable to seek professional medical evaluation and treatment. Many injuries are "activity-specific," for example, a contusion would be more common in racquetball than in a jogging/running program. By approaching exercise prudently and scientifically, one can minimize any misfortune. Many times the nature, cause, and resultant treatment is very individual, and it is possible to be your own doctor...sometimes.

# Doing Something Is Better than Doing Nothing—Keep It Going

Injury doesn't necessarily mean a complete breakdown in the exercise routine or exercise itself. Although altering your exercise program to accommodate an injury may be frustrating, good initial care will save days, weeks, and months of potential problems.

Most injury can be viewed as a "temporary inconvenience." The injury may not allow you to do what you always did but total rest is usually not necessary. You can "rest and treat" an injury, yet continue to exercise. An injury may force you to take a break from some form of exercise, but others are available. Someone with an ankle sprain or Achilles tendinitis may not be able to walk, jog, run, or do step training, but circuit training and swimming provide alternatives.

Unfortunately, people tend to resume their old activity schedule too soon when the injury is feeling better but not yet healed. This can be devastating and delay full healing. Remember, you can be your own doctor sometimes, but other times professional advice from physicians, physical therapists, and athletic trainers is the road to travel.

# Review Questions

1. To what does the acronym R.I.C.E. refer?

2. What is DOMS?

3. What is the difference between a sprain and a strain?

4. What is the difference between the two heat-related injuries?

# CHAPTER 10

# Making a Decision—Developing a Personal Program

## Where Am I Now? Where Am I Going?

You have come to a point where you should decide how you will be allocating the times of your life. A life strategy that includes time for exercise is one well worth pursuing. The particular exercise or exercises you choose should meet criteria that would provide a sense of satisfaction from your experience. Many factors will affect your selection and some are illustrated in the following graphic. All of these factors are interactive with some being more important than others at various times.

Of considerable importance in determining where you should begin is to consider the status of **the big five of fitness: cardiovascular fitness; body composition; muscular strength; muscular endurance and flexibility**. Based on your own admittance or evidence provided by some of the chapter activities the degree to which you need change or maintenance in any of the big five should dictate what, how much, how often, and how hard your exercise should be.

Your **present physical needs** will be based on your present level of fitness. Any attempt at beginning an exercise program should be based on what you are capable of doing at the present time. A running, swimming, or other cardiovascular program must be instituted at the proper entry level or you will be discouraged. Programs to improve muscular strength and muscular endurance will also depend on your present physical needs. Remember that inactivity will cause regression and you must start at a lower threshold.

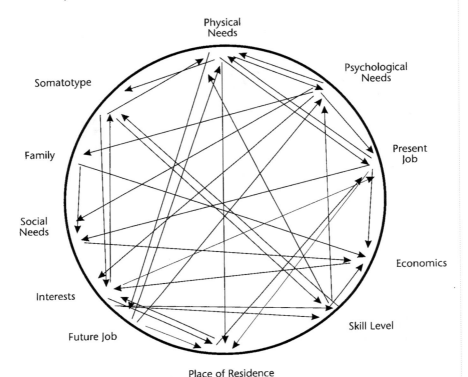

*Many factors affect exercise selection and they are interactive.*

**Social needs** of people are often satisfied through positive physical recreation experiences. Your interaction with others in sport and recreation will help develop and reaffirm friendships through enjoyable experiences. The communication aspect of physical recreation often allows an opportunity to develop social contacts.

**Present interests** are, by definition, transitory. Our adolescent interests are marked by an interest in activities that are group oriented (softball, basketball, etc.) as we desire peer recognition, and we are committed to being part of a group relationship. Our interests become more singular as we age, and our desires for personal satisfaction may cause our interests to change. Interests will also be influenced by present popular exercise forms (tennis, jogging) and by the interests of our friends.

**Your type of work** should influence your choice of activity. A sedentary occupation should be balanced by the choice of vigorous physical activity that contributes to physical and mental well-being.

Jobs that entail vigorous physical activity should be complemented by less energetic and more physically relaxing activities.

**Future place of residence** is very difficult to predict, since we are a rather mobile society and you may be subject to change of geographical area. Climatic conditions do play a part in the intelligent choice of activities. Activities are adapted to the physical and social climate of the geographical location. Warmer climates provide excellent opportunity for outdoor recreation throughout the year (tennis, golf, volleyball). Cold climates provide opportunities for a variety of activities (skiing, platform paddle tennis) and a need to build indoor facilities to satisfy climatic conditions (indoor tennis).

**Your present skill level** will influence your success in an activity. The complex activities will take more time to master. Indeed, you may be limited in your ability to utilize balance, power, speed, agility, reaction time, and kinesthetic sense. Most people can achieve success in a range of physical activities, although they may not achieve an exceptional skill level.

**Your body type** will be a continued influence on your general body weight as well as your ability to perform activities with ease and efficiency.

**Present emotional needs** are an important consideration as we recognize the catharsis that physical activity can bring during a troubled day. Articles depicting the emotional release achieved by joggers and long-distance runners have been numerous as have the positive attestments from psychiatrists that physical activity provides a positive release from emotional stress.

Consider all these factors and then embark on a planned program of exercise, for you have learned that exercise can be a dominant force in your lifestyle. The benefits of exercise can measurably improve and sustain the quality and quantity of life.

## Summary

Exercise, as part of a general life-style that includes proper diet, can contribute immeasurably to your sense of personal worth. Exercise may make you feel better and look better. Try it—just for the health of it!

## Filling Time or Killing Time

One phenomenon of our contemporary society is an increase in "discretionary time"—free time, sometimes called leisure time can be filled or killed—and all too often it is easier to kill time rather than be a participant, easier to be a consumer than a creator, easier to do nothing rather than something.

One approach to using discretionary time is to keep some of it for yourself. Invest time in yourself. Exercise is one such option that allows you to make such an investment. This investment can yield outstanding benefits—physically and psychologically. It may take some looking, some rescheduling, some excluding to find this "self-time," but it can clearly be accomplished. Fill some of this newfound time with exercise—sow an act, reap a habit; sow a habit, reap a lifestyle.

Exercise can:

- Increase heart stroke volume at rest
- Decrease resting pulse rate
- Decrease exercise pulse rate
- Increase recovery rate from exercise
- Increase ability to sustain one's self in an activity
- Increase the rate at which calories are burned off
- Increase muscle tone
- Increase muscle strength
- Increase muscle endurance
- Decrease emotional stress
- Increase survival rate from heart attack
- Increase recovery rate from heart attack
- Increase self-confidence and self-esteem

# Review Questions

1. List four factors that affect selection of exercise and analyze how they interact.

2. How do present interests affect exercise selection?

3. What may the difference between "filling time" or "killing time" mean to you and how can you find time for exercise in your time schedule?

# Index

energy equation and, 54–57
expenditure, 54–57, 137–40,
175–79
fat equivalent to, 52
intake, 40, 49, 88–89
Cancer
breast, 29
colon, 13, 29
deaths from, 6, 145
Carbohydrates, 79, 83–85, 86. *see
also* nutrition
Cardiorespiratory efficiency, 27,
28–29, 175. *see also* physical
fitness
Cardiovascular disease, 12–13,
145–46. *see also* cardiovascular
fitness
deaths from, 6, 144
defined, 141–42
heart attack, 142–43, 145,
153, 159–61, 163–64
risk factors of, 146–53,
159–61, 163–64
symptoms, 153
Cardiovascular fitness, 141–66,
245. *see also* physical fitness
atherosclerosis and, 141, 142
blood pressure measurement,
165–66
exercise for, 155–56
heart anatomy and, 142, 143,
146, 152
physical activity and, 29–32
Catalysts, 90
Centers for Disease Control, 34,
40, 49
Cholesterol, 48
guidelines, 150
HDL ratio and heart disease,
148, 149

heart disease risk and,
147–50, 159–61, 163–64
plaque and, 142
Circuit training (circuit weight
training), 195, 199–200
cardio segments example,
200
programs for, 213–16
Climate, 247
Cocktails, 123
Collateral circulation, 142–43
Colon cancer, 13, 29
Complex carbohydrates, 83–85
Compression, for injuries, 236
Conditioning, 2. *see also* physical
activity; physical fitness
Congestive heart failure, 141
Contusion, 238
Cool-down exercises, 172
Cooper, Kenneth H., 196–97,
210–13
Core strength, 202
Coronary artery disease (CAD),
12, 29
Coronary heart disease (CHD),
141, 155–56. *see also*
cardiovascular disease
Coronary thrombosis, 142
Cross-training, 195, 204
Crunch, 217, 223
Curl, 217, 222
Curves, 200
Cycling. *see* bicycling

# D

Daily Distress Test, 24–25
Dancing, aerobic, 212

Food. *see also* calories; fast-foods
    calorie counter
        overeating, 40
        reading food labels, 92
        sensible eating for health,
            122–24
Food Guide Pyramid (USDA),
    81–82, 84, 87
Framingham Study, 148
Franklin, Barry A., 52–53
Free radicals, 90
Free weights, 201–2, 214
Frequency, of exercise, 167–68,
    174, 209–10
Friedman, Meyer, 7, 8
Fruit group (Food Guide Pyramid),
    81, 84

# G

Gender. *see* men; women
General Adaptation Syndrome
    (GAS), 7
Genetics. *see* heredity
Geographic area, 247
Glucose intolerance, 48
Glycogen, 83
Golding, Lawrence, 52
*Goodbye Backache* (Imrie), 227
Gynoid fat distribution, 47–48

# H

HDL (high density lipids), 147–50
    exercise and, 152
    HDL ratio, 148, 149
"Healthy weight," 127
Heart anatomy, 142, 143, 146, 152.
    *see also* cardiovascular disease

Heart attack, 142–43. *see also*
    cardiovascular disease
        death rates from, 145
        risks (RISKO), 159–61,
            163–64
        symptoms of, 153
Heart rate
        aerobic fitness test and,
            189–90
        exercise intensity and,
            185–87
Heat injuries, 238–39
    heat exhaustion, 239
    heat stroke, 238
Height, ponderal index and, 46,
    67–68
Heredity, 12
        body composition and,
            39–40, 41
        genetic fat pattern, 47
        heart disease risk and, 147,
            159–61, 163–64
High blood pressure. *see* blood
    pressure
Hip flexors, 193, 228
Hippocrates, 10
HIV, 145
Holmes, Thomas, 7, 8, 21–23
Homocysteine, 145, 151
HRmax, 168, 169
Hydrostatic weighing, 45
Hyperplasia, 49
Hypertension, defined, 149. *see*
    *also* blood pressure
Hyperthermia, 238
Hypertrophy, 49, 202
Hypokinetic disease, 2
Hypothalamus, 41
Hypothermia, 239

# I

Ice application, for injuries, 236
Imrie, David, 227
Injuries, 235, 240, 243–44
    resuming activity, 241
    R.I.C.E. therapy, 235–37
    types of, 237–39
Institute for Research and
    Education, 11
Intensity, of exercise, 167–68,
    185–87, 201, 209–10
Interests, physical activity and, 246
Interval training, 195, 203–4, 227
Isocaloric balance, 54

# J

Jacobson, E., 25
Jenkins, David E., 35
Jogging, 57. *see also* running

# K

Karvonen method, 185
KFC®, 100–103
Kraus, Hans, 2

# L

Lateral trunk lift, 192, 228
LDL (low density lipids), 147–50
Lean tissue
    body composition and, 28
    lean body weight (LBW), 44,
    45–46
Leisure time, 248

Lifestyle
    developing personal fitness
      program and, 245–49
    including physical activity in,
      11–12, 14
    sedentary, 14, 39, 151–52
Light wave measurement, 46
Lipids, 85–87
Liposuction, 49
Long John Silver's®, 119–22
Long-term training effect, 29–32
Low back, exercises for, 227–28
Lumen, 142

# M

Macronutrients, 79
Maintenance programs, 183,
    210–13
McDonald's®, 103–7
Meat, poultry, fish, beans, eggs,
    and nuts group (Food Guide
    Pyramid), 81, 87
*Medicine and Science in Sports
    and Exercise* (ACSM), 175
Men
    aerobic fitness and heart rate,
      190
    body-fat ratios of, 41, 46–47
    cholesterol guidelines for,
      150
    desirable weights for, 66–67
    fat distribution in, 47–48
    HDL ratio in, 149
    heart disease risk in, 147,
      159–61, 163–64
    physical fitness program for,
      215
    skinfold measurements for,
      71

*Physician and Sportsmedicine,* 2
Phytochemicals, 80–81
Pizza Hut®, 112–16
Plan of Action, for exercise, 206
Plaque, 142
Point system, for aerobic exercise, 197, 198
Ponderal index, 46, 67–68
Positive calorie balance, 54
President's Council on Physical Fitness, 213
Progression, in exercise, 172
Progressive Resistance Exercise (PRE), 200–203
Protein, 79, 82–83. *see also* nutrition
Psychological inducements, food and, 40
Psychosomatic responses, 9
Pulse rate, 30, 31

# R

Raab, H., 2
Rahe, Richard, 22
Rate of Perceived Exertion (RPE) scale, 168, 181–82
Rathbone, Josephine, 25
Relaxation, 25
Repetitions, of exercises, 201
Residence, physical activity and, 247
Resistance exercises, 199, 201
Resistance stage, of GAS, 7
Resistance training (weight training), 195, 200–203, 216
    calculations for, 233–34
    exercises for, 217–23
Rest, for injuries, 236

Resting heart rate, 185–87
Resting metabolic rate (RMR), 49, 50
Retrogression, 173
Reverse cholesterol transport, 149
Rhythmically choreographed exercise programs, 199
R.I.C.E. (rest, ice application, compression, elevation), 235–37
Rippe, James M., 189
RISKO (heart attack risk), 159–61, 163–64
Rosenman, Ray, 7, 8
Running
    calories burned by jogging, 57
    for cross-training, 204
    maintenance program, 211
    running/jogging exercise program, 198

# S

Safety, in exercise, 173–75
Salt, 124
Saturated fat, 85–87
Schade, William, 25
Sedentary lifestyle, 11–12, 14, 39, 151–52, 246–47
Serving sizes, 81, 84, 87
Set-point theory, 40–41
Sets, 201
Sex (gender), heart disease risk and, 147, 159–61, 163–64. *see also* men; women
Sheldon, William, 42, 65
Simple carbohydrates, 83–85
Sit-ups, 191, 228
Skill level, 247

Tendinitis, 238
"10% rule," 44
Testosterone, 147, 202
Thermic effect of eating (TEE),
  50–51
Thirst, 238
Time out theory, 10
Total body weight (TBW), 44
Training effect, 9, 29–32, 167
Transcendental meditation (TM),
  25
Traumatic injury, 235
Treadmill exercise, 212
Triceps skinfold measurement,
  45–46, 69, 70
Triglycerides, 49, 147
"20% rule," 44
Type A/B Behavior Patterns, 8

# U

Ultrasound fat measurement, 46
University of Michigan, 33
Unsaturated fat, 85–87
Upright row, 217, 220
U.S. Department of Agriculture
  (USDA)
    Dietary Guidelines for
      Americans, 124–25, 127
    Food Guide Pyramid, 81–82,
      84, 87
U.S. Department of Health and
  Human Services, 3–4
U.S. Preventive Services Task
  Force, 155–56

# V

Vascular disease, 141, 145–46. *see
  also* cardiovascular disease
Vegetable group (Food Guide
  Pyramid), 81, 84
Very low calorie dieting (VLCD),
  60
Vitamins, 79, 90–91. *see also*
  nutrition

# W

Waist-to-hip ratio (WHR), 48, 75,
  127
Walking, 33, 55
    aerobic exercise program,
      198
    aerobic fitness walk test,
      189–90
    beginning program for, 230
    maintenance program, 211
Warm-up exercises, 171
Water soluble vitamins, 90–91
Weight. *see also* body composition
    control/maintenance, 39, 49,
      57, 66–67
    Dietary Guidelines for
      Americans (USDA),
      124–25, 127
    "healthy weight," 127
    heart disease risk and,
      159–61, 163–64
    total body weight (TBW), 44
Weight lifting, 200–203

Weight loss
  calorie burning and types of
    exercise, 55–57
  fat-burning guidelines, 58
  popular strategies for, 51
  yo-yo syndrome, 49–50, 51
Weight training, 200–203
Wendy's®, 99–100
Wescott, Wayne, 53
Wind chill index, 239
Women
  aerobic fitness and heart rate,
    190
  body-fat ratios of, 46–47
  cholesterol guidelines for,
    150
  desirable weights for, 66–67
  fat distribution in, 47–48
  HDL ratio in, 149

  heart disease risk in, 147,
    159–61, 163–64
  physical fitness program for,
    214
  skinfold measurements for,
    71
  weight of, 30

# Y

Year 2000 (U.S. Department of
  Health and Human Services),
  3–4
Yoga, 10–11, 25
Yo-yo syndrome, 49–50, 51

# Z

Zuti, William, 52